the JOY *of* CLIMBING

TERRY GIFFORD'S CLASSIC CLIMBS

TERRY GIFFORD

Whittles Publishing

Published by
Whittles Publishing Limited,
Roseleigh House,
Latheronwheel,
Caithness, KW5 6DW,
Scotland, UK
www.whittlespublishing.com

Cover design and text layout by Mark Mechan

ISBN 1-904445-06-3

Climbing is a dangerous activity and is the responsibility of the individual taking part.

Printed and bound in Poland, E.U.

DEDICATION

This book is dedicated to the partners who have shared these adventures, especially David Craig who started me writing by example and Norman Elliott who has looked after me on the crags for over 40 years. Others who deserve thanks for contributing unique qualities to my irregular climbs with them include Julian Cooper (vigorous conversations), Jim Curran (incapacitating hilarity), Harold Drasdo (ruminations around obscure Welsh crags), Pip Hopkinson (unfailing enthusiasm), Tim Noble (tolerance and drive) and Ian Smith (Picture Editor for this book). In America, Larry Giacomino first introduced me to the Sierras before I had some good climbs and fun times with Allen Steck, Steve Roper and Doug Robinson. In North Carolina Howard Mask was my weekly partner for a spring semester, whilst Jimmy and Lilace Guignard became life-long friends on and off the rock. Special pleasure has come from climbing with my son Tom and my wife Gill Round. The generosity and patience of all these characters have given me *The Joy of Climbing*.

An anthology of writers:
Terry Gifford, David Craig, Tim Noble,
John Baker.
Photo: Gill Round.

CONTENTS

THE JOY OF CLIMBING

INTRODUCTION

Should I apologise for this title, *The Joy of Climbing*? If you are expecting the climbing version of *The Joy of Sex* would you be disappointed? Well, this book does contain some hot tips and it does explore the infinitely subtle variety of what appears to be a relatively simple, even absurd, activity. It is also about an obsession that can get a little embarrassing at times and can lead to arguments with one's partner. On the other hand, it can lead to moments of sheer joy in doing what seems to come naturally. Perhaps entertaining writing about it can even come from people who are not particularly good at it. Welcome to *The Joy of Climbing*.

Actually, this title is stolen from a newspaper review of a book about the angst of climbing. The reviewer asked, 'When will I read a book about what I get out of climbing, the fun of climbing?' That reviewer may not be entirely happy with this book because I have to admit to cheating a bit. There is some angst in here too. It comes from getting scared easily on what many will regard as the easier routes. Actually, around the VS grade (and just below it) I'd say I'm quite competent, technically, with a little pre-stretching and visualisation exercises. The secret I share with the average climber is knowing that if you get out into wild places with idiosyncratic people, camping gear and a bottle of wine, interesting things happen.

So by now you know what you've got coming: epics on Diffs; relationship epics of the 'This is never Diff!' kind; angst on Cretan gorge walks, downhill of course, but in the searing heat of summer; epic walk-ins to the easier long climbs of Scotland; wine-fuelled epics on the less bolted routes of Europe; moving moments on the friction of the more amenable slabs of Tuolumne Meadows; routing in the woods with the crazy rednecks of North Carolina – the joy of climbing.

When I was a kid the highlight of our year was a week in a caravan on the bleak East Anglian coast. It was good training, looking back on it. My dad would borrow granddad's Morris Ten, strap the deckchairs on the back and launch out from Cambridge on a journey that would bring us to a windy clifftop of boulder clay above the North Sea. One year it was Cromer, another Hunstanton, until we seemed to settle for East Runton. Then a remarkable decision by my mum changed everything forever.

Actually, it was the Boy Scouts that started it. They took me to the Lake District and employed Des Oliver to introduce us to rock-climbing on Glaciated Slabs in Coombe Gill. He was a wonderfully mysterious smiling figure who let me carry the rope. I remember that he had a finger missing from some dramatic climbing accident. Des, as he let us call him, gave us the time of our lives on what seemed to us Fen boys an incredibly steep fellside. It was on this trip that we invented a touchstone phrase for this new uphill country. We knew we were in the mountains when we said to each other, 'I wouldn't want to ride my bike down that!' The first sight of bracken in the minibus headlights meant we were already in wild country, a world away from my family roots.

So I was hooked. I persuaded my mum that we ought to try a different kind of annual family holiday and my dad that the drive in the opposite direction was just as easy. Our week's holiday changed to a caravan outside Betws-y-Coed and my mother fell in love with the mountains. She knows the latest developments on the climbing scene in Chamonix better than I do. When my dad retired from his job as Head Gardener at Kings College, she found that they could get cheap off-peak trips to the Alps, catch a cable car up and walk back down, every day for a week, whatever the weather. For the last few years she's been looking more aged than she feels. Well, she is eighty-two. She told me that she caught sight of herself in a ladies' toilet recently and was shocked at how aged she looked compared with other women there. 'But I thought to myself,' she told me, 'I bet I'm the only one here with a subscription to *High* magazine.' My patient dad says she reads it twice, especially the latest news from places she knows like Chamonix.

'Don't stand so close to the edge, Harold,' Drasdo reports his mother saying to him on a recent walk as he closed his wry book of climbing memoirs, *The Ordinary Route*. It seems hard to believe now that my mother allowed me to hitch at the age of sixteen from that caravan outside Betws-y-Coed to beg climbs in the Llanberis Pass and Idwal. I have no idea who it was that picked me up on the roadside and took me to climb Crown of Thorns in the Pass with him. It was wet, as I now know it usually is, but it did have a crown of thorns to pull on at the top. (Jim Curran confesses to having pulled it off in a characteristic over-athletic moment.) I didn't tell my mother how scared I had been on that climb. I was now a climber, grateful to the climbing community that had taken me in. My parents continued to go to that caravan every year as they rambled through their own kind of hillwalking apprenticeship whilst I went to Sheffield to be a student and get a gritstone apprenticeship.

Apparently my mum is now a notorious mountain character in her own way, recognised, for example, at the ticket office of the Snowdon railway when she and my dad do their annual train up and walk down. Certain hotels in the Alps must dread the sight of that elderly couple who wait for them to open early for breakfast to maximise the mountain day. Certain pistefûhrer must be glad they no longer see that old woman in gaiters and a skirt leading her husband with careful ski-pole placements down through the end-of-season skiers.

'IF I CAN DO IT, YOU CAN DO IT.'

I settled in Sheffield, as more students do than in any other city in the UK. Twenty years and two children later, I was still climbing with my college partner, Norman Elliott, and joint family camping summers in France were enlivened by Pete Livesey's first English guide to climbing in France. After ten annual family visits to the magic Scottish island of Islay at Whitsun, I decided that I was wasting too much good weather not climbing in Scotland and began my first Whit climbing foray to the far north. At about this time David Craig started writing for the climbing magazines in what was to be preparation for his inspirational book *Native Stones*. He said to me, in that comradely way for which I am eternally grateful, 'If I can do it, you can do it.' I found not only that I could, but that I enjoyed the craft, so long as I wrote only when I wanted to revisit the experience. I was never tempted to become a columnist because I didn't need to. So every article collected in *The Joy of Climbing* was written for the sheer fun of it. They are offered to you here by way of passing on that bâton of David's, if you'd like to take it up.

Over the twenty years of writing about three or four articles a year, I've tried to vary the form and the choice of climbs. The earliest piece here, published in 1983, I called 'A Whale in the Forest' and is an extended metaphor based on a first visit to the *Classic Rock* route Ardverikie Wall. The latest piece, published in 2003, is the story of a first married row on the less popular Truss Buttress in the quiet Eastern Fells valley of Swindale. I quickly learned to look in the back of *Classic Rock* for that list of other good climbs that are not the subject of chapters in the book, but could well have been. Norman and I also learned to search new guidebooks for three-star routes that we'd not done, or that didn't have three stars last time. From Durdle Door on the Dorset coast to Wisdom Buttress in the Fisherfield Forest, I've been searching for the esoteric gems of British climbing. Check out Spinnaker in the hidden depths of Yorkshire gritstone. It's a rarity because, of course, neglected gems are hard to find in the most popular areas. And because I'm looking for a single climbing experience to celebrate I've not written much about whole crags. Hence there is little here on the relatively shorter routes of Northern England. I've really been seeking bigger adventures than those on my doorstep.

'SO IS THIS BOOK A HIT LIST?'

This book is not really a carefully selected hit list as *Classic Rock* is designed to be. It's really a sample of the fun available in our climbing culture. These climbs have, in a sense, chosen me. I haven't had to write about them, so they are only included here if they have produced some memorable experience. So, for you, perhaps they could be a hit list after all.

No one except the guidebook writer would call Pencoed Pillar in Cwm Cau a classic, but Norman and I had a certain degree of fun and frustration in discovering that it wasn't. You might have an interesting time discovering if it has changed with the traffic encouraged by that wicked guidebook writer, John Sumner, who gave it three stars. As you know, much depends upon who you go with to climb it, what birds you see from the belays, the pictures you bring back. That route led me on a search to find out just who the legendary Millican Dalton, its first ascensionist, really was. And that became another story, more about climbing culture past and present than particular climbs. The climbs are the central personalities celebrated in this book, but part of the joy of climbing for me is what surrounds it. In the end, it's the context that makes the whole experience the epiphany I'd like to explore through the writing.

'CAN THE EDGES DEFINE THE CORE EXPERIENCE?'

I think they do for me. I've usually allowed the contribution of the edges around the climb to give meaning to its core on the day: the spirits of place and of personalities, the history and the remarkable present, the flora and the fear, the little known writers like Elizabeth Coxhead and the famous painters like William Heaton Cooper, the chance encounters with delightful unknown people like John Taylor and the planned painting/poem trips with Heaton Cooper's son Julian. In fact, some of the greatest fun has been in going out to climb knowing that the edges are going to be interesting. Going out with a painter like Julian Cooper, or a photographer like Gordon Stainforth, who have their own professional agenda and observing them at work, supporting them in their work by brewing up and such like, but getting in a hill day or a long weekend with just one climb together, has often produced poetry as well as an article.

Climb with Jim Curran and it's the jokes you'll remember as much as the climb. Many times Norman has paused at a belay and said, 'Doesn't climbing get you into some brilliant situations?' I've wanted to let those situations sink in – the orchids, the peregrines, the jokes and the blisters – as well as the striking rock formations themselves and the challenge of reading them. Some of the contexts in which we climb can be disturbing or problematic. You don't have to be a hard climber to have to deal with death – if there's no risk, there's no climbing. You don't have to be an environmentalist to be horrified by the killing fields of Malta. The spirits of place and personality are not always of our choosing. But that's part of the adventure.

'ARE THESE ARTICLES OR ESSAYS'?

In order to be innovative with the richness of experience available in the climbing culture for an ordinary climber I've tried to experiment with the form of the 1000–1500 word article. I do think that this is *the* form for the rock-climbing experience. At first, I did try to make a different kind of book out of this material that was written for the magazines and journals. But the pieces have been so tightly and individually crafted that they have resisted being cobbled together for a book of climbing memoirs. This is mostly journalism, structured to work within the 1500 word unit of a magazine product. I could call these pieces 'essays' instead of 'articles', especially when I find myself to be more reflective than usual. To me they often have more in common with poetry in their play with language, their deliberate structure and their desire to mean more than they say. Sometimes they seem to have a lyrical intensity in celebrating a formative moment. But whether 'articles' or 'essays', their intention is to entertain a lot and enlighten a bit. Which art form they are matters little if they do those jobs for readers of the particular publication in which they are placed. This kind of journalism can be, I hope, as powerful a form of creative writing as poetry or fiction. As a matter of fact, there is a bit of fiction in here from time to time…

'ISN'T IT JUST PLAYING WITH FORMS AND STYLES?'

Early on, the writing of an article seemed to lead naturally to a poem. However, I learned not to use a poem as a coda to a magazine piece because it was so easily edited out. Embedding the poem, as in the piece co-written with Jim Curran on Fionn Buttress, is a better literary strategy to outwit the editor who is usually nervous about poetry. It's better to find a strong story and then play with form and style. In 'Down The Tube' I thought I might try the tense, dramatic style of the American writer John Long on climbs that would be unlikely to produce his kind of death-defying epics. In 'The Lady and the Raven' I was tempted to make a myth to handle what is really a love story. Alert readers will notice that, from time to time, I have adopted a few characteristic turns of phrase from certain writers by way of playful homage. In fact the reader might notice that the more unusual forms and styles have been offered to the *Climbers' Club Journal* because I've wanted to give friends some knowing fun from recognising the characters, or the style, or the sheer quirkiness. Club journals should be an exchange of surprises.

Latterly, I've been developing with Gill, articles composed of 'jointly gendered voices', as we called them when we slipped one into a presentation at an academic conference in America. We write alternate paragraphs, each partly in reply to the previous one, exposing our different subjective experiences on a climb together. We only attempt this when there is some tension to be explored between the 'his' and 'her's' voices. This might sound like earnest therapy (which, come to think of it, it might be), but we regard it as part of the joy of climbing and have got married since we started sparking off each other in this form. Although, it must be admitted, there was one long climb in Spain that was such an epic (missed descent route, multiple abseils to a path high across the mountain, an endless moonlit descent of scree…) that we've not yet brought ourselves to confront it in writing.

'CAN WE AVOID MOUNTAIN LANDSCAPE POLITICS?'

The BMC recently thanked people who had 'performed exceptionally well' in their contributions to the BMC Festival of Climbing. Among them were characters who do not appear in this book: 'a wall builder', 'a harness putter-on' and 'an isolation escort'. For those mystified by these roles it should be pointed out that this festival's notion of climbing is an indoor competition ascending leaning boards with little holds bolted onto them. Thousands pay to watch a few matchstick climbers get as high as they can before falling off, held by the rope above them. This cannot be watched by the poor matchstick climbers themselves who have to sit very still doing something called 'visualising' in isolation. The 'isolation escort' appears to have drawn the short straw policing non-climbing at a Festival of Climbing.

Someone, perhaps the BMC, should point out that it doesn't have to be like this. Even in December there's no need, if you're a climber of modest ability, to pay to be sitting it out in Birmingham on a weekend. Try the aforementioned Spinnaker. It's already beautifully built; you can hitch up the tension by putting on your own harness; you can be both the climber and the escort, which can be a delightfully pregnant prospect.

During the week in Spain when I've been working on this Introduction I've been out climbing twice with two different partners (Ian Smith, over from Sheffield, like me, for a week, and Pat Swailes who lives close to the crag), at two different times of day (early afternoon and at dusk), in two very different weather conditions (cloudless, then storm-clouded skies). The local Sella crag was the same each time, but we did different routes and talked about different things. It was all very jolly and some of the moves were interesting (some too interesting: I failed to lead a polished grade 5 with Pat). There was no route-finding, of course, since this was sports climbing. We followed lines of bolts into which we clipped our ropes for protection. But it was just good to be out in shorts, finding the finger-shaped incuts of easy limestone here again. This crag, like much of the rock of mainland Europe, has been lost to the bolt and my avoiding it was not going to change anything. There are articles here about partly bolted routes. But the routes of character that give the most memorable experiences are not of the bolted Sella kind.

I have juxtaposed competition climbing and sports climbing here to indicate that, although both are flawed forms of climbing for me, the outdoors experience offers much more interesting and varied edges to it. But if we are to retain the potentially rich experiences celebrated in this book we must be aware of the politics of the management of mountain and crag landscapes. If we turn our backs on the outdoors it will disappear behind some bureaucratic restrictions designed by those of goodwill to protect it for all our futures. This is not the place to go any further into the polemics of climbing culture. I merely point out that if you have an interest in the joy of climbing outdoors, you're involved in the issues of our climbing culture. To be in landscape is to be implicated in decisions about how best to be in landscape in a sustainable way.

'WHAT IS "THE BOOK OF THE BURREN"?'

So, in contrast to competition and sports climbing, this book opens with an isolated chapter on climbing at the Burren in the west of Ireland. This story takes us to the roots of our climbing tradition and its heritage, but risks an innovative mode of writing. It should be taken as a kind of literary frontispiece. It is a parable about a pilgrimage that should bring to life all that I've been saying in this Introduction. Enjoy the journey.

Terry Gifford
Sella, Alicante

From: 'A Stanage Year'
15th February 1987

The children play in the snow
At the foot of Crack and Corner.
Tom photographs his dad trying
To dance up Heather Wall. Hell,
It's so good I do it again.
Tom throws snowballs. Ruth yells.
I sort them out, then solo
Manchester Buttress better
Than last time with Curran.

He shook with fear at facing
The prospect of his address
At the Al Rouse memorial do
And I had to face my guilt
In the divorce court at midday.
Ian arrived to take my place,
Climbing for the first time since
Escaping from the hospital,
Now seeking Stanage the healer.

From The Rope *by Terry Gifford (1996)*

CHAPTER 1 IRELAND

The *Book of the Burren*

The two pilgrims paused at the top of the hill. They had come a long way. Now, below them, where the road wound down to the sea, where the Aran Islands could almost be touched offshore – there at last lay the Burren, the fabled limestone land on the western edge of Ireland.

They had come in search of a book. Many by now had been moved and uplifted by the *Book of Kells*, but few had actually seen the *Book of the Burren*. It was rumoured that the illuminations of the *Book of the Burren* were even more vibrant and more varied, skillfully linking the natural and the unnatural in images woven even more intricately around the text. Each spring, during the season of pilgrimages, travellers came from afar seeking the book.

The two pilgrims rested by the Labyrinth Stone at the top of the hill. Carved into the sparkling granite of the strange waymarker stone was a Celtic maze of concentric circles. It might have been a map of the landscape of lanes in the Burren below. It might have been a warning of the water-worn labyrinth that lay under the Burren. Or was it a sign to pilgrims nearing the end of their journey that showed them the meaning of the pilgrimage itself, a stone-carved symbol of their inner journey, one which could not simply end upon reaching the West? None knew the lost message of the Labyrinth Stone; it had come to be accepted as part of the mystery of the place. But, where within this limestone maze would Ronan and Kevin find the *Book of the Burren*?

Long after their return, Ronan had asked of other pilgrims they had met on those western cliffs, 'And what do you remember best of the Burren?'

'The dolphins,' said Stella.

'The Guinness,' said Johnny.

'And the rock,' said Stella, remembering that she spoke to a scribe of their stone-climbing sect. 'Quite technical but sharp-edged, with friction and fossils. Did you climb Pis Fliuch after we left? The only rightly recorded route we followed all week.'

'But someone should record,' insisted Johnny to Ronan, 'that those boulders at the bottom of the Mirror Wall have been shifted back by the storm tides. Few of those routes have been reclimbed by their new starts.'

The pilgrims had heard tales of the ferocity of the winter storms from Calvin Torrans as he sat in his tent between clifftop and road.

'You know,' he had said with his Northern accent and perpetual smile, 'sometimes you can

TG at the Burren, Ireland.
Photo: Norman Elliott.

arrive on a winter weekend and find seaweed being thrown up over the cliff and onto the road.'

Well, that Whitsuntide the sun shone at Ailladie, the main cliff of the Burren, where everything is less than a rope's length above the Atlantic. The way down the fluted limestone cliff is through grass studded with upthrust fists of purple and pink orchids, delicately spotted and ignorant of paths. In the micro-climate of crevices, rare ferns shelter and tentatively finger the air. At the sea's edge of this green world, a short steep descent leads to a wide nontidal platform. From here, when the weather is wild, pilgrims can at least do 'Gogo at Hard Severe', as their language has it, or if penance is due, follow the undercut traverse and razor jams of Mad Mackerel. But many travellers to the Burren seem to prefer to tune into the steepness of Ailladie by way of the awkward ramp of Bonnain Bui or the thin diagonal crack of Ground Control. It was below this crack that Ronan made a discovery he was later to honour in his chapbook:

> The fiddler of Doolin was sleeping
> But the pub window advertised
> 'Music Food Drink Crack'.

> Out there, in the bright early light,
> The Aran Islands slept, shifting a little,
> Uneasy in a chill Atlantic sea.

Through the green patchwork of cut
And uncut meadows, lanes tacked toward
The stepped white sheets of the hill
Where club-foot ferns crouched in folds and clints
And orchids bristled up through cliff-top tracks.

We were approaching a new crag again,
Sniffing out, as usual, signs of the descent,
Then balanced across cliff-bottom boulders
Reading cracks and corners from a thin book.

Following a ledge leading under a wall
That reared sheer and, seductive,
Suddenly we stepped on flowers,
Sweating under cellophane. 'For Simon'
Said the faded card pinned down
By stones from the crag that killed him
And that we had come to climb.

Reverence, mixed with a little unease, delayed the ascent of Ground Control until late in their stay. Then Kevin led it nervously, tiring himself by placing too many small wires and twice having to descend for a rest. They knew that the boy from the North had been killed on the harder crack to the right of their line, and anyway, their order demanded that life must go on. Rock must be engaged by the limbs of the living if they are to learn the awe and elation offered by the diligent reading of texts.

Ronan and Kevin marvelled at the memorable lines of the walls and corners of Ailladie. They watched Keefe Murphy at his oblations on Brother Gibson's inspired line up the center of Mirror Wall, making regular offerings of nuts to the thin crack called The Cutter. It was a lesson in steadiness on steep, unrelenting rock from the local maker of lines. To the left, a young acolyte had rushed halfway up Wall of Fossils and hand-traversed out onto the hanging arête called Fall of Wossils. He quickly clipped the peg and was girding himself for the long, unprotected ascent of the arête. At last he moved up, hanging first left and then right, off the straight edge. His cry at the top left no doubt that a pilgrim had found ecstasy.

Ronan found that his faith was tested by the bold step across a wide crack at the top of Moon Rill, one of the easier corners. But he transferred his weight and his trust across the void, finding unseen holds coming to hand as he did so. Then, preparations complete, the two pilgrims approached the final stations of their devotional journey. Afterward, they remembered this as the day of the trinity of visions, as much for the revelations of the sea as of the rock. This was the day they read three uplifting lines on Boulder Wall, each prefaced by a small epiphany during the abseiling ritual.

The first abseil brought them to a ledge just above a dark velvet sea, which appeared to be carpeted with diamonds that sparkled with the brilliance of a miracle. They turned their backs on this wonder to look up the arête at the left end of the ledge. Here lay the dazzling charms (they were now looking into the sun) of Doolin Rouge. A delicate slab led to a bulge where a dubious but necessary nut could also get in the way of a clumsy high step. If this nut rattled back down to the ledge, the piety of a pilgrim would be severely tested by the steep (and now totally unprotected) traverse across the top wall. Ronan was glad he'd agreed that they top-rope Doolin Rouge when his foot slipped from a small edge as he climbed badly over the bulge. He was ready to accept that the climb was better than this particular climber.

A glance down before the second abseil produced the vision of the jellyfish. Now the sea was translucent with floating pink ghosts, which had strangely vanished when the pilgrims stood again on the ledge. Kevin led off up a wide, black crack as sharp-edged as though cut by lightning only yesterday. This was Great Balls of Fire. An arm-bar and knee-bracing struggle suddenly turned into a fingertip traverse left to a steep crack leading up to the sunlight.

The third abseil was remembered for their discovery of the auks. They had probably been there all the time – this, the pilgrims were coming to realize, was the mystery of the Burren. Guillemots and razorbills, bobbing black and white on the water, had surely been watching them all the time, out on the margins of their rock-focused vision. Then they remembered passing above the chattering birdcliffs of Moher on their way to the Labyrinth Stone. But now they were confronting what was to be the most rewarding test of all: Black Magic. The key to deciphering this text was to escape each dark groove by moving up right into the next. High on the wall a horizontal break offered Ronan a rest to gather inner resources for the final soaring fingerlocks up a vertical crack to the top. These were magic moves out of the black wall and into the clear light of the Burren, with the doors of perception cleansed.

It is in the nature of a pilgrimage such as this that the opening of one door is the closing of another. Now that the climbers' eyes were opened, the sky darkened with rain. Still, they ascended the mountain, crossing the massive white pavements to worship at Murroughkilly. Their first climb, An Mhear Fhada, revealed a new texture to the rock, which seemed like white, fragile charcoal, until a falling stone drew blood from Kevin's unhelmeted head. An audience with The Cardinal over at Eagle's Rock had also been planned until Calvin had warned them of the dense, overgrown approach: 'You know, that is probably the very wood where Sweeney lost an army. In any case, the name is more impressive than the route.' Useful advice from Ireland's sage of the stone.

So, as the rain fell the pilgrims pulled up their hoods and made for the Ailwee Caves to receive instruction in their formation from the local guides. Then they pressed on up the road to the bleak plateau above where they prostrated themselves before the Poulnabrone dolmen, vying for the best vision in their lenses as it loomed stark against the dark sky. It was an unnatural rock form, but this neolithic burial chamber was as much a part of the mysterious power of the Burren as were its famous sunsets or its music.

It is the custom in the Burren that each evening pilgrims and pagans alike make their way to the inns of Doolin, where the Guinness is always already settling in pint glasses on the bar. The musicians of Doolin exert a westward pull felt throughout Europe. Their fiddles, guitars, pipes, and bodhran make music as intricate as a Celtic design and as clear as the light of County Clare. So, long after the colours have left the evening sky behind the Aran Islands, the inns of Doolin retain the colours and tastes of Ireland.

Halfway up the road out of the Burren, Ronan and Kevin sat down to look back. They had long ago forgotten their hopes of finding the *Book of the Burren*, that long-lost manuscript of fabled illuminations. And they knew they would not have the luck to find it now, buried beneath this field wall, these strange upright slabs against which they leaned. Kevin marveled at the squirls of the serpents fossilized in the famous Doolin Stone. To Ronan these relief shapes seemed to echo the carved spirals of the Labyrinth Stone, that mysterious waymarker on the bend above the Burren.

Before leaving on this pilgrimage, they had received a letter from Dermot Somers, the Wicklow hermit and teller of tales. 'An extraordinary area,' he had said, 'quite apart from the climbing, which you would lose in Pembroke, except for its rich cultural, archeological, and geological context.' Slowly the

The approach to Murroughkilly, the Burren, Ireland. Photo: TG.

Opposite page: TG on Black Magic, Ailladie, the Burren, Ireland. Photo: Norman Elliott.

pilgrims began to decipher the meaning of the fossil hieroglyphics on the Doolin Stone. They were reading a page of the *Book of the Burren*, bordered here by interwoven grasses and the delicate yellow heads of buttercups. The stone pages they'd read in the Burren had each been illuminated in the margins of their vision by dolphins and dolmen, the birds and the beer, the music of County Clare and the caves of Ailwee, the rare flowers amongst the rocks and the flotilla of jellyfish in the sea.

Indeed, this book may still be found by alert pilgrims who venture to the west of Ireland. For, better than the *Book of Kells*, the *Book of the Burren* is alive, its illuminations constantly renewed, its stone pages open to different readings every day.

CHAPTER 2 SCOTLAND

A Whale in the Forest: Ardverikie Wall

Open the car door and a scent like wild iris cannot be ignored, direct and delicate as the line of Ardverikie Wall we're peering into the hills to find. 8 a.m. in early August and the half covering of cloud could thicken to rain or be thinned by the strong light. The day is poised and we are drawn, or rather driven (Sheffield to Glencoe in six hours) by the reputation of this *Classic Rock*, desert island, three star, hidden climb with a name like a chant that's been growing in our heads with the years.

The MacInnes' (1971) spartan prose is just enough, as usual, to get you round to the back of Binnein Shuas. As you come to the lochan a whale begins to grow, its rounded back stranded above the shores of the long lochs. Barnacled with heather patches towards its tail, it eyes you from the overhang in its head. Between eye and tail a vertical vein of white quartz scars the smoothest section of its flank. Keeping just to the right of this lies a perfect line that nevertheless requires route finding, with what appear to be cracks that aren't, and unexpected threads in fine-grained rock. A riddle of a route, but how many fish fly in the forest?

The moves up the initial rib promise a steep and searching day. It's fun swinging gymnastically off the ground, but we ought to have known that the first moves can resemble the last. Stepping right onto a sandy ledge at 40 feet I belayed too low down at first. The big flake hidden in the niche above is needed to allow for the length of the next pitch. Swinging back onto the rib for his lead, Norman utters cries of delight, still high on the iris and orchids, until he's silenced by the steepness of the cracks that break onto the long slab above. Warming sun, soft breeze, and suddenly screams I haven't heard since Whitsun: a pair of peregrines shoot out above the crag chasing a raven. As I'm thinking it's late for young, the rope comes tight. It was on that slab of superb friction that we decided the rock of the Devil's Slide on Lundy came closest to these microgranite crystals and little closed cracks you can tiptoe up. Move to the right then to the left, or go straight up, there was always just enough to move on.

So facing the next pitch I ignored the Moac-width invitations of the hundred foot crack on the right and followed the guidebook of the Fox of Glencoe straight up the white line to the overhang. It's not as hard as it looks. Flat holds appear in all the right places for hands and feet. But when the crag is being benign the head must be alert. Flattered by the upward progress I forgot the diagonal needed to belay in line with the hundred foot crack, which left me with a thin high traverse to find the flake. I belayed not just on a tape round this but also a nut between the legs for Norman's lead of the crux, which he began by stepping down so that he started his 'rising traverse' on a top-rope! But he discovered a rising ramp and layed away, up and out over a void he finally stepped across to some quartz knobs big enough for runners. When he'd moved up a little and found a line of holds back left he was raving again about the rock, the route-finding, even the trees of the Ardverikie Forest. As we got higher we could actually see a few.

For the final pitch up to the terrace I was still following my 'or go straight up' policy, and nearly came to the climber's understanding of a dead end – well, not quite because it isn't in the nature of the rock to do that to you. Past the thread on which I thought he should have belayed, until the flake on which I was certain he should have done, I was drawn upwards between two glaring white lines of washing soda. Unable to decide which to follow I stayed between them on rock which was less friable, less blinding in sunlight, but which eventually bumped me on the nose. I stopped, contemplating two finger pockets leading right and over the top. An inspection, that turned into a move, going for jugs that weren't, produced an exit from the Wall that couldn't have been bettered, I decided, afterwards.

My memory of the easy scramble above the terrace was washed away by a swim in the lochan below. But those final moves characterized the route: delicate and open, well protected and exposed, always a vertical adventure. Of course, a whale's flank couldn't really be expected to lean back the higher you go, anymore than Ardverikie Forest is really a forest, because like the best of the *Classic Rock* (Wilson 1978), desert island, three star climbs it is greater than its literature. And how many whales fly in the forest?

Bright as Paradise: Arran, The Chasm, The Island

Walk through the stone door and bow before the mountain, only then will its summit visions be revealed to you. I remember registering an unspoken liking for a mountain that made you pass through the shadow of your own death, under a curve of granite like a dolmen door before reducing you a little later to the foetal position of a baby emerging from a cramped cave as you answered the questions of the path to the summit. We were probably off route. The sun was burning our brains and we were making progress through a mountaineer's dreamtime.

And then the view: sea and land, shores and summits, islands and inland hills layering away at every turn. Across spangled sea the white shores of the Mull of Kintyre, across the low Mull the Paps of Jura, beyond the Paps the Bens of the Isle of Mull. Turn round and draw your eyes from the Cobbler down to Bute and across the sun-singing Sound to the nearer pointed peaks of Cir Mhor, Goat Fell and A'Chir's alpine ridge. We were on Arran, the people's island, for May Day weekend, and it was, as Bill Murray (1951) promised in *Undiscovered Scotland*, 'bright as Paradise'.

You don't have to search for some far neglected fastness to experience your own undiscovered Scotland. The elemental qualities of the wilderness can be experienced in a special way sometimes in a well-known place. For me the view from Beinn Tarsuinn, which is probably familiar to thousands of lucky people, was a special vision on that day. It was my first visit to Arran. In a sense the undiscovered is waiting as much inside as outside every searcher after the mountains. In another sense the experience of undiscovered Scotland is still available to anyone in the newness of well-known places they have not themselves yet entered. The Chasm on Buachaille Etive Mor, the people's mountain, was one of the wonders of the world to me on a long day's discovery. But also there remain the little-visited areas which wait for anybody who wishes to search for them. They may not be true wilderness, but you won't find other people climbing there. Such places deserve to be left for everyone, without guidebooks and grades. I'd like to celebrate an evening's seacliff climbing in a place which will never become a good climbing ground, but which I'd like to leave unnamed for others to experience as I have done. In fact I'd like to suggest with these three examples from Arran, the Chasm and an island seacliff, the fact that, in at least three different ways undiscovered Scotland is still alive.

A view from a summit is not just all that lies before you, but all that lay before it. You have to touch a top to see the Sounds, but before drinking in the view you have to smell your own sweat and the odd dead sheep. Arran is so accessible, even to the English for a weekend, that it must be the people's island. But, nevertheless, on a May Day weekend there was room to pitch a tent up Glen Rosa out of sight of any other. And even in a drought the infamous bogs do not disappoint, grabbing you by the ankles in broad daylight, the stink of bog battling with the stink of sweat and a heavy pack producing more of both.

There must come a point for everyone who carries climbing and camping gear up Glen Rosa when the romantic simplicity of stepping from boat to island in empty-handed innocence, carrying all the necessities in ancient and honourable style on the back, begins to fade, when the delight of walking freely through the thousand-year-old Viking frontier town of Brodick begins to seem ages behind. When 'Just a bit further' began to fade we looked for a flat patch for four of us. I don't know why we went along with Norman's choice of site because it involved a wicked balancing act across wet rocks on the very brink of a waterfall. But it was well above the path on what should have been sponge. Instead it was a tinder box of dead grasses like woolshavings through which shone violet stars of Cranesbill.

Evening clouds touched the white pyramid of Cir Mhor, framed in the tent door, and closed down a spring day. We 'opened the bar'. When we woke it was a day of winter, dark and laced with a chilling wind. Finding ourselves first on the hill in the morning, we witnessed figures emerging from under boulders higher up the glen like the ragged remnants of a clan battle. I shivered on the stones of Sou'wester Slabs trying to enjoy the view. I had to blow on my fists before plunging them back into the frosted granite cracks that drew crystals of blood. Then we warmed to the humour of Caliban's Crawl, loving the adventure of its trail of suprises. A linger to look across at a pair climbing on the long laybacking line of West Flank Route, a traverse of the summit, a wild downhill run through the deer herds, and we sank back by our tents, sun at last lighting the slabby, scabby flanks of Goat Fell.

I woke to the sound of Norman snoring like the original goat. Outside it was a day of high summer that squeaked meadow pipits and sang skylarks. I gave Norman the message. Soon we had backs bent to the hill as we plodded up to the col left of Cir Mhor for a traverse of the A'Chir ridge and a look over the top of Beinn Tarsuinn. It was hot. The black peat had dried to a grey ash flecked with shards of quartz. I remember thinking it was like walking on a slope composed of ground kestrel pellets. The heat must have already been taking its effect because also I became fascinated with the idea of stepping into my own shadow, a sort of lead-booted doppelgänger in front of me who controlled my steps. I tried to live with him since he was me.

An orange at the col exorcised the ascent and from then on it was all rock. And big drops – the exposure of the polished moves we found ourselves climbing up made us respect the walkers who down-climb them, doing the traverse from the south. Descending laybacks in boots over big drops for what the guidebook calls 'a 14ft wall' are just not my speciality. But, ascending the difficulties, we were enjoying ourselves, lapping it up over the humps and onto the splendid summit block. Route finding down the other side was delightful for the rock's friction and its forms. Over slabs and under boulders we followed the footmarks of the generations.

It was only when the slope turned upwards that we decided to wander on towards Beinn Tarsuinn, through the stone door, crawl out of a hole and find a final climax to the weekend. It must be difficult anywhere else to find the elemental contrasts of sea and land on all sides, to see so many islands and yet see so well the peaks of the island you're on. From here you can see how Arran itself is an island of contrasts. To the east is that rocky cluster of pointed helmets we'd climbed, sharp and hard as the sound of Viking placenames, and to the south the lower land lies soft as the sound of the Gaelic language.

In fact the culture gives not just names but narratives to places. Ailsa Craig, for example, that looming plug dropped in the sea to the south, is the stepping stone made by Arran's gruagach, the giant

23

fairy who guarded the cattle, when she tried to step across to the mainland after having been offended by the people of Arran. Unfortunately a three masted ship, happening to pass between her legs, spiked her thigh. She lost her balance and drowned. Our stepping stone was to be the ferry, and it left in a couple of hours. We had to step out of this dreamtime, although I think we knew that we carried back a vision from this spot that would last a week or two of work, at least.

The Chasm was supposed to be an anti-climax. For years we'd wanted to climb Ardverikie Wall and finally, on a perfect day, we'd done it. It had been hot on the wall, so hot that we'd actually stripped off afterwards and swum in the loch below. So we found ourselves back in Glencoe fully satisfied, ambitions fulfilled by a glorious day and no idea what to do next. After a day like that I thought the obvious thing to do was to climb a waterfall. It would be drinkable, shaded and uncrowded. From the underworld of memory rose images of a black silhouette bridging under falling water in the depths of The Chasm hidden round the back of Buachaille Etive Mor. Norman wasn't so keen. It sounded like a long grotty gully, but he'd 'go and have a look'.

This was his first mistake. There are two reasons why you can't really 'go and have a look' at The Chasm. The first is that although routes on the Buckle are a step away from the road, it is not a roadside crag. You commit yourself to unseen moves on a mountain. Secondly you cannot guess the way The Chasm will absorb you, draw you in and trap your mind with its succession of choices, alternating with straight-jacketed demands. It plays you down its line like an angler with time on his side.

Then, with nearly 1,500ft of climbing above us, we couldn't get off the ground, couldn't even find the start in fact, caught out right away because we hadn't taken ourselves seriously and didn't really want to get wet. The first pitch goes up the watercourse pouring over the left edge of the house-sized boulder hanging above. To pull over the top you make your a arm a drainpipe. Blooded now, we began the first of several horizontal journeys into the mountain. 'What have you got me into here, Gifford?' started again, so I pointed out the brilliant ferns forking the air above us and thrutched up under another house to step awkwardly out onto the left wall and finally find another Disneyland journey into a grotto of level gravel.

It was a strange rhythm: puzzle a possible route up the right wall, turn to choose the left, thrutch up desperately, walk roped together towards the next waterfalls and prospect the right or left fork. I'd adopted the Wonderland attitude from the start, but Norman, expecting just a scramble up a gully, took a long time to settle to the fact that this was a *Classic Rock* route he couldn't simply flow up. A few recognisable pitches like the unprotected 90ft runout of the Red Slab gradually brought his mental approach in line with The Chasm. In the Hundred Foot pitch I found a shiny protection nut that came out so easily that it told a story of just how the pressure of The Chasm had affected a previous party. If you are expecting your eighth pitch to be Hard Severe it is steep, but enjoyable.

The strain began to tell. Below the Piano Pitch there was a little pool. I realised that I was in need of my only Mars bar, but it was hard forcing the chocolate down a dry throat. The sun had been shafting in on us all day, since this 'dank gully' faced south and also cut out any cooling breezes. Norman remembers looking down to see me sucking at a fly-flecked puddle. Above here the water gave out altogether. The famous Converging Walls pitch of the photographs was only slippery, but desperate, on steep thin holds until a final wide bridging move above the gully required a fall across to one side. The thought of the crashing swing into the back of gully if it didn't work out, focused the mind. An English outcrop mentality of easy gully scrambling had quietly fluttered away well below, so that finally, in the dark of the Devil's Cauldron, we half expected the 4b moves and their peg protection on the South Wall exit from The Chasm's mental grasp. When we reached the sacks in the gully-bed again it was 7.30 p.m. We'd first 'had a look' at 9.30 a.m. Smile only if you haven't yet discovered The Chasm.

After a weekend's climatic vision and an epic day on a mountain I want now to focus on a single evening's climb of less than 200ft on the coast of an island that's a wilderness of eagles and adders. When first I came onto the island as a stranger, I was told to ask at the garage for the climber. Pete and his wife had come on holiday once from Chesterfield and had come back to stay. He immediately took to walking the wild hills and discovering the cliffs, lying in the long heather, miles away from the nearest of his own species but surrounded by other presences. The Gaelic-speaking islanders regarded this as the madness of an English incomer who doesn't appreciate the ubiquitous and traditional dangers from the 'serpents', the adders that have a symbolic reputation in this Biblical culture.

Occasionally Pete persuaded friends to climb with him, but mostly he had soloed round the rockiest bits of coast, always at a modest grade, keeping his own notebook, but not seeking the publication of routes. 'People sometimes come and explore for themselves and go away again,' he says, happy to leave this bit of Scotland like that for others to discover. Not that Pete is sitting on a fabulous Crag X. Most of the rock I've seen over the years is short, scrappy, heavily gripped by green growths and densely populated by birds. But because this, too, is part of the range of experiences available in Undiscovered Scotland I'd like to celebrate a memorable evening on a route of Pete's that he calls Angel Edgeway.

Because it is such an exception, it was a shock to see the clean narrow ramp leaning easily-angled across a compact face, pink with recent rockfall. An eagle had lifted on the sea breeze as we had followed the goat paths across the moor towards the hill. Lousewort bunched its frail flowers underfoot. Some sundews opened their rusty mouths from clumps of sponge. It was a magical evening of pure island sunlight. Andy and I followed Pete down a slope to the top of a boulder-field which fell down to the sea. Half-way down this to the left was the start of the ramp, ribbed by horizontal lines like the roll of a tyre. It looked white, but in the course of the evening as the sun set, it turned orange and finally pink. A scramble for 50ft led to a peg which Pete placed with all the no-nonsense of a Scottish pioneer. The next pitch proved less deeply ribbed by horizontal ledges and the feel of the middle of the face began to grow like the chatter of fulmars below its edge. Pete placed a crucial peg belay below the long unprotected line of the top of the ramp. He climbed it slowly on fine friction at its seaward edge. A peregrine crossed the sky. A squadron of gannets patrolled the sea surface below. And he then sat astride its top edge balanced like a razorbill egg, unlikely on this raw rock.

I found it Hard Severe when I led it the next year, and recently I didn't find it at all because Pete's sea-traverse 'approach' through nesting rubber-necked shags and air filled with auks, took all night. Don't talk to me about magazines full of the latest new routes on Lundy. In Undiscovered Scotland, even on Arran or in Glencoe, you can be so far out nobody knows. At such times you'll see it, as the Master says, 'bright as Paradise'.

Red Slab, Rannoch Wall

I thought we were going up to the Rannoch Wall to do Agag's Groove. As we flogged endlessly up towards the ridges and gullies of the great cone of Buachaille Etive Mor I was savouring the steep line and fine position of a classic V Diff I'd been wanting to do for years. Really we were going to do Red Slab. Tim was psyching himself up silently to leading a serious VS that traverses into and then goes straight up the very centre of Rannoch Wall. That day I felt I could have followed Tim up anything, and this was only our second climbing trip together. After his amazing lead of most of Spartan Slab without a dry streak on it, stepping into little rivulets to find the famous Etive friction footholds, and our abseiling off only after a drenching downpour turned rock into water, I felt he was pretty well unstoppable.

The only problem was that I was tied to the other end. When we got to the top of Agag's Groove, on which the only pause for thought was caused by the looseness of the blocks on the exposed crux, Tim seemed to traverse left a little and began wrenching these other blocks to see how loose they were. I should have known by now that Tim is a man who never walks down from a climb. He called to a party gathering at the bottom.

'Is there a peg still under the overlap in the middle of the wall?'

'No'

'Well do the ropes reach the deck?'

'No'

So Tim set off. I had some slight reservations.

'What are you going to do when you get to Yosemite, Terry?' he said as I was still trying to persuade him not to go over the edge. Who had mentioned Yosemite? It was only Agag's Groove I'd come for.

Well, allowing for stretch and a little jump I suppose you could agree that the ropes had reached the bottom. But however well you've checked everything there is always, finally, the facing up to your faith in this thin strand of hope in the rope down an exposed abseil. And the huge view suddenly becomes a negative factor. When Tim said, 'Red Slab next', he must have known that I was still suffering from shock. I couldn't see any signs of a slab on the Rannoch Wall. Of course, it is a Scottish slab so it doesn't quite get overhanging. Except at the start. Once you've got off the ground and found the rhythm of bridging the steep groove of the first pitch it becomes really absorbing. I remember saying to Tim at the cramped stance, 'If it's all like that I'll love it'.

'Well it isn't', he grinned, 'it's better than that', and disappeared round the corner on to the long quiet loneliness of finding the line and not finding protection that is the experience of the main pitch of Red Slab. The belay behind me was a No. 1 Friend in a flared wet groove. My two additional nuts were psychological, as they say.

'Come low on the traverse.'

'Coming to the crux.'

'Cracked it!'

'This is what I love about climbing!'

Now Tim is a whooper, and not necessarily after a crux. He whoops pretty freely and was doing so now from somewhere high on Rannoch Wall. There was no choice but to get there too.

The start of the traverse right is a ramble which quickly thins to nothing, necessitating upward movement to an overlap. A hand traverse under the overlap leads to a point where you must continue to traverse over it. I could see the tiny square cut foothold to go for in a long stride, but crouched now under the overlap I couldn't find finger pulls. The long reach of exposure down to Rannoch Moor and out beyond began to be less romantic than when, at the top of the abseil I'd quoted Bill Murray on this view to a couple of bemused Brummies: 'Height and distance were a sparkling wine poured to the mind from a rock decanter' (Murray 1979, p. 32). I wished I wasn't so conscious of that height and distance now.

But, once again, in actually making the stride the hands somehow followed, the anatomy still keeping wonderfully together, and able to cross towards a poor runner in a corner. The temptation is to go straight up the corner, but its slightly bulging fierceness can be avoided, if that's the word, by little square edges to the left which lead to the vertical crux wall. It's protected only by a paper-thin peg. It felt steep and calf-quivering. The secret is to keep going and gradually it gets easier, though not easy, enjoyable, though a long way above protection. I felt like becoming a whooper, but it had already been done. And then that gulping great abseil again.

A couple of days later I was sitting at the bottom of a route called appropriately enough, Boomerang, when my raising the subject of Red Slab rather rebounded on me. We were chatting to one of those wizened, immensely fit Full-Time Scottish Instructors.

'Slab!' I said. 'That's a bit of an under-statement.'

'Well', he said, dead seriously, 'I did it when it was a Severe.'

I had thought we had gone to do a classic V Diff and I'd ended up doing this Scottish severe slab and had to abseil down the Rannoch Wall, twice.

How much does it actually cost to get to Yosemite?

Twisting Gully

German chocolate with a white yoghurt centre: hard, creamy and exquisite. One small thing, or rather the two squares of it that Marilyn had just passed me, seemed to tip our sense of delight into the excessive as we fastened our crampons in fierce sunshine on perfect snow in an empty Coire nan Lochan.

It was worth the early start, sitting in the car park watching a full moon blow clear of the black cone of Aonach Dubh as another car pulled in beside us. Its occupants emerged just as we decided the top of the Pass of Glencoe was holding the first light of dawn. We tumbled out too.

They had just driven up from Glasgow and were going for SC Gully, or so they said. Scots who are that keen are capable of anything. So we shot off first to find the bridge where it used to be necessary to do a Bill Murray – wade the river barefoot to step with relief onto the snow on the far bank. ('Circulation was soon restored on the uphill tramp,' Murray assured his disciples.)

Our uphill tramp was a warming pull towards a snowfield backed by blue sky. Yesterday's glissade grooves were this morning's slippery tramlines, making our progress a little like skiing uphill without skis. A small stream in a snowhole provided three delicious mouthfuls of icy water.

The steepening plod brought us suddenly into a bowl of crystal that hardly took the imprint of a boot. Sparkling in sunlight of alpine intensity, it was backed by the dignified broad buttresses that look like they sound: Stob Coire nan Lochan. At the border of sunlight and shadow we stopped and geared up. The yoghurt chocolate seemed an unnecessary treat.

CLEARING A COLD

The slope in shadow above us led up to the promise of Twisting Gully – the gully with a difference. SC Gully cuts a conventional straight cleft, deep between South and Central buttresses – hence its name. Twisting Gully twists its way uncharacteristically up the left of the crag itself.

The original route leaves the gully bed and further twists out of narrow walls to wind across more open ground. All this contortion on the first ascent cleared a heavy cold for Bill Murray, who was, in his own words, 'feeling like death' at the start. As we geared up in the sunlight, drank coffee, ate this amazing chocolate, we couldn't have felt more alive.

Soloing up the steep snow we rounded the left wall and entered the gully, moving up to the point where a twisting spine of rock starts to give it its shape and name. To the right, the tumbling icefall of the gully proper had been hacked into platforms. To the left, vertical rock and ice brought route-finding – the skill of Scotland – into play.

I placed a trusty Moac in the left wall, followed by a smaller one below it for an upward pull, and tied onto them. Marilyn led off to discover the first twisting moves across the left wall above. Bridging to the left she deftly brought her right foot across onto a ramp and stepped round onto the buttress above and out of sight.

'What are the placements like?'

'A bit sugary, but you've got to hang off them. There's a peg here!'

With no more hesitation she ran out a rope length before sending down the usual snowballs to bounce off my helmet. I knew I'd need a good platform at the next stance to get my heels on – my calves were about to be exercised.

I found the foot ramp across the left wall quite generous, but not the ice on the shelf at chest height. Trying to identify ice amongst rock and hacked snow for the first time in two years, was like trying to spot friction holds on limestone after a long layoff. Awkwardly I stepped onto the shelf and crept round left to find a perfect rib of snow dropping away into the bowl and the crowds arriving below.

Above the peg is a high left step, described as 'an awkward mantleshelf' on the assumption this is a mixed rock and ice route, as on the first ascent. With double axes and banked snow, it was just possible to reach the ledge with front points, then up through a gap in rocks to the snow slope where Marilyn stood, smiling, and belayed to a 'dead person' (no sexism in this team).

I gladly edged onto the belay platform and Marilyn crabbed across the right slope towards the rocks at the neck of the final snow fan. Below the rocks she found a platform so perfectly shaped that it demanded to be used.

Since we were having that sort of a day, she popped a big sling round a rock bollard above and rested indulgently at the commodious belay. Taking the odd runner as I passed, I pressed on for the sunlit rim of snow, uncorniced and tempting. As I was placing another trusty Moac in the last rocks of this revered climb, one of the natives came soloing by, all Terradactyls and Andean earflaps.

'Enjoying it?' he enquired, enthusiastically, as my Moac slotted home between rock and ice.

SENSUOUS SUMMITS

Well, all right, I was indulging myself too by placing a probably useless runner in a beautiful secret slot. Up and up, my calves ached now as I broke the crusted snow unnecessarily heavily with my axes. But it has to be said, there's nothing like that final vertical shaft-plunge over the top as you pull onto the level with a yell.

And there was half a day left, with windblown vistas, sparkling snow-slopes, sensuously shaped summits and the rest of the yoghurt chocolate.

So we leaned into the ice-flecked wind and stamped onto the summit of our mountain. From here the conical curve down to the col and the steep slope to the summit of Bidean nam Bian drew us on and into the worst of the wind.

It was a beautiful shape to walk, with small cornices on the left edge. But a hand to the face was needed for breathing and a foot lifted blew right from the knee like a marionette's. Walkers retreated past us from the summit. We crouched into the slopes, unable to stand in the strongest gusts. We passed straight over the top and went down to Bealach Dearg at the head of the Lost Valley.

The wind still staggered us. To descend the Lost Valley we backed over the rim, double-axing and feeling for a foothold, until we were out of the turmoil on a sudden, steep, stillness of snow at the head of the trough. Its great ravine lay before us with the black seam of the stream down its centre. Time took us to its flat floor.

Ambling along I heard someone call out my name. I looked across to a group and there were the sparkling eyes of Julie Calvert and the freckled smile of a woman I had taught in Sheffield when she was 11-years-old. They're delightful, those half embarassing, unexpected meetings in the mountains with ex-pupils who've known you at your best and your worst. How self-assured and full of life they always are.

Julie Calvert sparkled wickedly, knowingly, in the snow of the Lost Valley. The meeting was the taste of yoghurt cream at the end of a day: hard and exquisite.

Marilyn and I wandered off through the trees and boulders, out of the disguised entrance to the Lost Valley as a helicopter flew over our heads. Twisting Gully had given us a day of sheer delight in being alive. Elsewhere, unknown to us, at that moment Marilyn's friend, Adam Gordon, was being carried down to Bridge of Orchy with a fractured skull, his dog lost on the hill until we found it days later.

On our day of bright living, the killer wind took the lives of four people in Scotland, two in the Lakes and two in Wales. All made their judgements for themselves. For us, it had been Twisting Gully on a day with a sad twist in the tale.

Gordon Stainforth in the Cuillin

It was clagged in thick cloud. With hoods up we stepped off the road into the bog that is Skye in February. The rain threatened to turn into snow as we plodded across the rising moor towards goodness knows what for the day. Gordon Stainforth was heading into the hills again to work on his next book, *The Cuillin* (Stainforth 1994). In his 30 lb rucksack was his usual photographic equipment and a duvet. Oh, and a Mars bar. He hadn't room for a flask. No, we couldn't really carry any gear for him, but we could carry flasks if we wanted to. We wanted to rather a lot. If we'd known then that it is possible to stand for two and a half hours mostly not taking photographs on a summit in February we'd have carried a bit more.

So why had Julian Cooper and I driven all this way to be trudging across this uphill bog into the clag with Gordon? Because we knew things would happen. When Stainforth's fired up for photography on the hill it's like looking over the shoulder of Turner in the Alps working fast before the storm actually hits him. Gordon's favourite word for good weather is 'moody'. 'The best climbing days are often bad for photography,' he says. 'They're too hazy. The changeable days are best for filming.'

Well, we were plodding into mist, 'entering the Cuillin by the back door' for the Stainforth promise of 'an incredible shot of the Ridge and 360 degrees of mountains'. Typically meticulous planning from a detailed survey of the topography was taking us to Stainforth's 'inner viewpoint' of Ruadh Stac. As we bent our backs towards this little-trodden knoll a black storm overtook us before we gained the top. Suddenly all was spindrift and follow-my-leader. As we became aware that we were on a summit the snowstorm, just as suddenly, thinned away. The landscape unrolled on all sides and the sun came out. Stainforth had arrived.

Here we stayed for two and a half hours as snowstorm after black snowstorm tried to freeze us or blow us away. Here the patience and receptiveness of the mountain photographer was revealed: the preparedness to wait and the ability to recognize the moment when the defining photograph should be taken. Of the 130 pictures in *The Cuillin* two are from that day's work, taken three minutes apart: one of Sgurr nan Gillean from an unusual location; the other of clearing spindrift and light on the sea loch below us. They are both visions, not just in the dynamic sense of what can be seen from that place at that time by anyone daft enough to hang around that long, but they are Stainforth's paintings from his distinctive planning. 'The image should be fresh, as if never seen before, as a child would see it.' Open to what the elements offer in place and time, Stainforth also adjusts his camera with an inner vision of what these mountains are about: 'the Ridge and the sea'. And his sense of what those simple words mean is informed as much by climbing history and Gaelic culture as by being out there, in among them, 'getting the wobblies' in the words of the book.

On our second day we were setting out into white mist with a film director rather than a painter. Stainforth called this a 'shoot' and the aim was to get a shot that he had designed on his computer after a recce on a bad weather day. Supposedly some people do climb the south ridge of Blaven on its crest, but the shot on page 56 is of two figures who had, according to the Director, been avoiding doing just that. They are actually being shouted at by the Director over the walkie-talkie to stop eating their lunch and get scrambling up those iced-up rocks because the light has just hit them after hours of positioning and waiting.

Stainforth's mountain landscapes are peopled, unlike some, by climbers, fellrunners and suckers like us. Mike Lates, a local fellrunner, is photographed setting off to run the greater traverse of the Ridge, and again on the top of Blaven at the day's end, no picnic for the photographer either. Then, there was Stainforth's bad hassle with the Hasselblad on the famous Bad Step. After waiting all day for someone to cross it, Stainforth had to compose a self-portrait on it, risking his precious Hasselblad above the sea as he set the timer and scrambled down for the shot. This was after four days in the Coruisk Hut cut off by storms and a rising river.

But it was on the Ridge, the main subject of *The Cuillin*, that the loneliness was transposed into something else: 'Savagery, size, exposure, scale' are words that Stainforth spits out with awe and respect as he talks about the making of this book. 'In the end it wears you down,' he says. This book is in the tradition of praise-song for the Cuillin that Stainforth quotes from the Gaelic poet Sorley Maclean. It's also an invaluable resource, containing the most detailed guide to the Ridge published so far. After eight trips from his home in Derby during one year and 150 days on the hill (on 71 of which the Ridge was clear), he has produced an inspirational vision of a book. He doesn't like it being referred to as a book of photographs. The text here is less peppered with quotes, more strongly his own voice ('like a preacher', he admits), and more integrated into the design then the previous books. *The Cuillin* is the result of not just commitment, research, judgement, technique and a Mars bar, but of listening to the mountains with a photographer's ear. Open *The Cuillin* and you'll see what I mean.

The Enigma of Doctor Collie

At a time when we do not yet know the full impact on the sport and on the crags of the full-time commercial rock climbers and their need for sponsors, competitions and publicity, it is worth pausing to consider the case of Norman Collie. As a Victorian young man he was torn between two careers. He might achieve brilliance in both or they might destroy him, literally, since both were more dangerous than he knew. In the days before the motor car his dilemma was made no easier by the fact that one career was to be made in London and the other lay in Skye. Norman Collie's two fascinations were with the two newly developing fields of chemistry and climbing. Although he was appointed Assistant Professor at University College, London when he was only 31, his professor complained at the way 'he bolted when the session was done.' Collie was standing on the summit of Mont Blanc on the day his lab finally isolated the gas argon. The Professor Collie who died at Sligachan in 1942 had actually made major contributions to both of his fields of interest. The facts bear this out. Yet a biography which carefully assembles the facts, fails to get under the skin of that ultimately lonely, enigmatic resident of the Sligachan Hotel.

Christine Mill's (1987) biography is called *Norman Collie: A Life in Two Worlds* (Aberdeen University Press) and counterpoints the discoveries of the climber with those of the chemist. Collie is best known as the leader of the team that first ascended Tower Ridge, but he also played a leading part in the team that first discovered the existence of the noble gases, argon and helium. The Collie who constructed the Collie step in Moss Ghyll — that famous chipped hold which he later came to regret — also constructed the first neon lamp. The man who discovered and photographed the Cuillin's famous Cioch was the man who first saw metal inside the human body by making an X-ray photograph. The climber whose steadiness, bridged between an icicle and one wall of Great Gully in the Wasdale Screes, enabled the boots of another to climb on to his shoulders and out to the top, was the man who was famous in his London labs for the discovery of what was known as 'the Collywobble' — a three-dimensional model of the formula for benzene.

Collie took part in most of the areas of mountaineering exploration of his time. In 1889 he opened his long career with the first ascent of Am Basteir in the company of the local gillie who became his closest friend, John Mackenzie, reputedly Britain's first rock-climbing guide. In their seventies the two men were said to sit for hours in silence together, satisfied simply with each other's company. In the Alps Collie climbed and named the Dent du Requin. Climbing with Mummery on the first traverse of the Aiguille des Grepon Collie carried two large stones for the purpose of lassoing the summit spike and ensuring that it was officially surmounted. In 1895 he climbed with Mummery on the Diamirai Peak of Nanga Parbat. After Mummery's disappearance whilst taking an alternative pass to join Collie for an attack on the north side of Nanga Parbat itself, Collie revealed that, although an impressive ice-climber 'Mummery was not a good mountaineer. Now Slingsby was a magnificent mountaineer.'

The abilities of being able to judge not only the best and safest way up a mountain but also 'knowing when to turn back' were Collie's definition of a good mountaineer and were, in fact, the abilities Collie himself possessed. For two summers he combined his own qualities with Slingsby's to climb a dozen new routes on the Lofoten Islands of Norway. Collie's mountaineering discipline was undoubtedly based on his scientific approach to the mountains themselves. Maps, even of Skye, in the 19th century were rudimentary. Wherever he went, Collie undertook survey work and early in both his careers he designed his own portable mercurial barometer with which he proved that the highest point of the Cuillin was Sgurr Alasdair and not the Innaccessible Pinnacle as was thought at the time. It was in the Canadian Rockies that Collie made his greatest contribution to mapping and climbing unnamed peaks with unknown approaches through dense, mosquito infested bush. He was the first person to see whole glacier systems such as the Columbia ice-field, and in 1902 joined forces with his rival, the Reverend James Outram, to climb the beautiful and much-coveted Mt Forbes (11,852ft).

At one camp on this latter trip Collie was seen mumbling to himself and pacing about with a compass until he finally dug up a bottle of whisky and a bottle of brandy he'd buried there five years before. Such a meticulous and secretive man might well find a factual biography entirely appropriate to himself. But what of the Collie who told the tale of his being followed by the Big Grey Man of Ben Macdui, who ran 'with an intolerable fright' away from the footsteps that threatened to come right up to him on the summit? 'No power on earth', Collie said in all seriousness, 'will ever take me up Ben Macdui again.' Was Collie frightened by his own imagination? He would actually have rejected this psychological explanation. He was a collector of Chinese jade and of books on alchemy and the mystical. He believed not only in the Loch Ness Monster, but in the spirit of each mountain, to whom he and Mackenzie would pay silent homage after a first ascent to a summit. 'A wanderer's dreams are happy dreams,' he wrote. 'He should sacrifice often at the shrines of the Gods of the Wilds, for they are pleasing Gods when they whisper to one in the dusk.'

If he was fascinated by the mystical he was not beyond parodying it, at least earlier in his life. To the editor of the *Scottish Mountaineering Club Journal* he described his write up of the Tower Ridge first ascent as 'a pseudo Rabelaisian alchemistic attempt.' It is entitled 'On the Divine Mysteries of the Oromaniacal Quest' and the final section, in which Collie refers to the inhabitants of the Ben Nevis Observatory coming out to offer the climbers a cup of tea and a draw, gives a flavour of the style:

'So at last they came even unto the very topmost Point, and were aware how that Priests from the heavenly Temple, which is placed on the top of that mountain, had come forth to guide them, to the gates of the Temple itself... Then did they drink the mixed draught, the comfortable potation, joyously, philosophically and with discernment, for they had at last attained to the divine Secrets of the Philosophers, even unto the mystagorical Delight, the great Fulfillment of the Spagyrick Quest of devout Oromaniacs.'

But at the same time the editor of the *SMC Journal* received writing of a rather different kind in a private letter from W. W. Naismith.

'The Sassanachs have indeed taken the wind out of our sails maist notoriously I wull say that if their bit hillocks could be detected with the naked eye we might still get Gibson to pull himself together and astonish them on their own ground. Couldn't he do the Houses of Parliament by the Clock Tower or a traverse of Beachy Head?'

There are, it seems to me, two aspects of the enigma of Norman Collie that have a strikingly modern relevance to the SMC. The first concerns the fact that until 1989, the year of its centenary, the club still maintained its ban on women members. In 2003 there are still only ten women members of the 440 total. Collie preferred to remain unmarried, but certainly climbed with women as many of the photographs, some of them previously unpublished, in Christine Mill's book show. On a trip to Norway in 1901 he went out of his way to meet up with the President of the Ladies' Alpine Club and her husband. Collie may have been a bachelor but he appears not to have been a misogynist, and it is doubtful, on the evidence here, if he would be objecting to female members in the 1989 vote to admit women that was passed, according to one member present, 'by a hair's breadth majority'.

The second point re-enforces the SMC policy of leaving some areas of Scotland out of their guidebook plans for others to discover for themselves in wilderness climbing. Collie objected to describing new lines 'like railway timetables' and was particularly enigmatic about his climbs on Skye. Listening to plans made in the Sligachan Hotel, Collie would chuckle to himself and mumble, 'They'll find a little cairn there – when they get up.' It's a pity that the SMC, in a desire to sell its journal, includes there details of all new routes in Scotland despite their leaving some areas unrecorded (for wilderness climbers) in their guidebooks.

Of course, we can only guess at what Collie would have said on these issues. In his last years, visiting climbers found it hard to get much out of him. Perhaps on some occasions he was reflecting on those dangers he'd underestimated in his two careers. He certainly improved his belaying technique, holding a dramatic fall on an ice slope on Diamirai Peak. He may have reflected on why his old professor had died of cancer of the nose after a lifetime's work on radium. Sometimes his gaze out of the window from what was known as 'Collie's Corner' in the Sligachan would be interrupted. On one pouring morning two ladies tried to penetrate his thoughts with the question 'Oh, Doctor, what kind of a day will it be?' The silent gaze continued. When they repeated the question Collie continued to stare out of the window, but said, with perhaps not unkindly advice, 'Can't you use your eyes?

Fionn Buttress (by Jim Curran)

Surrounded by mountains and high above the rushing river, I'm completely out of control, utterly useless, a gibbering wreck. Help – press the panic button. Full Red Alert – I'm definitely going to fall off – no I'm not – oh yes you are – get a grip – concentrate – you're going to kill yourself.

It was, in my defence, my first cycle ride in over 30 years, and this was on an overloaded mountain bike wearing a heavy rucksack and big boots. Luckily for me, after only two miles of uncontrolled panic, contrasted with fits of giggles and what felt like a pile driver up my nether regions, the deer fence of the Letterewe Estate abruptly foiled further progress/damage. 'No bicycles whatsoever' proclaimed the sign on the gate, amongst a long list of other prohibitions. Feigning aggrieved frustration I slung the bike in a gorse bush next to Terry Gifford's, who locked them up. Nine miles of walking beckoned. I doubted that we would ever see the bikes again and wasn't sure if I was sorry or not.

It had been Terry's idea for Whit weekend. 'Fionn Buttress', he had enthused. 'Bike in, do the route, bike out, completely painless and the best VS in Scotland.' I agreed to go, with the proviso that we had a 'no poetry' embargo on the whole weekend. 'No rhyming couplets' I insisted, before remembering that none of Terry's poems rhymed anyway.

> Fionn freedom
> comes from a journey not a fight,
> steady patience,
> savouring acceptance
> of the ever-wet, the elusive distance,
> the commitments of flesh to place:
>
> Wester Ross
> Poolewe
> Carnmore Crag
> Fionn Buttress

bikes, boots
big sacks
plasters
bothy, tent

So it was that two footsore and weary old men reached the halfway point and breasted the gentle rise that concealed the longed-for view of Fionn Loch and Carnmore Crag. I had been here once before many years ago, and was suitably shamefaced when Terry pointed out that we had been staring at our objective for the last hour or so.

As we slowly gained the end of Loch Fionn, Carnmore Crag took on the ferocious aspect familiar from many photos, with its huge roof of Gob and the Cenotaph-like walls of Carnmore Corner high above. On the left side of the crag Fionn Buttress looked long and wonderful, nine pitches of sustained and intricate 4b/4c climbing. What's more, the weather was perfect and seemed like staying that way for ever. What more could we ask for? Not having blisters, burrowing sheep ticks, and great rucksacks sprang instantly to mind as we plodded over the causeway and round to the bothy below the crag, passing several more notices reminding us that we were in a wilderness area.

It was indeed a wilderness. Surrounding Carnmore Lodge were rusting oil drums and wheelbarrows, sheets of corrugated iron, cement bags and broken barbed wire fences. They contrasted incongruously with orders not to camp and respect the countryside. Sighing yet again at man's seemingly complete inability to recognize his own folly, we settled down to a late afternoon of eating, brewing and crag watching. The sun sank slowly, lighting the buttresses of Beinn Lair and the endless vistas of more mountains and lochs stretching away to the west.

In late May we were spared the ravages of midges (though not the aforementioned sheep ticks) and the necessity of an early start. Carnmore faces southwest and doesn't get the sun until mid morning, which then stays on it until late in the evening. So we actually had to restrain ourselves from leaving the bothy until 10.30, and walk gently up to the narrow path skirting the great sweep of slabs and overhangs above. We deliberately decided to take it slowly, savouring every move of each pitch.

I had waited 20 years for this route, and wanted to perform the ritualistic celebration of fluid movement, to become part of the crag, to lose myself in its rough embrace – oh my God what am I writing? Surely just being on a climb with Terry doesn't mean I catch the creative writing bug. I'll be signing on for one of his courses next, or writing about sphagnum moss and dead rowan trees. What I meant to say was I started up the first pitch (phew, that's better).

It wasn't particularly distinguished and the next, which was Terry's, was even less so. It led to the foot of a short pedestal leaning against an immaculate slab of pale grey gneiss (that's granite to you and me). The pitch could have been specially designed to the specifications of a fully paid up member of the Byron Slab Climbing Club (BSCC), a title originally coined by Steve Bancroft to describe that august body of elders and obese gentlemen who frequent the hostelry of that name in Sheffield, and who all share the common ability to perform as adequately on rock the right side of vertical as they do the opposite when on the wrong side (do I make myself clear?) The slab in front of me was supplied with perfect and unexpected letter box shaped slots that led to a final steepening and a few committing moves to the sanctuary of a good ledge and belay.

Ego suitably boosted, I dismissively waved Terry through to cope with the next pitch which led to the crux. He took his time, not, I soon came to realize, because he was battling with the desire to knock off a couple of stanzas before lunch, but because it was wet, hard and badly protected.

limestone letter boxes
reward a blind reach,
Etive edges
enlighten a long stare,
wet pocket
dry pocket
wet pocket
slap and step
The Overhang

Thankfully the crux, which now loomed above looked dry and well protected. We took stock and sorted out the gear.

Now Terry is methodical and racks his gear in order of size, purpose and stage. I suppose all climbers do nowadays. It gave him the look of a man in complete control. That is to say it would have, were it not for the fact that such meticulous attention to detail was offset by his attire, which consisted mainly of an ancient helmet and a similarly vintage pair of underpants, Terry having left his shorts in the bothy. Consequently by the end of a long day the negative image of his harness was stencilled around his upper legs, set off by a large acreage of rather fetching lobster-pink sunburn. A sight of sore thighs, you might say.

Unable to put off the moment any longer and encouraged by Terry's supporting presence, I left the belay and sidled unobtrusively across to the big overhangs hoping they wouldn't notice me. The route sneaks through at the narrowest point, which seemed to bristle with big juggy flakes. Surely even a member of the BSCC could manage it? Well yes, and no. After a modicum of nervous teetering and some complex conjugglements of rope and runners I realised that 'if the deed were to be done twere best done quickly.' Feet up high, undercut jam and reach the first flake, great, now a big heave, get your feet up higher – reach with your right – aagh, it isn't a jug – too late now – pinch it and get your right foot up – judder, shake, done it, quick get a runner in. 'Piece of piss actually'. Out came the ritual cliché.

After a few more easy moves up and round a little corner I reached the perfect post-crux belay, braced on bombproof large nuts and a Friend, while perched on a sloping slab and looking down into a quite respectable void. Terry made short work of it and then set off on what appeared to be a mind-blowing traverse. It was inexplicably ungraded given its wild situation. Luckily it wasn't desperate but it did involve two long steps across and down, a classic second's nightmare. Thankfully Terry put on runners after, as well as before, the bad bits, so that I didn't burst into tears once.

On the approach to Carnmore Crag from Poolewe. The Letterewe Accord allows bikes to go where vehicles can go, so we would now lift our bikes over this fence. Photo: a passing Dutchman.

Opposite page: Jim Curran on Fionn Buttress, Carnmore Crag, Scotland.

'You have to want it'

this move
this route
this place

traverse the wilderness
step across the wild space
on gneiss holds
to the soaring alternatives:
slab, wall, arete
and somewhere a step left'

I joined him perched on the very edge of the buttress. Above was a vertical groove and some very grown-up looking country indeed. 'I thought we'd done the hard bits'. Nervous and slightly weary, I found leaving the ledge both awkward and strenuous. Then perhaps as a result of the heat, euphoria and fright I failed to make sense of the route description, and went very wrong indeed.

Lured by a beautiful pale grey crozzly (crossed by cracks and rough lines) slab I climbed to its tapering crest and came hard up under a vertical wall topped by an overhang. I should have hand-traversed left about 30ft below, but unfortunately the guidebook still made some sort of sense. To my right was a huge nest, surely belonging to a pterodactyl. Luckily the owner wasn't at home. Straight up was out of the question which left the vertical wall and arête to my left. Gulp. A good small Friend in a horizontal break gave me a bit of Dutch courage and I hauled up on to the first flat holds, stood up and just managed to reach the arête with my left hand.

Now I am 49 going on 50 and it crossed my mind quite forcibly that heel-hooking with my left foot was an absurd and poseurish thing to do at my age, like going to an acid house party, wearing an ear-ring, or trying to grow a ponytail. But if I didn't do something p. d. q. I would be off, and I am certainly far too old to entertain even the thought of a leader fall. I wasn't entirely convinced that heel-hooking wouldn't simply make airtime a certainty, but it was all I could think of doing. 'Watch the ropes' I squeaked down to Terry, by now so far below that it didn't much matter what he did. By pressing with my right hand, piano playing my left up the arête and pawing ineffectually round the corner with my heel, calf and anything else, I lurched upwards and at full stretch grabbed a superb incut slot with my right hand. Dry mouthed with terror, I peeped round the arête. Joy of joys, big holds appeared only just out of reach. Rather neatly, I thought, but from Terry's vantage point in blind panic, I tiptoed across a steep lichenous slab and grabbed the jugs. As I did so a rope jammed solid. Give us a break – I wrenched furiously, to no avail. At full reach I could just place a comforting Friend 3, clip the other rope and tension back down. Ironically the rope had jammed in the life saving incut slot. Relief swept over me as I freed it and hauled back to big holds, ledges, easy angles and bombproof belays.

Terry came up quickly, cold and stiff from his windy vigil below. I was pleased he slowed down for the last bit, but maybe he was just trying to please me. Poets can sometimes be like that. As all his other pitches had been ungraded and mildly desperate, we hoped that the next pitch, given 4b, would be much easier and so it was apart from a curious pull up on colossal blocks apparently completely detached, around which Terry threaded slings presumably to act as extra ballast to his not exactly petite self should he and the blocks part company. After that a short juggy wall, then my turn again. The last pitch up really easy ground, slabs, a little traverse, a last wall and suddenly – hey, no more crag.

Bemused, I pulled over into a horizontal world, full of great bubbling joy at the best route of its grade I'd ever done. In the cloudless late afternoon Terry emerged rapturous. I could have forgiven him if he had addressed me in blank verse in Latin at that moment, but even he was lost for words. (That didn't last long.)

rising wind
drooping sun
white slab
rising wall
flat grass, suddenly,
and the best walk off in the world
complete with drinking drip

the best dram in the world
is backs to the bothy wall now
feet in mud, bums on 'sacks
sun setting sideways
and Fionn Loch winking back

first light through tent skin
snipe drumming and drumming
greenshank shrilling up from the bog

and the walk out
past sparkling wind-scoured water
over the narrow causeway

cairned at each end by cement
and a metal sign declaring:

No camping
No litter
No fire anywhere

Walkers keep to footpaths

No mountain bikes
No fishing
No vehicles except on estate business

Please help us preserve
this precious wilderness

To put icing on the cake, the way down was simplicity itself. We skirted the base of the crag to our 'sacks and watched tiny figures high above us whose voices we had occasionally heard during the day. They were actually doing the pitch after the traverse the right way. But now it didn't matter, nothing mattered. In a trance I strolled down to the bothy lost in my dreams. Blisters, sheep ticks and big rucksacks, the rest of my life, could all wait until tomorrow.

PS. Well I'm dashed. He's smuggled the poem in anyway. Next time I'll do the frilly bits and he can do the writing. And I'll try and make it rhyme.

Back to Bienn Eighe

You know what they say about how good it is to retreat with dignity and all your limbs intact? Well, it isn't exactly true. Your head stays damaged a little, especially if you haven't even set foot on the route – and Central Buttress is clearly the route on the majestic Triple Buttresses of Bienn Eighe. These north-facing buttresses rise for over 1,000ft above the chill mirror of Loch Coire Mhic Fhearchair. You see them suddenly as you climb over the lip of the corrie. A beetling base of 300ft of red sandstone guards access to the soaring quartzite crests that are calling out to be climbed.

When I first saw that magnificent mountain last year, after a walk of only one hour fifty minutes from the car, I knew I had plenty of time to study its stark, complex beauty. We were carrying camping as well as climbing gear and we settled in on a knoll that projected into the loch. There had been a long dry spell and the sky was still clear so Julian and I answered the call of the triple goddess, first finding the best scramble to the long ledge where, way above the loch and some steep rock already, things actually began. Or should have.

We found the start of Readymix, a recommended route up the sandstone. It is vertical, rounded and obviously has complex route-finding. Suddenly we were cream-crackered from carrying all that gear. So, thinking we might prefer to savour it next day (you know how the argument goes) in less of a rush, we passed along the ledge to the wet chimney start of Howett's (1990) version of Eastern Buttress. The new guide says it 'has been climbed in summer (Very Difficult), but is wet and loose'. Since neither of us could get off the ground past a dripping bulge of loose chockstones, we passed along the ledge again until the angle eased back and we could at last make upward progress, with some delicate moves, through the sandstone tier to the green band that marks the change to quartzite and sharp, positive holds.

At the far right end of the grassy band we launched up a white slab inset into the grey quartz. For 700ft we led through on slightly too easy, slightly too ledgy Diff rock that suddenly levelled out on to the top of the mountain. Honour was restored for the retelling, but not really fulfilled for the frank remembering. Down on the bold lines of the Far East Wall a different class of deeds were being done by several teams in the evening sun. We watched with vicarious exhilaration as a leader pulled through the overhangs on the brilliantly named Ling Dynasty at E5 6b. (In 1899 Lawson, Ling and Glover did the first route on the mountain.) Finally from the summit cairn we drank in a landscape of sea lochs cutting into the mountains of Wester Ross.

While the hot Scots did their impressive Far East climbing on Beinn Eighe far into the last of the light, I cooked a curry and Julian worked at his sketchbook. Julian Cooper had made the crag drawings in 1972 for the Turnbulls' (1973) guidebook and he now wanted to make a large oil painting from these new sketches. He was really into it: 'It's not just the forms that convey the power of these buttresses,' he was enthusing, 'it's the violence of twisting that's gone into the making of the rock itself.' We glanced back at deer silhouetted on the lip of the corrie against a red sunset out beyond Skye. Then, magically, the Triple Buttresses were lit by an orange afterglow that was slowly cut away by the shadow of seaward mountains creeping across the great buttresses one by one, closing them down. This is why you carry camping gear.

In the morning a single cloud drifted across the face, drizzle turned to Scottish rain and suddenly the triple goddess had disappeared before our eyes. This is not why you carry camping gear downhill, although limbs may be intact.

Exactly one year later, after another long dry spell in May, Julian and I were heading back to Bienn Eighe, this time without a tent. Snowfields below the crag, as well as in the gullies, gave the north facing buttresses even more drama as they reflected in the sparkling loch. We hid rucksacks under a boulder and racked up in the warm sunshine. Walking up the edge of the snow disorientated me and I traversed off too early on a lower grass ledge. Julian found the right scramble. Suddenly a chirpy female voice came up to us: 'Are you going for the classic Severe?' A woman and two men were hot on our heels. A breathless 'Yes!' and we were on the correct ledge moving along to where we knew the exact start to be. They scrambled up directly below the start and we arrived only seconds ahead of them. All we had to do was uncoil ropes, change boots and the lead was ours. But something in the friendly banter at the start of this epic climb, and the chortles of anticipation of the young woman gearing up for the lead, made me do the unthinkable: 'Do you want to go ahead of us?' They could not believe their luck.

'Oh well, if you're sure,' she said. 'We were going to have seconds climbing together anyway. Thanks.'

'The sun comes on to the last pitches in the evening,' I confessed, with a pretence of smugness. Actually I was relieved not to have the three of them snapping at our heels.

The young woman swung off the terrace on to the steep red rock with impressive speed. At 30ft she was stopped by an awkward corner, put gear in and followed suggestions from below to step blindly left. It looked delicate. When I came to do it, I demurred at the smooth sloping surface for the hands and instead pulled, slightly desperately, up the wall of the corner. The rest of the pitch just flowed for her, punctuated by occasional giggles of delight: The Craggiggler. We knew we were on route thanks to The Craggiggler ahead of us throughout the day.

When the rope came tight a young greyhound raced upwards, with his friend literally on his heels, making it obvious that we would have held them back. I found this pitch intimidating. The right leaning crack-line, which the corner gives access to, has rounded jugs on a vertical to overhanging wall. Some steep bridging, and an ability to look round the corner, finally got me to the exposed belay ledge. As I was tensioning two tiny nuts against each other The Craggiggler climbed over me with a wicked giggle, I'm not sure at what exactly.

Julian was so impressed by the first pitch that he offered me the next lead too. The quality of this route will be hinted at by the following words: 'step down from here and make an exposed traverse right.' The feeling that, in fact, this was not too difficult, was just the opening of a trap to be sprung in two stages. At the end of the traverse the route goes back left across a broad ledge that is low enough to make you think you can step across to it using the pocket in front of you. I couldn't do it. The obvious holds were all in the wrong places to fit together for the move. In the end, with a deep breath, I leaned down, got two hands on the edge of the ledge and swung myself below it. Once committed to the mantelshelf straight up, it all fell into place but at the far end of this shelf I was stopped again. Another long step left seemed to be required, above a gaping drop. Fine if there's something to pull across on. As I tried to escape this second trap a voice came down: 'You're going to love this classic layback.' Everyone was enjoying this climb and I wanted to too, if only I could climb it. Once again a commitment to one of the options was ultimately rewarded with holds and the layback was indeed delightful because it was unusually positive for this subtle sandstone. A third pitch of cracks and walls led into the final few feet of a chossy (loose rock, mud and scree) chimney that indicates what Piggott's Route, coming up from the right, is really like. Readymix requires a readiness for a mixture of everything.

As I was on the second stance I had noticed a single climber scrambling up the base of the cliff. From above my head The Craggiggler shouted down: 'Come for a climb, John.' Whilst Julian was joining me on the green band at the top of the sandstone strata, a soloist climbed up beside him. When we wandered across to the start of the quartz arête he was roping up in order to partner The Craggiggler. It was John Chadwick, whom I knew from the Climbers' Club, joining his friends who were apparently from the Cleveland Mountaineering Club.

As we were chatting, Julian pointed out a curtain of rain charging towards us. The forecast had been for 'fair-weather cloud' all day. Well, here it came, suddenly drenching everything with Bienn Eighe's form of fair-weather cloud. John set off up rock running with water. I considered waiting for the shower to pass (it did not pass), retreat (hard snow filled the gullies at each end of this terrace), and the steep, wet way upwards which was now slowing down even the fast four with what seemed to be technical difficulty.

'We don't think this is Severe,' came from the upper pair, now in the mist. Julian urged me upwards and once again, of course, it wasn't too bad, mainly because the rock is brilliantly flat, sharp and more solid than it looks. However the next pitch, straight up, was definitely causing problems, so I looked round the corner (the key, I was learning, to Scottish route-finding) and found a slab I could romp up. Julian quickly joined me. Feeling better, if wetter by now, I launched straight up the wall above, only to be stopped again. I backed off and went walkabout along the terrace to the left. At its end there was a Friend stuck solid in a horizontal crack. This omen of desperate retreat, my sodden condition, the mist and its echoing raven, the crux still to come, together with the uncertainty of our outcome in this lengthening day, sapped my spirit. My thoughts on stances had been wandering towards a possible cornice and then the problem of finding the descent gully in the mist. We were going to be lucky to get out of this. Then suddenly there was a horrendous rockfall in the gully to our right. It rang with that eerie presence of the forces of destruction out of control right beside you. We hoped all was well above. At this point Julian produced his secret weapon. He unclipped his Ziggy bottle and offered me a drink. It was the best whisky I had ever tasted.

Then, miraculously, a little more looking revealed an easy line breaking back right towards where the final tower should be. Sure enough, a giggle echoed down to me and I could just make out a figure through the mist, hunched in the bottom of a chimney like a gnome. After checking that the rockfall had not touched them, I took some advice on the line of this crux pitch at the base of the tower. From the right I climbed on top of a huge detached flake. The crux is stepping off it. Hidden to the right I found a fist jamming crack. Getting into it, with feet in the right order, was awkward, but after that everything came to the right hand in particular, if it felt round the corner.

I'll look forward to actually doing this pitch in the evening sunshine one day, and the further 220ft of amazing chimney climbing that follows. Out on the top Julian pointed out that, a year later, the mountain had tricked us into having to climb it in the rain anyway.

The next wet day we went down to Loch Maree's Tollie Crags to see if any climbing was possible before the drive home. Walking out of the trees towards us was The Craggiggler and one of the two lads.

'Weren't they great conditions to do that route in?' she enthused. Well, I had not thought of it like that. It was still too much of an epic in my head. As the rain came on again, Julian and I decided to take the road home, but that clinking through the trees was the Giggler, off to lighten up another wet crag.

Thanks, Joanna Newton. Yes, they were great conditions and I hope you're there next time I'm quietly having an epic in them.

Wisdom Buttress

In the bright evening light at Carnmore bothy climbers relax after a day on the bold famous routes above them – Fionn Buttress, Cob and Dragon – Scottish VS and HVS every inch of the way. But as they lean back against the bothy wall they see the dying sun catch the majestic architecture of Beinn Lair's north face across the other side of Fionn Loch. They half wish they could allow themselves the further uphill walk for the lowly grade of Wisdom Buttress, the most remote quality V Diff in Britain. The upper arête of this narrow tooth glows in the sun as the yearning is displaced to another trip, and recedes even further at the thought of a 14 mile walk in for a V Diff.

I was that climber four years ago when Jim Curran and I, gloating after getting up Fionn Buttress, promised ourselves Wisdom Buttress 'next year'. Well, that didn't happen and yesterday I was 'unfaithful' as Jim quaintly anticipated. Today I am lying in the heather under Wisdom Buttress gloating again. Actually I am snuggled in a bivvy bag (it is Whitsun, but this is Scotland) beside a roaring stove, doing my bit as support team for the second project of this trip – the north face of Beinn Lair is having its portrait painted. Somewhere over the rise further back from the crag Julian Cooper has a huge canvas pegged to a peat bank, bulldog clipped to the alloy frame he carried in a ski bag round his neck. In it, along with the roll of canvas, he also carried his secret weapons – metre long brushes that could only be acquired by a special Channel Tunnel trip to Paris. You can see that for him the climb is only another kind of preparation for the real thing, which he is working at now. I'm not supposed to look while he's painting, so I'll tell you about Wisdom Buttress in between the spitting mists that drift over these craggy teeth like bad breath, slightly smudging these words. He's working in oils, so he's not worried.

First of all, getting here. You don't have to walk in all of those 14 miles. We now have the Letterewe Accord negotiated for us with the Letterewe Estate. 'Mountain bikes are only allowed on vehicle tracks.' So you can ignore the sign on the gate, lift your bike over it, and take at least two and a half miles off the walk. It's on the way out you appreciate it most, as you free-wheel back to Poolewe. This time I left my bike hidden in the heather beyond the farm. The other good news is the new keeper, who has moved up recently from Wensleydale. He actually suggested I left it even further on, in the larch trees. (Julian had declined to use the bike I'd borrowed for him after a little trial ride the evening before had left him in a ditch with a scarred face and, even worse, a bruised painting arm.) Unfortunately, tyre tracks in the moor on our walk in showed that some people cannot accept a reasonable compromise patiently negotiated on their behalf. I wish we'd met them. But there's another way to reduce the walk in to Beinn Lair. Past our camp (yes 'low impact' camping is now accepted under the Letterewe Accord) there walked a lone Scottish weekender who had walked from Kinlochewe to Letterewe House above the north shore of Loch Maree and in, through a good track over Bealach Mheinnidh. This must be most pleasant approach and is only 10 miles.

I keep having to retreat inside this bivvy bag and zip the showers out. But I've got a whole day to write with the crag right in front of me. The climb itself is a masterpiece of route finding up this narrow soaring buttress of interlocking slabs and overhangs. It feels intimidating because in its 700ft there always seems to be an overhang above you. But the incut horizontal strata of the hornblende schist gives constant encouragement against the equally constant exposure. Right from the start there's also an overhang below. That's assuming you can find the start. So you're into Scottish route finding before you leave the ground, with a distinctly tight-lipped description from the guidebook, (Howett 1990).

I made two attempts to traverse the steep gully wall on to the undercut buttress, but I couldn't even get started: 'This isn't V Diff,' I kept saying, and 'this can't be right,' as I moved further up the gully. I was about 30ft above the chockstone in the gully before I found a traverse line left that was anything like V Diff. I see from the *Climbers' Club Journal* that Hamish Nicol approached Wisdom Buttress as 'a VS Scottish V Diff' and just accepted that the start was an overhanging finger traverse on rounded holds that I'd rejected.

My down-sloping footholds and series of sidepulls higher up gave entry to a huge slab of incut strata and a nut belay that was not to be missed. This route's reputation as having poor belays and little protection had sunk in and so did my old Moac. A rising gale threatened to rip us from the stance. I raced on now, anxious to make up for lost time. The cruise leftwards up the slab ran out a rope length in which only two runners were possible, but a belay appeared at the right moment. Then the rain struck.

'Are we committed, now, to doing this in the rain?' asked Julian, remembering last year's epic ascent of the Central Buttress of Beinn Eighe when the upper tier was awash and the outcome slightly uncertain.

'It does say the rock gets greasy in rain,' he added, anorak flapping in the wind.

'If we can find a route at V Diff we can do it in the rain.' I said. I was motoring on these holds that were hidden from below because they dipped so delightfully inwards.

'The rock is certainly absorbing the rain,' Julian observed, as the amalgam grey of the Wisdom tooth turned black before our eyes. Julian recognised that our luck was repeating itself as, after a fortnight of dry weather, just when it broke we were committed on a big route again. This was not a place to slip on greasy rock. Although runners did, in fact, appear before every crux, people pass beneath this crag rarely and getting a rescue team here would take a day. I looked up. I'd belayed below a small overhang on the left edge of the buttress. This was the natural place to end up since the ground to the right steepened considerably. From our little platform we looked out through the rain upon acres of unpeopled emptiness. This is the fabled Last Great Wilderness of mainland Scotland into which we'd come all this way to climb.

So I pushed on up, turning the overhang on its right (good nut here) and gaining entry to a smaller slab. As I pressed on the rain stopped, rewarding the climbing spirit. I was gaining Wisdom, slowly. Another steep step right was rewarded with a final slab capped by overhangs. I followed a weakness on its left and stopped on a ledge, feeling the need to regroup. Thank goodness I'd not been tempted to lighten my load for the walk in. A crack by my knee whispered 'my old Moac nut'. It was more than friendship it wanted. It was love at first sight. I turned away. Now I could relax.

Julian has just come over for a cup-a-soup lunch and the painting is going well apparently. Now that he's returned to work I'll tell you about this key section of the route. I was 20ft below the roof and a traverse line out right seemed possible. I called down to Julian as he was climbing to ask if he had a big overhang to his right. I sensed that this might be the crucial place to cut right between overhangs. It was. The traverse out to the edge was sheer joy. I even got a runner in early on. Side pulls and a toe ramp led up to the edge. A look round the arête was disheartening. More overhangs. But a delicate step across to small platform above the void was again rewarded with a comfortingly solid block belay. I called round the arête to Julian: 'You've got to be bighearted to get up these Scottish crags. I can't believe there's a way through above here at V Diff.'

But when it came to it, of course there was. The overhang was turned on the right once again by steep pulls on great holds on its right wall. I cut back left on to the very nose of the buttress where exposed climbing led to a huge unexpected sloping platform. Here I persuaded Julian to take the lead, not realising that this was the crux pitch. He barely paused to put in gear under another small overhang before swinging leftwards under it and romping up the crest of the ridge to which the buttress had now narrowed.

As I came up to him I looked past him and exclaimed: 'Yet another feature. This route is amazing.' The guidebook's casual 'Continue up the crest of the buttress' suggested a scramble, but here was more steep rock. The incuts kept a-coming and the position was the closest you'd get to an eagle's view, soaring over the wilderness. Heathery blocks led to the top, which could be the only reason for giving this route two stars. But that's the last memory and not typical of the route as a whole, which provides all the holds. It just keeps you guessing as to where they go.

The rain is setting in again. Can't write any more. I'm going over to look at that painting.

That Painting
took 3 days, 6 Vesta meals and a 28 mile walk
to make.
It was in black and white (and grey): lead white,
storm black,
on a 6ft by 5ft primed canvas on an alloy frame,
bulldog clipped,
carried on a rucksack rolled up with brushes in a

ski bag.
Two litres of turps sloshed about in the rucksack with
light pegs
for anchoring the whole sail on a heather bank
a butt,
under the most majestic, neglected, inaccessible crag
in Scotland:
the north-east face of Beinn Lair. Hornblende schist
gleams grey,
bristling its beautiful forms: Butterfly Buttress,
The Tooth.
We climbed Wisdom Buttress in the spitting teeth of
a gale,
the artist's fingers feeling their way up the earth's
hard core
a long way from rescue, a pint, a car, all other oil
painters.
Back up next day at 11, position chosen, charcoal
outline
in the frame, a wild mile of rock reduced to its
incisors.
The painter does not think of commitment courage,
the risk
of failure on a large scale in big mountains
for out
which the later sunset down Fionn Loch would not
pay for,
nor the evening rainbows above the tent and Dubh Loch
because
at 3 o'clock in a deluge that painting was washed
away.

Julian Cooper: Hands of a Painter

Two days after the mountain painter Julian Cooper arrived at his Base Camp in Peru, a runner arrived with the news that his father, William Heaton Cooper had died. It was the end of an era. The kindly painter whose prints softly glow from the walls of urban Lake District lovers throughout the world (I last saw one in a home in Salt Lake City) and from whose crag drawings a generation of climbers had learned to read the crags of the Lakes, was being laid to rest in Grasmere churchyard at the very moment when his son was beginning a new phase in his own work. Ironically, William had missed the funeral of his father Alfred. On Julian's departure for his first visit to the Andes, he knew he was saying farewell to William for the last time. Such are the painful choices mountaineers sometimes have to make.

We had talked about the Peru trip at our camp under Beinn Lair the previous Whitsun. Julian, like his father, prefers a hands-on, fingers-in-the-cracks approach to painting portraits of crags. That was why we had climbed Beinn Lair's Wisdom Buttress, the Central and Eastern Buttresses of Beinn Eighe and The Great Ridge of Ardgour on our annual Scottish trips. At that camp Julian had explained his view of mountains as outcroppings of the earth's inner forces – the way rock formations speak of those huge energies whilst at the same time eroding, decaying and changing before our eyes. 'As a climber you're looking straight in the eye,' he said, 'the process that we are at the other end of. The hands that climb the rock are at the other end of evolutionary time.' The position of the climber's hands in his painting 'Wharncliffe' catches the delicacy of evolution's achievement, just as the pylons in that painting, like the railway and bypass, remind us of what those hands have done to the natural environment.

The ice and snow mountains of Peru, Julian said, would offer a more active field of ice, snow and rock on a larger scale. As it turned out it was more active than he had bargained for. Working from a Base Camp on the Andean watershed he carried 40 tubes of paint, a 7ft x 6ft canvas and its alloy frame another 1,000ft higher to his painting position on a moraine edge. He was facing the complex West Face of Ranrapalka. For five days he fought against the altitude to make a painting whilst seracs cracked off, stones fell, glacial dust was blown up from the cliff below and cracks started appearing in the ground behind him and in front of him. 'Slicing off like salami, the earth eroded right up to my canvas.' He decided it was too dangerous to stay.

Add to this three nights without a sleeping bag, which the local agent had forgotten to supply for a crossing of the Andean watershed and the need to continually forage for firewood due the agent's faulty stoves, and one can understand how suffering for his art on this lonely two month sojourn turned into a familiar climber's sense that the mountains might be out to get him. In fact the stresses of painting in the Andes – altitude, logistics and weather – resulted in two of his four large canvases being brought back unfinished. But he had discovered a deeper part of himself and 'made progress in attention to the quirkiness of these particular mountains.' He even managed to reach the summit of Pisco (5,900m) in the cracked plastic books he hired.

In an essay titled 'The Mountaineer as Artist', (Mallory 1914; extract in Gifford 1997, pp. 34 – 36) George Mallory argued that mountaineering is less a sport than an experience closer to the enjoyment of painting or music. But he does not separate out special moments as heightened aesthetic experiences. His argument might sum up the work of Julian Cooper as a climbing painter.

'We do not think that our aesthetic experiences of sunrises and sunsets and clouds and thunder are supremely important facts in mountaineering, but rather that they cannot thus be separated and catalogued and described individually as experiences at all. They are not incidental in mountaineering, but a vital and inseparable part of it; they are not ornamental but structural; they are not various items causing emotion but parts of an emotional whole; they are the crystal pools perhaps, but they owe their life to a continuous stream'.

On the climb of Tophet Wall the climber might feel lost in a vast complex of angles and planes, light and shadow, air and rock. Julian Cooper's drawing shows a leader belayed unconcerned whilst the second is crucified on the crux, almost invisible in the 'continuous stream' of stresses swirling high on Great Gable. It is as though the climber's concentration achieves an integration with the forces of the rock forms. The drawing was actually made with lumps of rock, chunks of graphite scavenged from the Elizabethan spoil heaps in Borrowdale.

Julian has been an artist-in-residence at Keswick's Cumberland Pencil factory, the business which historically grew out of these local plumbago mines. He followed up discoveries such as one made at Stanage some years ago that thick charcoal on a large scale is the ideal medium for getting to grips with gritstone. Again, the climber swinging on the lip of his 'Flying Buttress' is dwarfed by the stature and bulk of the crag, but heel-hooking on to its dipping lines, small but integrated – if he gets up it. The human presence, humbled but active, in even his high Andean work, is symptomatic of a view of nature that includes the human, both the climbing animal and the maker of pylons, barbed wire, Sellafleld.

Sir Arnold Lunn wrote that 'there is the mountain that we climb, the mountain whose rough granite is woven into the very tissue of our skin, and there is the mountain that we dream of.' In Julian Cooper's work the powerful, beautiful mountains of dreams are actually the slowly decaying granite that is under his Lakeland skin. Those knowing hands make a more knowing mediation of the mountains.

Great Ridge of Ardgour

'I suppose we're going to make a meal of this start again,' Julian says as I look round the bulge to find that the expected handholds do not appear; I back off. He means me, I'm not very good at finding the starts to these long Scottish routes that somehow always turn into epics just getting off the ground. He's reminding me about Wisdom Buttress on this Whit trip last year.

So I forget the direct start to the Direct Start, go 10ft right of the laid-back curving corner like the book (Howett 1990) says, make a long step right into the vegetated grotty crack I'd wanted to avoid, and gain the ramp at last. The corner crack is wet with seepage from the vertical wall on the left and both hands have to use it, so it's a bit awkward. But for the feet the ramp has fine friction from rough-grained silver rock that rises in little waves like the exposure. A wedged Wallnut winks from the crack and I accept its offer of a belay. As I clip in, my belay device drops, bounces off the ramp and goes on and on into the boulders way below, a grey metal Tuber somewhere in grey rock. Perhaps I shouldn't be telling you this. I've only done this once before (your honour) on a long abseil in the Alps and I caught it between my knees. The reach down to it took years off my life. Whilst Julian searched the boulders more years were ebbing away. Okay, so when did you last belay with an Italian hitch?

Amazingly he found it and was soon on the ramp. 'Intimidating isn't it?' he said as he was making the slightly off balance moves up the increasingly unnerving ramp. 'Well you can definitely lead the next pitch,' was his only comment whilst handing over my Tuber. Since we'd only done the first pitch of 1,000ft of climbing I raced off up the steepening ramp, clipping the peg that betrayed the first belay of 1952 and soon faced the block that walled off the ramp.

A big sling for the big swing round to find the huge hidden foothold and standing on top of the block brought two airy choices. To continue right seemed to require more faith than friction but to step up left demanded a commitment to wet, compact slabs. I went left, then across right with the rope-drag over the rough lip below lending each unprotected step an increasingly ominous sense of gravity. Somehow seriousness had just seeped in through my wet fingertips.

Ropeless and dry, it might have been a romp, but for the invisible presence of a plumbline I'd already tested with my Tuber. I was getting very severely frightened on a V Diff. Another tug for free rope, another step up and another pull backwards at the hips, just when I should have come into a relaxed state of balance. I didn't want to pause to consider every wet move, but the rope was playing games with my head. As one voice said: 'get a grip, keep going', another replied, 'this is serious, do everything right'. Caught between cursing and staying calm, mental balance was pivotal. Tug free, step up, pull back, wobble, tug, step, pull, wobble. Suddenly grass appeared at eye level and a Friendly crack for the grovel on to gravel. Sport climbers can have no idea how good it feels to sink a Moac into a wet crack, blind, at full reach, against a rope that's on a mission to get you killed. Now that's a clip to sigh for.

Seconding was apparently a doddle: 'a great foothold round the corner,' 'all there' etc. I grabbed gear and stepped round the left corner to find great holds and an easing angle leading to a grass ledge and the flake chimney we'd spotted from below. I charged up it, hand over hand, to belay behind the huge flake. The ice-cap on Ben Nevis had risen into view. But out there beyond the Ballachulish bridge, galloping down Glencoe was the rain that had been forecast for the day. 2,000ft below, the sea was disappearing. Julian had already felt the first spots which I'd been too absorbed to notice. But it had to get easier now, so he headed straight up the wall above, which turned out to be Severe with wet jams, and landed on the grassy rake below the magnificent and much foreshortened Great Ridge. Now we could delight in 700ft of 19th century climbing, courtesy of J. H. Bell and W. Brown.

This must be one of the truly great ridges of Britain. Thrust out from the mountain into space, its structure is always fascinating, offering an arête, a crack, a wall, a chimney in continuously rough rock that just rose on and on above. From large ledges it seemed to lean back, only to rear up again excitingly further on, forcing a choice of lines with varying degrees of airy views. Rope drag kept the pitches shorter than the rope as we led through with a rising enthusiasm that seemed to even hold the rain at bay. I was still climbing in traditional style, if one looked no lower, than my thermal vest and wool shirt. (One might feel slightly guilty at moving fearlessly now in sticky boots, having lost the art of nails. Wearing rubber-soled rock boots J. H. Bell (1950) pointed out: 'one tends to get a false sense of security, attempting things beyond one's ability without the careful placing of feet which is essential with nailed boots'.)

But here's a wall of rounded knobs to step up. Then I teeter up a wet slab again and Julian bridges across a steep corner pulling on sharp edged jugs. We lead through on as brilliantly breathless a bout of climbing as we can remember. Eventually I have to put my jacket on as wet hands are giving me the shivers and the rain soaks in. We seem to be above everything around us, but it still keeps coming. A vertical wall of little ledges topped by holds rounded for the hand lands me on a platform and what must surely be the summit above. Julian is not so sure, believing that we're so high and detached that there may be an abseil into a neck to escape the ridge. He carried his coils apprehensively towards what is, in fact, the summit. It's six o'clock. We started walking in from the road at ten past ten.

From the col below we watched a party profiled on the start of the Great Ridge. The rain is setting in. Their calls are echoing and serious. They're having a great day too. You can tell.

The Gates of Death: Hanging Dyke Route, Coire Sputan Dearg

'My grandfather must have been here.'
'Did you know him?'
'Since he died in 1929, no.'
We were at the Linn of Dee, that bend in the road beyond Braemar where wildness began for Queen Victoria and for those who followed her fashion into the Highlands. Following them was Julian Cooper's grandfather with his easel, brushes and paints, trying to make a living at what he loved. A biography *Alfred Heaton Cooper: Painter of Landscape* by Jane Renouf, (1997) describes how Julian's grandfather had escaped from the waterworks department in Bolton Town Hall to eventually paint the tumbling peat-brown waters of the Dee, complete with mist-shrouded deer, for homes rather different from that of his mill worker parents who had worked long hours to set him on this road. This was the road we now travelled to climb (and paint) the highest crag in Britain, Coire Sputan Dearg, on the southeast side of Ben Macdui.

The SMC *The Cairngorms Volume I* guide (Fyffe and Nisbet 1995) is helpful in hinting that a bicycle might be used, in the spirit of the Letterewe Accord, to cycle the tracks of vehicle access on the approach to this crag. (I have the words of the Accord from *High* 136 (Gilbert 1994) taped to my crossbar, should a keeper come upon my discreetly abandoned bike, woven in its three yards of chain and padlocked as securely as any estate gate.) A bike will get you to Robbers' Copse (grid ref. 015938 OS sheet number 19), having taken five miles off the eight and a half miles to the crag. Some folk had camped there (and in earlier spots) and two bikes were locked to the deer fence that protects the copse of regenerating Scots pines from the over-population of deer. You might argue that if we have to put up with deer fences out here, they might as well become bike stands. I prefer to hide mine from the sightlines of tracks, which is not that difficult.

Now Julian has this funny thing about bikes. They're out to get him. Even without his carrying, as he was this trip, a rucksack of climbing and camping gear, plus a smaller one of painting gear attached to the big one, a bike seems to behave like a wild bull contriving his sudden death in a ditch. If this sounds a trifle melodramatic, artistic, irrational, you should hear him argue coolly, at some length, about that bike I lent him for the trip into Beinn Lair three years ago – how it threw him viciously into a ditch on his first, unloaded, trial run, damaging the shoulder of his painting arm.

So I cycled in alone then, and I cycled in alone now. Except that the roadway into Derry Lodge is so flat that I was able to dump my sac occasionally and return to ferry Julian's multiple load forward, thus offering the painter an unladen view of the landscape under the benign light of a Whit Saturday afternoon sun. Yes, it was one of several Sassenach weekends in Scotland (New Year, February half-term) when the helicopters get lots of practice and haggis sales rocket. Everyone on the path was English.

As though this was an expedition, like our sacs, of Himalayan proportions, there appeared, soon after turning north beside Luibeg Burn, a distant massif of high black buttresses protruding from gleaming snowfields: (dis)Concordia. The guidebook had teased us with a crag with 'an unusually friendly atmosphere, quick to dry, not the place for the hard man (sic) there is no better place in the Cairngorms'. The only catch was now obvious: it is in the sky. It appeared to be alarmingly detached from Scotland. It is not very friendly of the SMC to omit this small point. How are the English to understand what 'a cliff base at 1,100m' means when we are still learning what a Scottish Very Severe, Càrn Ballach and Blàs na Beurla mean?

The entrance to Coire Sputan Dearg is guarded by the deceptively 'friendly atmosphere' of the meeting between the Luibeg Burn and the Allt Càrn a' Mhaim (Stream from the Summits of Mayhem). On the left bank ('looking Scottish Magnetic North at 113.5m from the friendly confluence', as the modernized SMC guidebook might say) a future EU-granted Helicopter Heritage Tour landing site can still be used as an unofficial camp site. It was free of any evidence of previous English campers, I'm glad to report. (German walking and camping tours were also not in evidence – yet – although Julian did find Dutch shotgun cartridge cases littering the hill above at his later painting spot.) I had brought along my American orange plastic camper's trowel for obvious reasons. I hope that the National Park Rangers here in the future will be empowered to shoot-on-sight any camper or bothier who has not bought one from the dispenser attached to the Derry Gates parking metres.

And so we came to approach Grey Man's Crag in Coire Sputan Dearg where 'the routes are short (30 – 150m) and descents are quick and easy'. It soon became clear that the reason the routes are short is due to their being almost engulfed by the surrounding snowfield. Despite evidence of glacial shrinkage in recent years – the green rim across the bottom 19.3m of the rocks – this permanent snowfield demanded a trying period of careful stepcutting and skilful use of our shock-absorbent, adjustable ice-dagger/ski poles. A step across the bergschrund brought us to a ledge one could imagine being designed in the future, with a little chipping and belay bolts, for the change into sunny rock-shoes. But we were in a boltless corrie, a European museum of climbing, more important than any that could be constructed indoors in exhibitions such as that at Rheged, Cumbria.

'No problems starting this one,' said Julian, alluding, in the friendly atmosphere, to my usual difficulties with Scottish V Diffs. In fact, he offered to lead the first pitch of Hanging Dyke (Very Difficult 120m), a groove in a slab, which was toothed with the square fangs of a pegmatite dyke. He climbed so fast that he continued up the parallel cracks above before the rope ran out. When I came to the cracks I was reminded of how rounded and blind these can be on Cairngorm granite. An ancient jammed nut exhibited itself in the museum. Everything suddenly got a little delicate with rounded side pulls and toe-stubbing across the cracks.

Then, at my lead, the dyke steepened as I bridged its groove on the crystals' flat planes. This was cordial, windless but midgeless, and punctuated by the throaty rattle of a ptarmigan flying about the corrie. I came to the arête which gave the Hanging Dyke its name. Although the holds were small and the position 'the backbone of the buttress', an easy groove close by and the need to step right into cracks to place protection detracted from its purity. This climb, we came to conclude, had been starred because it was a rare specimen in the museum – a V Diff in the Cairngorms. As we scrambled out towards the top of the ridge it became clear that no-one could have given this route a name like, say, 'The Gates of Death', unless it was to suggest the dangers of navigation on the summit boulder-fields of Ben Macdui to which it gives access. This crag is indeed no place for the SMC's 'hardman', or muc sheòbhaineach fhireann.

Passing several spectres of The Great Grey Man, we visited the summit *table d'orientation* as the map calls it, rather than *càite bheil* as it would if it were in Wales (if you see what I mean). We decided to return to do another short but highly starred route. Looking down the solid white descent gully we realized that descents there can indeed be all too 'quick and easy', so we came down the side of the corrie to find ourselves facing another long glacier approach to climb the tiny Crystal Ridge (90m) that is loaded cunningly with stars in disproportion to its length. The search for a painting viewpoint on the slopes of Derry Cairngorm seemed more attractive and a ramble turned into another summit as a bright day turned into stinging cold rain. We reached our tents soaked and in need of the inner warmth from Scotland's other aged museum gift to the world.

That night the rain turned into a storm of surging violence funnelling down the Allt Càrn a' Mhaim. At 11.30 p.m. (or 23.30 hr SMC time) we were woken by the single pole of our lightweight tent bowing down to our faces and springing up again. The mayhem had hit us and passed on.

In the misty morning Julian set off to attempt a painting. I remained blister-bound to review Ian Mitchell's (1997) latest true mountain stories faked as fiction. Apparently Julian had been about to give up as the rain had soaked his watercolour paper more than his paint had, when the sun came out. He came down for lunch with a sketch of water surging over rocks. He went up again, knowing that by evening we'd be supping a pint amid the Highland hospitality of the Fife Arms Hotel in Braemar. Later that afternoon I photographed his two-page portrait of Coire Sputan Dearg out of the wind in the tent entrance. Mission accomplished.

The walk out in the evening light was as memorable as any part of the trip. The Derry Flats were like the Serengeti as deer herds grazed right up to the track. From the woods came the romantic roar of a sad stag trapped inside the deer fence. All that remained was the hospitality being prepared for us by the Braemar hotel which Julian thought it likely his grandfather had also visited. Little were we to know that the band that had played for his grandfather was, indeed, still there. Removing their blazers, the drummer and two accordion players set up for their gig. What was fascinating was how they played with a minimum of fuss – a minimum of movement, in fact. The drummer sang without moving his lips and in the long gaps between numbers he looked out of the window into the street, arms folded. 'And now we'll have a modern waltz,' was the extent of their languid interaction with the audience. This, I suddenly understood, was the musicians' equivalent of The Great Grey Man.

'You can imagine that this is the band that plays you through the gates of death,' I suggested to Julian, realizing that I had not only discovered the band's name, but the perfect dramatic title for an article about a delightful aesthetic outing to a disappointing climb 'in the lower grades' on the highest crag in our United Kingdom.

CHAPTER 3 THE LAKE DISTRICT

'Lord Baker' in Langstrath: Cam Crag Ridge

> There was a lord who lived in this land
> Being a lord of high degree.
> He left his fort for a ship's board
> And swore strange countries he would go see.

Langstrath sounds like what it is - a flat valley floor as wild and 'lang' as a border ballad - and I'd never set foot in it. I don't know how that had come to be the case. It's a bit of an embarrassment really in a mountaineer with a hairline well in recession. (Until last year I'd never walked up Ennerdale either.) If you're always going to crags you can miss out on some fine valleys even in Borrowdale. So wanting to be a lord of this land in some degree I 'swore strange countries I would go see'.

Resting my fully extended rucksack against a wall to check the map at the first bridge across the beck I found that the midges tend to take a bite at midday here in July. I was sweating already and knew that with camping and climbing gear, not to mention wine aboard I'd soon be slightly extended myself. Norman, Kevin and Barbie were already well ahead, but I find that sailing up the motorway from Sheffield can actually weaken your legs.

> He travelled east and he travelled west
> He travelled south and the north also
> Until he arrived into Turkey's land
> Where he was taken and bound in prison
> Until his life it grew weary.

It was a bit early to grow weary since I'd only walked from Stonethwaite's cottages and through the campsite, a magical grove that used to be romantically known as 'Fairy Glen' in books with titles like *Odd Corners in English Lakeland*. It certainly is an odd corner nowadays, though perhaps with fewer fairies. Who knows? Crossing the bridge there was a last glimpse of Eagle Crag round the corner to the left stuck out of the fellside like the end of an upright piano. Music seemed to be in my head as I followed the others into the unfolding long journey that is Langstrath. Whole herds of rustled cattle could be hidden in the pastures of this strath, knives could be drawn here, Turkey's daughter ('as fair a lady as the eye did see') could rise from bathing in Blackmoss Pot to cut Lord Baker's prison bonds and lead him to a ship harboured in the narrow black zawn of Sergeant's Gully. It's that sort of a valley.

The track, keeping close below the little broken walls of Heron Crag, brings you up to a flat-topped tower called Gash Rock which all but blocks the path. Below it is the green pool known as Blackmoss Pot where Harry Griffin, in a memorable entry for *The Guardian*'s 'Country Diary', recommended bathing where 'neither costume nor towel was needed', although he did admit that 'this becomes too popular in heatwaves for my sort of dips, being too close to a well used track'. Above the track at Gash Rock the black cleft of Sergeant's Gully rises up straight as a sword.

In O. G. Jones' first pitch by pitch guide to the Lakes of 1897 the Abraham brothers contributed a grainy granite-textured photograph of the difficulties on the fourth pitch of this climb. A wild beard of woodrush, the eagle's favourite nest lining, overhung the chockstone. The steep left wall offered the solution. Jones wrote, 'From a short distance this appears to be a smooth vertical slab; even on close inspection the holds it offers appear to be of the most minute dimensions'. Bentley Beetham's guide of 1953 commented: 'A very difficult pitch but no longer incommoded by vegetation'. It looked to me a great winter classic that holds the snow well and long. It's only given one star in *Winter Climbs in The Lake District* but this valley promises more than can be described in stars, words or grades. It needs music; it needs pipes for carrying on the long rush of air it contains.

At last, after passing above several notable alternatives to Harry Griffin's Blackmoss Pot, which almost tempted us to rashness, we saw the tent of friends we'd come to camp with high up the fabled strath. They'd left their tent on the big bend above all the deep pots and plunging forces at a point where the river braids into little rolling plaits of water. By the time we'd pitched our own tents they'd appeared from up the valley and we all saw, looking back down the dale a soaring hump of rock, unnoticed on the walk in. Cam Crag Ridge stands clear of the green fellside as a slightly stepped, rounded spine on the skyline. Barbie was into the discoveries of the new scrambling guide after a long experience of fell walking and trekking. She vowed she'd climb the white back of Cam Crag Ridge, and this is the valley where vows are strong:

> They made a vow for seven years
> And seven more for to keep it strong
> Saying 'If you don't wed with no other woman
> I'm sure I'll wed with no other man.'

Roused by the force of this we grabbed slings, rope and torches just in case, before stalking off through the grass, boulders and bracken to keep an appointment with the horizon.

Now it's in the nature of scrambling that a description in a guide cannot be as well defined as for a rock climb: you're finding your own way through uncharted wild country. If you accept that, you can pass below the jumble of boulders that probably provide a very interesting start to the ridge, and see instead the raven's nest round the corner, perched on a block, trailing a long bit of binder twine down into space. At the first platform on the ridge we began to savour the rock we were vowed to climb. Andy found a way, Barbie followed searching for holds with a clarity of purpose the ballads are made of. I threw more words and tunes to the wind behind, whilst Dave, forgotten at the back, enjoyed a new experience. Kev drifted about between us, focusing and refocusing his black Cyclops' eye from Japan as if the oral tradition had never existed.

Years seemed to pass as the ridge steepened and reclined, steepened and reclined in front of us. A little wall always gave to an open scoop, a top edge would reveal solid jugs to an easing slab up to a grassy break which we'd cross to a wall to start again. One steep section was littered with loose flakes which required care but mostly the rock was clean and sharp or leaning and rough, without tricks or traps. The final wall weakens with a groove and crack beside a tree. This last problem sharpens the enjoyment of hold-searching before a final rush to the flattening top of the ridge.

Barbie was pleased with her achievement, quite rightly. While I was babbling words she nodded silently, her eyes screwed up in that deep, inner, staring smile of hers. It was a great spot above the length of Langstrath with route-finding problems solved behind us. I was pleased to be part of it, but I was really married to the rock routes I realised that day, much as I'd enjoyed this scramble too. That night in the tent, well after dark, when all the bottles lay empty on the turf outside (temporarily) I sang what I could remember of the ballad of 'Lord Baker', how Turkey's daughter had searched for him when those seven years and seven more were over and done, finding him at last on the very day he'd taken a new bride in. When she sent a message that she was at the door asking for a piece of his wedding cake 'and a glass of your wine it being ere so strong',

> He took his sword all by the handle,
> Cut the wedding cake in pieces three
> Saying 'there's a piece for Turkey's daughter,
> Here's a piece for the new bride and one for me'.
> And Lord Baker ran to his darling,
> Of twenty one steps he made but three.
> He caught his arms round Turkey's daughter
> And kissed his true love most tenderly.

The next day Norman and I walked down the valley, Bowfell being in mist, hitched to the Bowder Stone car park and rediscovered the delights of pure rock moves which had been our true marriage all along; in this case the surprisingly neglected moves provided by Quayfoot Buttress, directly above the car park. Aberration (MVS), appropriately named for us, deserves to be better known since it rivals Ardus (Severe) on Shepherd's Crag for its delicate leftwards traverse on the top pitch. All that remained was a lunchtime pint in the Scafell Hotel with a warm lad who gave us a lift, a celebratory exchange of good routes yet to be done, and we'd both seen strange countries and found our true passion in the way of the narrative of things lived and sung.

Bonfires in Borrowdale: Jackdaw Ridge, Glaciated Slab

I looked down the first pitch from my stance beside a tree and braced my feet firmly apart to take a fall. The rope ran down in a straight line but disappeared over the top of the steep wall at the bottom. How reassuring the ritual calls are when you're out of sight of each other. Tom's head soon came into sight, and his hands, feeling over the rock, testing holds. 'The trouble with these trainers,' he said, 'is that you have to be careful not to catch them as you lift your feet, or the velcro lifts and they might drop off!'

At the start of the next pitch I placed a left foot high in a groove and made a huge pull, wondering if Tom could find the solution to this problem. I needn't have worried. He didn't hesitate to discover an alternative to the left, and in the polished groove of the third pitch, followed by the foot-jamming crack of the fourth, before the final wall of the fifth Tom kept coming, talking all the time. On the Belvedere I coiled in the sunshine whilst Tom removed the belay before we moved across to peer over the edge a few feet further to the north. Another team were starting the final pitch of Little Chamonix, the leader spreading fingers and toes across the steep top wall. Tom's eyes lit up. Well, we'd come to that. Tom had just done his first route in the Lakes. When you're seven there is plenty of time to feed bonfires.

In fact that very night, instead of dreaming routes ahead, time turned backwards as the young climber blacked his face with the rest of his family and swinging a fearfully grinning turnip lantern set out singing the Lyke Wake Dirge to trick or treat the 'shepherd's house' below Shepherd's Crag. Later that night, the excitement over and young climbers fast asleep, a rustling at the window brought us peering out into the dark to glimpse a witch in black plastic bags riding a beesom round the corner of the cottage. Tempted closer, after our shock, the disguised shepherd of the crag offered us a drop of 'real dragon's blood' to calm our nerves. His little lad, Jason, watched these pagan rites from behind a car, as we brought out the turnip's and the pumpkin's flickering faces to see them off again to their home under Tom's high viewpoint of earlier that day.

Tom's route, Jackdaw Ridge, makes a final jagged fling and tumble of rock through the trees before Shepherd's Crag disappears round the corner into the hillside and a marvellous walk up to Watendlath. For connoisseurs of Bentley Beetham's detailed explorations of Borrowdale, and this end of Shepherd's Crag in particular, the Jackdaw Ridge actually starts up Beetham's Ant Highway, which matters little. Tom claimed it like a new route and climbed it again next day together with a 30-year-old who had never climbed before, but knew someone else who would love to do it.

However, the following afternoon Kev and Barby arrived for Tom and I to guide them up Knitting Haws. It's a scrappy scramble, but Tom led up all the bits of boulders and little walls that we could find as, unroped, we strung rock and heather together. By far the finest descent is to turn north and follow a track below a wall to a smoothly grassed spur. We fell through deep bracken towards the lights of Grange as dusk closed in.

A wet day and we were pulling fallen branches out of the fields, dragging them down the road to a growing bonfire opposite the Borrowdale Hotel. And still Little Chamonix was receiving continuous ascents. In an afternoon of clearing weather, Tom and I, with three-year-old Ruth, walked into the great bowl of bronze trees that leads to Black Crag. Voices came from Troutdale Pinnacle, a valley route with a big-crag feel that Tom could look forward to climbing at any time of year. I memorised the elegant line of a parallel party on the Superdirect as we slowly explored the orange fell below Greatend Crag. In full autumn colour this is a magic corner of the Lakes, not far from the road. Rowans explode in bonfires of berries along the paths.

November the fifth and I wanted to take Tom on a nostalgic climb in Coombe Gill. I must have been 16 or 17 when I did my first climbing here. We were awestruck working class kids from a Scout troop up Newmarket Road in Cambridge. Des Oliver (creator of Troutdale Pinnacle Direct) introduced us to rock-climbing on his afternoon off from the grocer's shop where he worked in Keswick. I've never forgotten Glaciated Slab since that day twenty years ago when we Fen boys flogged up the bouldered fell towards this whale's back 100ft high. As we youngsters were introduced to the concept of Old Man's Pace up that slope I remember someone stating what became for us the Cambridge definition of steepness: 'I wouldn't ride me bike down here!'

The top of Glaciated Slab is the top of the fifth pitch of a Bentley Beetham creation called Intake Ridge, twelve pitches of Mod that wander up the east side of the entrance to Coombe Gill to the top of Bessyboot. Beetham is supposed to have made these linked scrambles for the initiation of kids into climbing. Glaciated Slab is itself perfect for the purpose as Des Oliver obviously knew. He lit something there that was becoming a recurring ritual. Tom silently soloed up the easy scoop at the top end of the slab. I followed at his heels. Next David Craig, who had come up to Borrowdale for Bonfire Night, started out in big boots up the face in the centre of slab declaring it clearly V Diff rather than Beetham's grade of Diff. Tom tried hard to solve the problem of the thin crack in the middle, but finally traversed across to find an easier way up for his short reach. The chimney also proved good fun, taking us out to the open left edge of the outcrop. Finally, David and I soloed the excellent break just round the corner that finishes at the top of the chimney.

And then to the bonfire, with fireworks provided by the film director Ken Russell. Anyone who has seen just one of his films can imagine his delight in setting off bigger and better displays of pyrotechnics. The rockets shot up like flares, lighting Little Chamonix. The first Guy, top of the pile of branches and beds, was quickly consumed and so we then brought on our crucified straw man whose candle eyes flamed from the front of the fire. As his body burnt, the turnip head rolled safely out of the fire for a second or third life beyond Halloween, the Celtic year's end.

The shepherd passed round his tatties from a tin hooked out of the heat of the fire to challenge the bonfire toffee already circulating. We stood facing the heat in the comfortable neighbourly atmosphere.

'I took our Tom climbing in Coombe Gill today on routes that have all got the old sheep counting names, you know. Trod, Yan, Tan, Tethera, Methera .... Do you know them?'

'No, I've never used them.'

'They were named by a guy called Bentley Beetham.'

'Now I remember him. I gave him a lift once. He used to stay in a tin hut beside the road beyond Rosthwaite. He was getting on then, maybe in his eighties, and he could hardly walk along the road. He said he'd climbed a route up Bessyboot that you could walk up either side of.'

'Intake Ridge! That's where we've been today.'

'Aye, and I remember him saying "They'll never stop me till they nail me down".'

'Well I hope I'm around when our Tom takes his daughter or son up old Bentley Beetham's routes in Borrowdale!'

As the fire died down at last and we drifted away, the crag bulked black above. It held in the promise of darkness one of Beetham's best discoveries, made a month before I was born. From Halloween to Bonfire Night, Little Chamonix had literally hung over us like the future, to be savoured when it comes .... the spikey corners, airey stances, the engaging of toes on the slab, the revelation over the knife blade, the unfolding of incuts on the testing top pitch. Well, Tom will come to that in his own time. Some routes are worth saving to savour in the fired light of leading.

Millican Dalton: Professor of Adventure

We are coming to the end of an era in the history of rockclimbing. First there was the gully era, then that of arêtes, followed by the steep faces, until the era of bold, overhanging and sometimes loose rock. Today bolts, climbing walls and competitions are clearly going to put an end to the era of risk and adventure in the history of the development of the sport. We are in a transitional stage. It seems a good time to look back on the life of a character who epitomises the spirit of anarchic fun to be had in the outdoors before the sport turned away from nature and became intensely po-faced.

I first met him on Pencoed Pillar, the Hard V Diff that gets you to the narrow summit of the Matterhorn of Mid-Wales. He was chuckling to himself as we sat there looking across the cwm to Cader Idris and Norman was saying, 'Brilliant line, crap route'. I glanced behind Norman to the lean grinning figure with the pointed beard and broad-brimmed hat with a pheasant's feather. His obviously homemade clothes were of leather, like his face, and his heavily nailed boots were sockless. He sucked on his Woodbine as if it were oxygen.

'What did you expect?' I whispered to Norman. 'You're talking about a route put up by a Professor of Adventure who was noted for fresh air and fun.'

The leather man lit another Woodbine.

'Not that Millican Dalton character,' Norman shouted, 'the one dressed like Robinson Crusoe? No wonder this route's more mud than rock. That eccentric guy who lived in a cave in Borrowdale? That's where Sumner should be, for giving this route three stars!'

I glanced over Norman's shoulder, but the Alpine gnome had disappeared. It was to be the first of several uncanny meetings over the following years as each visit to the Lakes included a search for signs of Millican Dalton. In 1903 he'd climbed Pencoed Pillar at the age of 36, just after he'd packed in the London office life and moved in to a hut in Epping Forest which was to remain his winter home until he died at the age of 80 soon after it burned down. At first he spent his summers in a tent beside Shepherds

The belay technique of a Professor of Adventure: Millican Dalton.
Photo: Alan Hankinson collection.

Crag, then he moved into the cave under Castle Crag which is still known locally as 'Millican Dalton's Cave'.

My next encounter with his spirit was in the twinkling eyes of Harry Griffin, a man who still refers to the Lake District as 'the district'.

'Yes, I used to bump into him before the war in Rosthwaite, coming out of Plaskett's with his shopping. He'd hang it from the crossbar of his bike with the ropes and bits of camping equipment. He used his bike like a wheelbarrow. He was a genial, kindly man who would be glad to talk about anything. Born in Cumberland, of course, at Alston. Do you know it? No? You don't know the district very well, do you?

Well, I'd seen his picture in Keswick before I first met him. He had posters in the Abrahams' photographic studio and in Arden's bookshop advertising himself as "Professor of Adventure" offering "Camping Holidays, Mountain Rapid Shooting, Rafting, Hair-Breadth Escapes". He can't have been the first professional guide in the Lakes because there was Gaspard, the Dauphiné guide, at the Wasdale Head before the First World War, but he'd take people up the Needle or into Dove Nest Caves. That was his favourite place. He wrote a guide about it for the *Fell and Rock Journal*.'

Millican Dalton climbed new routes there in 1897, although they're no longer recorded since rockfall has rendered the place unsafe. His friends called this 'the rock gym' because they could practise so many different techniques within '150 feet square'. Yes, they trained, took their skills seriously in order to do daft things in all weathers on real rock.

'I've written most of what I know of Millican Dalton in *Still The Real Lakeland*. Now you will mention that if you use it, won't you, because I think it's only fair, you know.' It was obvious that in this 80 year old teaser the spirit of Millican Dalton was not dead.

Meeting Alan Hankinson, the respected historian of Lakeland climbing soon after this, at the opening of an exhibition in Cockermouth, was pure luck. I was introduced to 'Hank', as he's apparently known locally. At a mention of the name Millican Dalton, Hank's big white eyebrows suddenly shot up and he fixed me with a historian's stare. 'Did you know', he said, 'that Ken Russell wanted to make a film about him with Spike Milligan in the part?' We both burst out laughing. Here once again was that warmth generated by Millican Dalton's ghost.

'He's my favourite local character', the white-haired historian confessed. 'He was vegetarian, teetotal and a pacifist, and in 1942 he wrote to Churchill from his cave in Castle Rock, asking him to stop the war.'

In his writing about Millican, Hankinson emphasises the balance between a fun-lover living off the land and a serious thinker who carefully considered his own life-style. Millican's Quaker education led to an admiration for George Bernard Shaw and then, at the age of about 30, a life of self-sufficiency exchanging hand-made camping equipment for food, and adventures for cigarettes. He preferred to avoid money. He slept under an eiderdown and knew where the best hazel nuts grew beside the River Derwent.

His clients were instructed in both knots and philosophy. They often came back for more. One of them was Mabel Barker, who eventually wrote a memoir in the *Fell and Rock Journal*. Alan Hankinson had hinted that her nephew living in Caldbeck had family photo albums. There Millican Dalton came to life again in amusing family folklore.

Mabel Barker was a teacher who, in 1913, hired tents from the Professor of Adventure for her pupils coming up from Saffron Walden for a camping holiday in Borrowdale. Millican offered to take them climbing - and Mabel too. So began the climbing career of the first woman to climb Central Buttress on Scafell. She eventually came to know Millican well during her life running a school in Caldbeck. Now Arnold Barker, her brother's son, was showing me his parents' wedding photograph. It was tiny, the size of the original negative. I had an enlargement made for him and could see Mabel, at the back of Rosthwaite church, rope over her shoulders, standing next to her brother, with rucksack straps pulling back his tweed jacket. His new wife was sneaking a hand into his pocket. Next to her Millican Dalton, the best man, stood fag in mouth, rope under his leather jacket and full sac on his back, itching to take them all climbing. The night before, Mabel had camped with the bride beside Shepherd's Crag, whilst the groom had slept in the cave with the best man. Millican, Mabel wrote, 'cooked the wedding breakfast - a chicken boiled in a billy can - in the slate caves, and we spent a happy day climbing in and around the quarries'.

'Mabel always used to say,' her nephew remembered with a wry smile, 'that Millican got dressed up for the wedding. He put socks on. But he sat down on the grass outside the church and took them off again straight afterwards.'

The official Fell and Rock obituary reveals that Millican 'somewhat scandalised his generation by introducing mixed camping tours'. In her memoir Mabel Barker wrote about the Professor leading just such a camping trip to the Zillertal in 1922 when 'five of us - four women and Millican - got caught in a blizzard and benighted high up at glacier level above the Alpenrose, and spent a very uncomfortable night out in the snow. A violent thunderstorm added excitement to the situation, the lightning striking on our ice-axes, while drops of water on our hair shone strangely, so that for once at least we wore halos. Perhaps we deserved them, for though drenched to the skin before we gave up the attempt to get down, and all very cold, we sang songs and told stories through the long night, and nobody "woke up dead" '.

Her nephew produced Mabel's photo album of that 1922 Alpine trip. It reveals the sockless Professor, fag in mouth, leading his clients across glaciers like a Pied Piper. They are remarkable period pictures which have never been published and they catch the infectious fun that seems to be running along the rope between them.

An unexpected meeting with Millican occurred in Little Langdale Post Office. It is run by Marion, the young daughter of Vince Veevers, best known as the unintentional author of a popular Severe called Ardus on Shepherd's Crag. He'd recorded it as Audus, to preserve the maiden name of his new wife, Elizabeth. 'He always did have terrible handwriting', Marion says. 'Just before he was killed he'd been talking about reclimbing some of the routes he did with Jim Birkett. He was still very fit.' Vince Veevers was killed in 1989 by a runaway lorry that rolled, driverless, down a lane in Shropshire where he lived.

A casual mention of the magic words 'Millican Dalton' in Marion's Post Office produced a family story from the late 1920s: 'Dad had cycled to the Lakes from Bolton and was carrying his bike over Styhead to Wasdale when he saw someone climbing on Kern Knotts, so he went over to have a look. A voice called down, "Can you tie a bowline?" Dad shouted up "Yes!" Actually he couldn't. He had to ask a passing climber to show him. That was his first climb, Kern Knotts Chimney, and when he got to the top of it he met Millican Dalton holding the rope. In fact, he didn't get a chance to climb again for some time, but he was sure that he definitely wanted to take it up after that first introduction.'

But where was Millican's cave? 'We could tell he was at home', Mabel wrote, 'by the blue smoke curling among the trees, easily seen from the Borrowdale road'. I searched downwards from the top of Castle Crag until, almost at the path, on the north-east corner, I found some quarries. I noted an amazingly colourful 'painted' wall to tip off Gordon Stainforth for his *Lakeland* book, wandered up to a big cave and hit a roadway leading up to another, in the high corner of which was a hole. This appeared to be 'The Attic', the Professor's cave. Confirmation came as I passed a wall to the outside. Unforgivably cut into the rock is Millican's now historical enigmatic message: 'Don't! Waste Words, Jump to Conclusions'.

From here the Professor took clients sailing on Derwentwater under his famous red sails, rafting down the rapids of Borrowdale on 'Rogue Herries' made from rubbish scavenged at Grange tip, climbing and caving by candlelight in Dove Nest, tree climbing which he called 'Tree Boling', gill scrambling up Lodore Falls in spate and camping with instruction on the best woods for fire lighting, all laced with a philosophy that was actually being lived out; but you won't meet Millican's spirit of adventure any longer in his own larger cave where the litter from overnighters makes it just like any other urban quarry. You can, though, meet him in other people and other places in the Lakes, still, I hope.

Overhanging Bastion

It's strange how a route's reputation as a psychological breakthrough can still affect minds generations later. I had a thing about Overhanging Bastion. For a decade I thought I could not climb it, although Jim Birkett had first broken its barrier in 1939, seven years before I was born. Of course the name helped - Overhanging Bastion - it's so true to the lie of the line across the dark face that the route leered its challenge every time I travelled past the twin guardians of Castle Rock and Raven Crag into Thirlmere.

I had grown to dread a return to the arm-stretching steepness of Castle Rock's North Face ever since sampling the guidebook's 'best introduction to the North Crag.' My enthusiastic leader, John

Driskell, had persuaded me it was time I was climbing VS. Today was the day, Zigzag was the route. Didn't the guidebook say, 'the difficult moves are close to stances and the climb is less exposed than the other routes here'? I spent ages trying to move off-balance up the narrow ramps, missing the fingerholds above and the footholds below the ramps themselves. On the steep crack at the top, the exposure overtook me and I was all rubber fingers on the ends of seized-up arms. I was dragged up, gibbering. 'Less exposed than the other routes here'? Overhanging Bastion went out of the question for what became ten years.

Jim Birkett's routes are all in steep places. The quarryman from Little Langdale had the finger strength of a worker with slate and nerves like the nails in his preferred rock boots. He was as at home on overhanging rock as the peregrines whose nest ledges he abseiled or climbed to for the purpose of marking their eggs under licence. Referred to in Derek Ratcliffe's book on the peregrine as the 'veteran all-round naturalist and master cragsman', Jim Birkett knew of more peregrine territories in the Lake District than any other man. And it was the discovery of rare plants that he recalled as providing his most exciting days in the high steep places. It must be difficult for modern wall-training new-routers to appreciate than the man who pushed forward the standards of Lakeland rock-climbing for over a decade probably had more interest in what he discovered to be living on the crags he climbed. The man who, with Bill Peascod was the first of the working-class climbers, quietly made his contribution as a naturalist at the same time as ascending the Overhanging Bastions of his day.

In fact Overhanging Bastion was only the fourth of the forty-eight new routes that Birkett put up in the Lakes. Although he may have improved on the quality of his 'nesting rope', protection was confined to slings on spikes. So it was the sheer commitment of this line across the North Face of Castle Rock that led climbers at the time to feel that a psychological breakthrough had been made. And something of that respect and awe more than lingered on for me, compounded by my previous 'introduction' to the crag. I'd heard that there is a good nut at the end of the big ramp, if you can find it. I'd also heard that the flakes on the steep wall that follows are now getting suspiciously loose.

But when David Craig discovered I'd not done it, that was it - a route he wouldn't mind repeating each year, he said. No lingering at the Thirlspot pub for more than sandwiches, up through the greens of grass and larch shoots to the crag. It was a day in early April, too, when Birkett successfully approached O.B. Some lads were starting Harlot Face (so named by Birkett because he'd found it hard). I looked up at the slanting edge of a ramp cutting across the top of the wall. Memories came seeping back from the last time I was here, ten years ago.

The Wound

Thirlmere
soft as meadow,
larch, or alcohol.
Castle Rock of Triermain
hard as Harlot's Face,
steep as Overhanging
Bastion, the scar across
the clean north face
that, once seen,
sears the mind.

Pulling past the holly
carefully, contained,
I seek to seal the wound
of panic on this crag
ten years ago.

The wall's small sharp holds
seduce the fingers,
a seeping corner draws
the rhythm and the confidence
of comfortably bridged feet
to a ledge above the larches
green fingering the spring air.

What follows is simple therapy
a relaxing rehearsal
of the crux above
from tempting ramp
to testing step
blind round a block
to land on the platform
of dreams, pinnacle anchored.

Great Eastern Route

The scars are beginning to heal. They are not the heroic scars of the hands like you can get from The File, as well-named a warning against bad technique as ever there was. (As I write I still stare at those deep scars on the pen-holding hand.) No, these are the embarrassing scars on the tops of my toes that necessitated a week in flipflops. My raw toes were too tender for shoes, but there'd only been a brief period of doubting whether it was worth it. That was during the last slithering stretch from the top of Scafell back to the bottom of Esk Buttress in pinching, skidding, rockboots. It had been a daft impulse, and although Davie had readily agreed to it, I didn't appreciate at the time just how cannily prepared for it he was.

As we sat in the sun at the top of Esk Buttress it had seemed a seductively short walk across to the East Buttress of Scafell. I was feeling particularly good. It was the first weekend in July and I hadn't climbed since Easter when, on an especially tough assignment for *High* to review the Jersey guidebook, I'd buggered my left knee descending all those sea-cliffs. Actually it had been the jogging to get fit for Easter that had really done the damage. And on a recuperation trip with Gill we'd camped just over the top of Mosedale, halfway along the 'quick' route to Esk Buttress, and watched the sun go down behind Scafell East Buttress, a crag I'd never set foot upon. We'd driven home after another dry weekend without climbing. I'd even bought a mountain bike to strengthen the knee without jarring.

Now here were Davie and I waiting for Tim, Renny and Ian to follow us up Arthur Dolphin's Medusa Wall. The Wiltshire mountain bikers from our campsite had actually arrived at the foot of Esk Buttress after hours of fine-tuning with spanners and sprays. (They were so knackered that they didn't even finish their route and were entirely exhilarated by the ride back down.) But on Medusa Wall I hadn't felt a twinge, so when Davie said 'East Buttress doesn't look too far away, does it?' and I said, 'Let's go for it', it hardly mattered that he was already wearing his trainers. Being a canny Scot of a

Cumbrian climber he carries them clipped to the back of his harness. It had occurred to me that this was a ploy to have the benefit of boots on both sides of the Square Chimney whilst back and footing, but actually Davie goes to great lengths to avoid cheating, as you shall hear.

So stepping like a fox across boulders I padded in rockboots across the fellside until a path brought us opposite the formidable dark diamond of East Buttress. A glance at the structure of the whole cliff tells you what the holds are going to be like. As on a diamond, all the surfaces slope diagonally. This was going to be different from the square-cut holds of Esk Buttress. When we got under the crag there was a more significant difference. Water dripped out through the chill, shadowed air. We had picked out the slabs sloping left and then right to the top of the cliff. Great Eastern Route, we reckoned, could not be following one of these dripping drainage lines. What we had not noticed were the little vertical steps, every one of which was increasingly wet.

On the easy scramble left at the start of the route two things became apparent. All the rock was covered with a thin film of lichen and the ground immediately swings away under you. The combination of these two factors renders positively dangerous the *Selected Climbs* combination of MVS and 'no great difficulties'. Next time I climb here I'll make sure I'm carrying prusik loops.

Uncertain that we were on the right line, Davie hesitated at a suddenly steep corner. 'Well I suppose it could go, and the nut placements are perfect, but it's a little damp. I'll have a look.' Davie stormed the corner and shouted down, 'The rope's running over an edge here, so I'll belay.' The corner was an overhanging layback with sloping footholds and long reaches for good holds. The final reach upto the left was for the edge of a slab that, when you pulled onto it drew your eyes off into the void beneath it. Running down left along its top edge was a thin crack. Davie was belayed on hexes jammed into the top end of this, but he was sitting in his harness since there were not the slightest of edges on which to stand.

I immediately put in two Friends, tied into them and tried to relax. 'Well, if you must go thrusting those devices in ...' he mumbled. It's not just that Davie regards these 'devices' as cheating on a route like this, which was first climbed in 1932. He declares himself to be a Luddite, and against the corruption of free climbing by these machines - 'They have moving parts!' Needless to say, he doesn't use chalk either. At this point, to put Davie's abhorrance of chalked-up holds into historical perspective, I'm afraid I must report that our friend Norman Elliott, in the early 60s, reaching up for the final jug that is the edge of this slab, found to his horror that he had put his hand in human excrement. Thus was delayed the early development of the dyno move, and Norman's youthful dynamic go-for-it style reduced to the cautious 'Watchme! Watchme!' of today. And some people complain about chalk.

So, in this slumped rather than hanging belay, trying to keep my head and my bowels under control, I watched Davie hand-traverse downwards along the top of the slab, put a hex in a corner and deftly step up left to pull onto the next short slab. Frictioning up the rib beyond he was a silhouette above space. Something was dripping from between his legs. It was just more jewels of water-drops from the joints in the diamond's facets. Following the plumline of drips I noticed Tim and Rene followed by Ian heavily laden with photographic gear, toiling up the scree below. Any smugness about my earlier foxtrotting across the fellside in rockboots received its reward a few hours later.

When Davie called me onwards and downwards there was a nut swinging on the rope between me and the corner. But the finger crack kept open just enough and I'd worked out the sequence of footholds for the bulging high step left. The little surprise in store was that the crucial finger hold on the slab, with which to pull onto the left foot, was a rounded dip into a puddle. 'Commitment is sworn brother to grim necessity', as Di Johnson said, so I pulled anyway and flapped my right hand blindly up right to discover another facet of this climb. It goes in the wet.

But 'jams are the greater comfort to the gritstoner', as Richard The Second said and Terry The Second shouted up to his leader, belayed on the start of the slabs running right. By this time the wet gunge in the twin cracks that provide comforting fist and foot jams, was the least worrying potential stain on the second's yellow Troll trousers. Ian shouted up that the trousers stood out well and the route looked 'exciting'. Obviously he could see something I couldn't. It was simply scary. Even as Davie was stepping up onto another stage of the slabs going right, and saying, 'The worst must be over now', he was heading for the worst, wettest, wildest overhanging step between slabs.

After adding a Friend to his single nut belay beside this crux, I watched Davie try several ways of avoiding hanging onto a single wet finger hold with feet astride the void on sloping wet little slabs. But this was the way it went, and I had not the slightest doubt that I could follow. Davie disappeared round a corner at the end of a farther traverse right. For the next half hour calls between us were relayed by Ian, on the screes photographing Tim and Renny on Mickledore Grooves.

Above the one finger hold, all others were out of reach and dripping. If I went for it and found only sloping holds, like most of this crag, I knew I wouldn't have a second chance. The rope ran out right and space was sucking hard out there. Davie lengthened his belay so that he could look round the corner and tell me that he had actually reached right and hand-traversed a horizontal crack line. I had already touched this once, but recoiled at its wet smooth edge. Girding my loins and all else for a go, I may well have uttered something to the effect of 'Watchme! Watchme!' The trick was to reach farther right where the edge was better and get macho, yellow trousers notwithstanding. It went, of course. 'Stop apologising', Davie smiled, a Luddite with generous patience. (Only once had it really been tested, when I took ages on a tight rope getting his hexes out of The File.)

'Stop apologising', Davie said again, as I burbled on the first large relaxing stance we'd come across. It wasn't quite over yet. An awkward crack led to another exposed steep step and then we followed a gutter up through a kind of Japanese rock garden of mosses with running water. Stand as we descended for that trek back to the foot of Esk Buttress.

Of the rest, little needs to be said - of Davie pointing out how the setting sun was 'printing the mountains on the landscape', of the slithering agony of the toe-pinching descent to the foot of Esk Buttress, of reaching the road at 10.15pm, hobbled by the hill. As I said, the scars are beginning to heal.

Boot Strata in Newlands Gully

May Day and the trees are still dripping outside. In this mist the mountains could begin to rise just beyond the garden, a glistening black outcrop in the next street, or lie, as of course they do, a motorway away. While I'm thinking again 'Did I do right not to go?' I remember that it was a day just like this that David Craig actually persuaded me to set out with him for Miners' Crag, carrying a rope. Cynically I splashed through rain runnelling the turf of Newlands' long glacial gutter. Missing the high path off to the left I scrambled up towards the crag over boulders like the backs of dolphins. Sweating rain I panted round to the bottom of a hidden cleft. Stacked up the first few feet of Newlands Gully were three generations of Lakeland pioneers, roping up together.

'I didn't think you wore a helmet,' said Young Bill to Old Bill. Old Bill grinned wryly up towards his two pals from Carlisle who had just completed the first pitch. Seven of us were preparing to get wedged like chockstones up this drainpipe. Even in the days of big gullying parties there were just the Rev. Woodhouse and G.F. Woodhouse on the original ascent of this first recorded route of the valley in 1913. I wished I hadn't fallen for this ski hat fashion.

Actually, as gullies go, Newlands Gully is a surprisingly good route – clean, steep and not a pull on a heather root needed. The chimneying is never thrutching back and foot stuff, but of the elegant bridging kind. The escapes from under its series of chockstones usually demand wall climbing on the right flank, and the V Diff-sized jugs come just when the steepness is telling. There are not exactly the route-finding problems that face you in the depths of The Chasm, but then there isn't much of a waterfall either in Newlands Gully. Stances are undercut platforms of walled isolation with only a slight seepage of water in the small of the back if you choose to recline in the gully's chilling arms. Here you can look down at the orange caterpillars crawling up and down the path below, until your second's hand comes flapping over the chockstone searching for the jug.

You emerge from the tight clutches of the gully as it opens out and lies back to accommodate a tree. Fifty feet behind this the gully again constricts to offer a final thirty foot chimney. We preferred the open rock on the right where, under a steep lee an alcove of dry rock enabled us for the first time to savour its texture, a quality that ensures that the neglected classics of Miners' Grooves and Corkscrew on the upper end of the crag are never desperate, despite their openness.

The wet black rock at the start of the route was nothing to savour and it was glancing up then that I had noticed three strata of boots, three generations in the evolution of boots and of routes ranged up the gully above. They seemed to be aeons apart, although they were worn by Lakeland pioneers of three rock-climbing eras spanning forty years : the 40s, the 60s and the 80s. Nails glinted like the teeth of a miner, narrow French vibrams carried the romantic name of Terray, and plastic white-shells were the product of the space age. They were not being worn for nostalgia, but were each climber's best judgement for a wet day in Newlands Gully. And they were not together for some filmed reconstruction, or telereality, but out of simple friendship. Bill Peascod, Chris Eilbeck and Bill Birkett were not being beaten by rain on a Sunday, not being holed up behind windows where the rain soaks only the memory, and a climber's legs twitch foolishly like a lamb's on May Day.

William Heaton Cooper outside The Studio, Grasmere.

William Heaton Cooper

A buzzard drifted over the roof of the Studio of W. Heaton Cooper as I walked down the lane from the Youth Hostel to call on him. It was early evening, a fortnight after Easter, and it would be light late. The Studio is in the centre of Grasmere, facing the village green, and its gallery is visited by thousands of people each year who buy paintings, prints and cards with those familiar tones of colour that together make a distinctive vision of the Lakeland landscape. It is W. Heaton Cooper's vision of the Lake District that hangs in homes across the nation and across the world. It was W. Heaton Cooper's vision of the crags of the Lakes by which I first learned to read them as a young climber, from his sketches in the little brown guidebooks first edited by Harry Kelly in 1935. In fact, if you buy a guidebook for Pillar in 1988 it contains crag drawings made over 50 years ago. Only with the series of FRCC guides currently in progress have Heaton Cooper's portraits of the crags given way to the work of younger artists. These days they have to carry so many routes that they are referred to as 'crag diagrams.' It was the story of the first guidebook crag sketches that I was curious about. But when I came away from that house a little later, I had a sense of having heard, not just history recalled, but of fresh discoveries recently made.

Opening the door of the house he had had built alongside the Studio in 1938, there stood a genial 84 year-old, straight and brown with fitness, smiling and firm-handed with a warm grasp of life.

'You'd better sit in the throne whilst I take care of the coffee', he said, pointing me towards his newish leather armchair. While he poured the kettle I asked him straightaway about the guidebook sketches. Had they been a special commission?

'Yes, out of the blue Harry Kelly asked me to do them for the series. His feeling was that photographs didn't really give a 3D effect. So I had to invent the idiom, catching the whole crag with the greatest economy of line.'

'Had there been any models of guidebook crag sketches to draw from?' I wondered.

'I hadn't seen any, certainly, but my training in drawing the human form made it easier. Art School training had certainly given me economic drawing skills. Choosing the position from which to draw the crags was a problem, though - to draw them from below, as a climber would see them using the guidebook, or from further away? I decided that further away was best, at right angles to the rock face. Of course, some crags were easier than others.'

'Did you ever have to cheat and draw something which could not actually be seen all at once?'

'The only place where I did that was for Pillar's South Face of High Man when I had to look round the corner and then draw from memory. Harry Kelly was very witty about that when he saw that I'd drawn it as though Pisgah wasn't there in the way: "A perfectly respectable bit of mountain appears to have been moved by Heaton Cooper!" I climbed with the guidebook writers to get to know the lines of the routes, not all of them, of course - some climbs were too stiff for me. Then I did a pencil drawing which was reproduced by photogravure. In a separate printing the black ink routes which we marked on transparencies were done by letterpress printing, off metal, to give a 3D effect. Later reprints of the guides tried to economise by doing them both in one printing, the result being completely useless.

I was surprised, when they were published, at the response to the aesthetics of the drawings. I'd thought of them as merely functional diagrams. I didn't see them as part of my work. I just gave them to the guidebook writers, or if people wanted to pay for them I'd say "£2.50 ought to cover it." Sid Cross has rather cornered the market in them now.'

Talk turned to Lining Crag in Borrowdale below which I had camped last year and discovered Heaton's routes on what he called in his autobiography, *Mountain Painter*, an 'insignificant piece of rock that no-one had bothered about.' How had he first come across it?

'For me the painting always came first. I had been painting in Langstrath one day in 1934 and I walked back down to Eagle Crag to have a look at it. Further up Greenup Gill in the evening I came across what I realised was a fine little crag. I soloed Greenup Arete that evening for fun. I liked the texture of the rock which seemed like Gimmer. I took Jim Cameron back two years later and we did Evening Wall. We just did these climbs for fun, you know, and then later Jim Cameron wrote them up.'

'A rather different spirit from that of today?' I suggested.

'Oh yes, we didn't descend, for example, by an easy way off, or abseil, in our day. We climbed down the same or another climb. That's why lead climbers in our day did not fall. They didn't climb what they couldn't reverse. I think the art of climbing down is needed now, don't you, in world leaders for example? But I liked the last line of the poem you sent me about Evening Wall and the painter, "In the evening of life amongst the crags." '

'I hope you weren't offended by that.'

'Why should I be? I'm well past the evening. It must be nearly midnight. I can't live for ever!'

'Well you certainly seem joyously full of life to me.'

'Actually I suffer from terrible depressions and I have just come out of a year's depression. This Easter weekend has been a personal renewal for me. I am painting every day. I get up at six o'clock, look at the weather, look at the glass and decide where to go today. The marvellous thing about the Lakes is that it's very small. You can get anywhere to paint and be back for evening. This morning I walked up Easedale and found a subject.

Tomorrow, if it's fine, I shall go out with a sheet of half imperial sized paper on a board, with an easel, and do a very detailed drawing in pencil or biro. Then I shall come back to the Studio and work from memory.

This last year, when I've not been able to go up any height, I've learned that now I can trust my memory. Memory stores the colours, tones and the effects of light because it all goes deep enough to stay in the subconscious. Form is the intellectual objective content which I have recorded in the sketchbooks. These days I'm going back to the sketchbooks more and more. The result is that there's more of me in the painting than a copy made on the spot. I was glad to be free of those guidebook crag copies.'

I mentioned that the paintings of his that I prefer are those in which there is some dynamic force at work, a storm about to break, or a movement of light. These seem to me to be more emotionally expressive.

'That's because they're from here.' (He taps an 84-year-old heart.) 'It's taken me all these years to learn what's important.'

How, I wondered, would he describe his own style?

'I always hoped I would never get into a style. I don't like the idea of trying to fit Nature into a style. Every painting ought to be a new adventure, letting the landscape dictate the style.'

Outside it was completely dark and, thinking of this young-at-heart mountain painter getting up well before me in the morning, I prepared to take my leave.

'This spring,' he said at the door, 'has been wonderful for me. I have got really excited about it. Isn't it marvellous that at my age I can still get excited about spring?'

Evening Wall, Lining Crag
for W. Heaton Cooper

Fingers are fine brushes
for dipping into wet dabs
of mosses blobbed on the palette
below the canvas of the crag.

Feet are the pointed ends
of sharp pencils, shaped
for toning strokes across
the grain of the crag.

Eyes trace the steady growth
of the composition, the length
and proportion of the line
on the page of the crag,

Sun holds the source
of shadow for the painter
and delight in the evening
of life amongst the crags.

Ruth's First Rock Climb: Seathwaite Slabs

I don't remember ever approaching a crag before with a climbing partner who insisted on singing hymns in the car. From the gleeful glint in Ruth's eyes, I knew she was winding me up rather than her courage. As a matter of fact it was the sceptical grin with which she fielded my well-argued points of view that made her so attractive.

'You'll find it's like walking upstairs', I'd said.

'Oh yes', she'd said wryly with that glinting grin again which made me feel we understood each other for what we were.

Young Tom, my 11-year-old son, shouted suddenly 'Look, rivers of purple!' Ruth and I looked, and then smiled. Flowing down the flanks of Cat Bells, starkly lit by the bright morning sun, were purple strips of heather that flowered against the broad burnt patches on either side. Tom was into linguistic discoveries. Already on this journey down Borrowdale Tom had spotted on a tractor 'Flat Caps Rule OK'. What did it mean? Then on a National Trust warden's landrover he read a sticker declaring 'I Support Dry Stone Walling'. It took Ruth all the way to Rosthwaite to help him sort that one out.

As we approached the little bridge just beyond Rosthwaite I introduced Tom to a bit of climbing folklore. 'You see this row of houses beside the bridge? Well, in the 1940s a climber called Jim Birkett used to ride his motorbike so fast over this bridge that he registered his speed by the number of front doors he passed in the air.'

'How long ago did he die?' asked Tom. 'He's still alive.' I said.

'Oh really? After how many accidents?' Tom joked back. Ruth and I laughed at the knowingness of the age of 11.

We were bound for another area of climbing folklore, Seathwaite Slabs, first found by old Bentley Beetham, who was into linguistic discoveries himself. I did my first rock-climbs as a Boy Scout from the Fens on Glaciated Slab, high above those Rosthwaite cottages. Bentley Beetham had named the climbs there with Cumbrian sheep-counting numbers: Trod Yan, Trod Tan, Trod Tethera, Trod Methera. For Seathwaite Slabs he transposed the names into a different area of tens. Ruth was to climb Smoot Methera, Smoot Pimp and Smoot Sethera. Bentley Beetham cleaned and climbed these lines on outlying rocks for the purpose of providing ideal first climbs. I'd never climbed on Seathwaite Slabs before, but I trusted his judgement like Ruth trusted her own.

So we set off up the steep path beside Sourmilk Ghyll, Tom carrying the rope, more out of stylishness than gallantry. Ruth's determination soon took her ahead. (It's good for morale if it doesn't expose the leader's unfitness too obviously. 'Looking up ahead is better than looking down at heels,' Baden Powell might well have remarked.) I panted up behind in the rather strong September sun. With a late spurt I came over the top, where the floor of Gillercombe opens its choices, just in time to shout for Ruth's return. On our right Seathwaite Slabs lay back among the grassy knolls across the Sourmilk stream.

Whilst Tom and I stood looking for a series of boulders to step across on, Ruth had taken off her trainers and was walking across, underwater as it were. Stretching for a foothold underwater she suddenly slipped, lost her balance, put a hand down into the stream and at the same time gave me one of those 'What-have-you-got-me-into-this-time?' looks. But before anything could be said she was up, across and walking straight through the boggy bit that Tom and I hopped across, failing to keep our feet dry.

Thus came Ruth's firm decision to do her first climbs in bare feet. I tried to argue her out of it, but not with much expectation of success. Well, I just thought it would be increasingly painful. In fact her toes found holes I wouldn't have been able to get the toe of my boot into. When her turn came she simply climbed. Her slender fingers found thin cracks. (I'd not even attempted to suggest she might remove her rings.) Her bare feet read the dimples of the slab faster than the glance of an eye. Her look never rose to me, but reflected the rock surface. She didn't need speech. She moved in a sequence of self-made narrative. Difficulty didn't enter into it. Rock-climbing was taking place, the discovery of a new language of self-expression.

Ruth climbed three of the hundred foot routes that aren't even named in the current guidebook. They've been lost to the new esoterics of the latest dug-out crags. History repeats itself, but differently. Ruth and I lounged in philosophical mood in a little dell at the top of the slab. The September sun still shone on my shorts.

Tom soloed up with the sandwiches and we listened to his banter. 'Are you any good at burping?' he asked me. I had to admit that I'm not. 'I'm not either, but I've been practising for ages.' he said solemnly.

'Strange boy,' Ruth said quietly to me.

I reminded her about it when I saw her last Tuesday. This was only a fortnight since her first rock-climbs, but it appears that the world has now changed. Somehow, during September, an era has passed. 'But they were Infant hymns,' she told me last Tuesday, 'not Junior hymns like we do now.' Now the world is Junior and as big as the hills.

The Lady and the Raven: Corvus

It was a raw day at the back end of the year. Only the highest red fells were lit by the sun of the winter solstice. It was the time of omens, hanging like ice in Coombe Gill between darkness and light, a year's death and a year's birth, between the salt-lick and the lambing, between scavanging and nesting. The Lady was heading for Raven Crag, Borrowdale. I thought it was time they met. Big Tim, the shaman, agreed and when you're setting out to climb with a man like that you know you'll get up the route, or have a strange tale to tell. He makes things happen, drawing on powers he gains from journeys to the high mountains of the East, often undertaken, some say, in the shaman's state of trance. The Lady smiled silently to herself as Big Tim joked, 'Of course, I'm a greater ranges man myself,' beating himself like a bear-hunter to keep warm.

The path was a river of ice and the slope up to the crag a steep stair of frost. We knew we'd arrived at the foot of our route, 'Corvus', and were sitting on the sharp claws of the Raven because the primitive icon of the bird was etched on the rock at the start of this journey upwards and into the very spirit of Corvus corax. Old Bentley Beetham knew his birds. In the summer of 1950 he had named our route 'Corvus' before, solo as usual three weeks later, he added 'Corax' on the right to make the start of our route specifically the left leg of the Raven: corvus corax.

And a scrawny notched crackline it is, leaning back at an angle to support the dark bulk of the bird above. The leg was more grey than black and it was blebbed with ice like blood which had dripped onto the slab from somewhere above. I wasn't tempted by our sacred brown Beetham book to cross into the gully on the right. Big Tim was already there, impatient to be climbing behind us. I continued left to stretch a rope up the full length of the natural line. The steeper crack above is absorbing as you feel for a jam under a chockstone to enable a high-stepped entry. From here long reaches find jug after jug inside the crack. 'The Lady's going to love this old bird,' I thought, and shouted down to her as she stood waiting to start this encounter with the largest of our native crows and her first high mountain climb. 'Yeh, yeh!' She seemed a little sceptical.

But how her eyes sparkled as she pulled onto the big ledge at the top of that first pitch. I made her turn and take a look out over far fields white with frost, to the end of Derwentwater and the sunlit snows capping Skiddaw. It was an open enough aspect for a Raven's nest-ledge, but not as overhung as the cunning crows prefer it. Being the earliest birds to nest, they line their nests with sheep's wool and bury the eggs in it. The Lady seemed to need a warming cuddle at that point, just a stirring of the ancient energies of rebirth you understand, to see us through this chilly encounter with the bird of death. And lest you think this melodramatic, let me point out that the belays on this stance were none too good.

From here you traverse across the body of the crag, across its bulky blocks and broad feathered ledges where you can choose to step out onto the very edge of experience, finding small hidden footholds whilst fingers close over flake after flake. So, without realizing it, you are drawn into the depths of the crag. A corner lined with disguised holds leads into a narrowing chimney where suddenly it gets steeper and you realize that you've journeyed a long way. You can see in the narrow vent a welcomed spike embedded like a heart you know you must grab to ease the pounding of your own. You are reaching deep into the spirit of the bird that savours the placenta at lambing time, 'sucking death's mouldy tits', as our former Poet Laureate once put it. You are half in the mountain and half flying in the raw air searching for holds both inside and outside the dark vent.

The Lady came through it like a rainbow, grinning, faintly coloured, and good to see again. It was the step off this stance that proved a wicked test. It took some time to realize that a start too high to reach round for a rib had invented this mysterious crux. On a journey of this kind you make your own.

But whilst I was belaying the Lady as she climbed this rope-long rib, the shaman summoned up Ray MacHaffie, Borrowdale's famous scavenger of new routes and neglected crags. Suddenly, across the other side of Raven Crag Gully, in the centre of vertical rock just below the summit of the mountain, appeared a grey-haired solo climber in old bendy boots. The shaman shouted across to him.

'What's your route called, Ray?'

The figure turned, gazed round calmly until, seeing Big Tim with his one good eye, croaked back,

'Summit Route.'

We watched as he showed what he meant.

The Lady, I thought, could probably lead the spectacular hand-traverse out along the wingbone of 'Corvus'. It's a continuous upright handrail and there are always little feathers of rock for the feet on which to stand in balance. But when I went out to have a look at it I found my fingers stubbing ice in the trough behind the bone. So I just kept going until I finally flopped onto the flat ledge round the end of the wingtip. The Lady cruised across and agreed that she could have led it, had I given her the chance.

Chastened, I turned to find that an icefall filled the groove exit from this embarrassing situation. A bridge up and a long pull brought easy scrambling towards a final scoop which is shaped like a beak pointing skywards. On its broad massive base the Lady slipped, but Big Tim held up a hand and she stayed on. (I forgot to tell you about his huge hands.) As the Lady came up to the narrowed point of the beak it seemed to have opened to emit a single 'Prurk!' of applause. I looked up and there was the Raven flying above us. I turned to tell the Lady, but she was at the top beside me. She had seen it already.

And suddenly there beside us too was Ray MacHaffie, known in the valley folklore as the original Jaws of Borrowdale, passing it on his way down. He stopped for a croak and a crack as we coiled the ropes, telling us how Columba's Gully across the valley was a good ice-climb, how he'd done the first winter ascent in 1950 and how he'd come up Borrowdale today on his bike and it'd got no brakes and only one gear (top). He explained how the climber who named this crag was told by a Raven that his girlfriend was seeing another climber, so, in a fit of anger he killed her and hid her body in

Doves' Nest Caves over there, but later he regretted it and got back at the Raven by blacking his white feathers so that he was as black as the crag he nested on. He can tell tales like that for hours, until at last the chill begins to bite and he flies away down.

After he'd gone I found the Lady looking at me long and hard. What she was seeing and what she was thinking, perhaps I'll never know now. She said nothing, but I could tell she knew she'd met the Raven that day at the turning of the year.

Truss Buttress, Swindale

If it's spring, it's Swindale. If it's a Bank Holiday, it's even better. The Barrow Boys knew that and were ahead of us on the race up to the crag. They had come all the way round from the west coast of the Lakes, following their local knowledge of a quiet corner for a busy May Day weekend. We had burned up the motorway and were surprised again by how easy it is to slip off into Shap and across the open moor into this unspoilt valley.

But we were delayed behind the Barrow Boys by two misleading signs. The first said, 'No parking beyond this point'. Well, maybe things had changed since I was last here. And I'd like to be sensitive to the delicate issues of access. So we pulled over, stepped out and filled our lungs. In the morning sunshine we sorted ourselves out, loosened up from the drive and a buzzard drifted free of the rocks above us. Cowslips littered the lane that led to the traditional car parking ledge above the river where there's room for only five cars. Three were there already. Behind us, a sparrowhawk circled the wooded bank of the valley. As we crossed the full flowing river on the old footbridge a dipper sped downstream on silent hurried wings. A grey wagtail darted out at invisible flies. Before I got to the climbing, I couldn't help but be reminded how much I just love Swindale in the spring.

The second notice was deliberately misleading and could have turned us back. 'A climbing restriction has been agreed for this crag.' You may have noticed that we enjoy all aspects of the climbing environment, including the birds. We would not want to disturb nesting peregrines because we enjoy their part in the climbing experience. Every year, since before a neolithic Dennis Gray probably, the British Mountaineering Council (BMC) has agreed that we will restrict our climbing in the spring in Swindale. And, of course, passing this sign and therefore knowingly disturbing peregrines, would leave you open to prosecution by the hidden RSPB representative. But I had done what the Barrow Boys had also done, as it turned out. I had telephoned Needle Sports in Keswick the day before and checked that the negotiated restriction applied only to one of the four buttresses of Gouther Crag, Swindale – the North East Buttress at the left end of the crag. English Nature's sign implies that the BMC has agreed, on our behalf, that we won't climb anywhere on the whole crag. For the rest of the day we watched pairs of climbers approach this notice and respectfully volunteer to turn back.

So after a pause for a fulmination along these lines against the righteous alienation of climbers by the bird protectors with whom the BMC had agreed a reasonable compromise, we watched the Barrow Boys reach the toe of Truss Buttress ahead of us. But they were interested in the steep routes on the right flank of the buttress, so we could uncoil ourselves and our ropes below one of the most delightful V Diffs in the Lakes. It was greasy. The first time I led this route, with a friend's son, tiny Tim Harbour, on a dry day in early March, I'd noted in my guidebook that it was probably only a Diff. Today, with the winter lichen still green from a week of rain and damp clouds hiding the golden eagled peaks yonder, I discovered just how plentiful is the opportunity to place protection on what, on a dried day, would make a great first lead climb.

Truss Buttress looks an easy angled climb, the soaring arête on the right edge of a friendly slab. But with a slippery feel it is less of a push-over. A little jigsaw puzzle of moves slightly left of the arête uses sharp edges and demands occasional high steps. A sudden steepening at two cracks calls for finger locks and momentary foot friction before a few jugs ease the way to an exposed belay on the edge of the arête.

I forgot to tell you that this was our first married climb and it was therefore to be our first married row on a route for Gill and me. It would have been easy to get nostalgic about this climb, pretend it was some honeymoon experience, but the truth must be told. It was only a few moves off the ground when our 16-year-long whirlwind romance came under threat. It was a row of the 'You call this a Diff?' kind. In my enthusiasm for this route I'd neglected to convey the actual guidebook grade. A little lichen can threaten even a marriage of convenience. Perhaps Gill would get access to my pension earlier than I anticipated. My life expectancy was certainly being shortened by the silent tension that followed the withering question. Here I was Getting It Wrong Again, just as I had as an unmarried man. After a little rope movement and more silence, a voice cut the innocent air with a razor tone.

'Could you ab off and get this gear out yourself?'

I looked back at my two Friends. We were supposed to be saving money by getting wed, not leaving it lying around the crags for our friends to introduce themselves to our Friends.

'Not really. Try looking left.'

By now a light drizzle was in the chill wind.

Well, necessity was the handmaid of invention and Gill arrived to extract a confession. I had probably broken a vow, the punishment for which is Wrath and probably the Wreaking of Revenge. Anticipating which, I made sure I enjoyed the next pitch, linking the two short pitches in the guidebook. A slab leads into a recess from which ledges leading left bring you to a steep little wall on the front of the buttress. A pull up this reveals an open groove and traditional flake belays. On this pitch, for Gill there were no impediments to a marriage, merely a few satisfying pauses for thought – a renewal of vows possibly. Or possibly not. Only the peregrine's voice cut the air on this pitch.

The grassy terraces hereabouts were sodden and I could see that a descent in rock-shoes might inhibit the full enjoyment of one's own pension. A passing Barrow Boy, who was unlikely to be a man of the cloth, nevertheless clearly seemed to sense that charitable pity upon this rocky young marriage of the misguided middle-aged was called for and offered us the use of his abseil rope. It was round a tree down a gully to our left. The descent to the tree down wet slopes did not appeal to my wife. So we took the sodden slippery path of possible perdition over the top of the crag and down knee-banging, ankle-wrenching scree to its right.

My further invitation to Fang Buttress for the fine slab of Kennel Wall (HVD), or even the neglected gem of The Fang (HS), was declined. But I would recommend The Fang especially, which I climbed ten years ago for Gordon Stainforth's camera one cold morning in early May. It's deliciously exposed and steep, but with very positive clean holds. But that's the story of another seductive spring day in the inviting arms of Swindale, comparatively early in our affair.

CHAPTER 4 NORTHERN ENGLAND

Windgather

To come up out of Manchester eager for an evening dose of that adrenalin-pumping hands-on experience of the nearest gritstone is quite different from the way the Sheffield climber approaches the nearest grit. From Sheffield you sneak up on Burbage from behind, creep over the shoulder of Stanage and suddenly there's a line of routes at your elbow waiting to be re-discovered. Racing out on an evening you're driving, or cycling, right into a setting sun guessing how much time you've got. You're high before you hit the crag.

Manchester climbers have the sun behind them and the crag hanging beckoning above the last crowded street. The evening will be endless and even after the sun's gone down Windgather Rocks will be oozing heat like a hearthstone. And that's just what these rocks have been to generations of Manchester climbers. To the unknown, the famous and the infamous Windgather Rocks are their home-hearth, the teeth on which they cut their hands, a nursery initiation on the intimidating Viking prows breaking through waves of green ridges.

For, like no other crag I know, this is the crag of the Diff. The VS routes are really space-filling boulder problems. The V Diffs each go through overhangs excitingly enough, requiring boldness rather than technique since they find jugs rather than jams in the crack lines they follow. You don't actually use the grain of rock you've stepped up to climb. But the obvious lines of the crag are all, with one exception, flying, exciting, improbable Diffs. Every arête, prow and fang is a Diff that provides tiptoeing up rounded points in windy positions for the grade. Every leaning-back line up the steepening slabs is a Diff with a difference. Graduates of Windgather who have passed away into the Es would miss the different demands of technique in the trio of Diffs on Middle Buttress; the jams in Chockstone Chimney, the foot friction on Central Route, the leaning out on jugs either side of the chimney at the top of Wall Climb.

It's the fine mesh of the rock that has been rippled by the wind which makes Windgather's incuts so welcoming in winter. I first came to Windgather Rocks in a January when snow powdered the ground and I was caught in its net of dipping holds for frozen fingers. This was before the days of winter climbing walls when on a Sunday we preferred the cold of the crags to the cold of the town. On a Diff at Windgather in winter you can find yourself in a position that gets the blood flowing a little faster.

Take the misnamed Zigzag for example, which goes straight up the slabs right of that orange horizontal hole which looks like the place where they excavated the goddess of the crag. For a moment there, just above the level of the hole, one toe is on a Windgather tooth, rounded and undercut, the other stubbed on some sandpapery stuff somewhere, and as you look up, an overlap protrudes from a steepening wall of rounded ripples. But then every reach reveals that dip of the fingers deep into the strata of the earth that only Windgather can give.

For this reason North Buttress Arête is the route of the crag and the Severe exception to the run of Diff arêtes. The move off the ground is amazing as a pinching between two pockets on the left becomes an undercut when you friction your feet above the initial overhang, holding the arête itself in tension with the right hand all the time. Then the upward grasping of the layers of the arête provides the essential joy of Windgather. In summer, when the crag is a sounding-board of hill-top bird-song, a gatherer of windless sounds, that ascent of North Buttress Arête can have you burbling with the curlews, shouting out loud with the lapwings and, as you pull over the top, meeting head-on the exhilaration of swifts' wings razoring the air by your ear.

Jim Perrin said to me one evening at the crag; 'Everyone who comes to Windgather comes to play.' I thought of the nervous banter between the sexes as novices waited for their first climbs, the young lads discussing girlfriends between routes and the pair of PE teachers who'd come out after school to solo and hold hands along the top of the crag. There's something primitive and mysteriously powerful about the place underneath its playfulness. I was in Cambridge when it came to me, the way that power at Windgather works through play:

> He approached the teeth
> of the wind, those
> black fangs, forced
> through soft green gums.
> He found a net
> of stone, sagging skeins
> billowing back between
> anchored arêtes
> gathering wind,
> netting the spiders
> climbing across the fine
> strands of its web.
> He stepped into
> its sensuous symmetry,
> was hooked on its edges,
> swung from its lips,
> and he knew,
> even as he savoured
> the evening return to her,
> he was caught here for life.

And what has become of Windgather's willing victims as the years have passed? What of all those other less infamous Manchester climbers of the Rock and Ice era, for example? One summer evening recently I noticed a wiry grey-haired man carrying a crash-hat and a carrier-bag. Back bared to the sun he pulled through for the top edge on Portfolio (VS 5a) in one long lunge which I failed to do when I top-roped it later. He was Ally Cowburn, a Windgather resident who used to give Joe Brown a ride to Wales on the back of his motorbike.

'I could out-bike them to Wales,' he said, 'but they could out-climb me when we got there. Once Joe was on the back – he was always relaxed on the back, you know, some people were a bit nervous – and it was a fortnight before he was due to go to the Alps with Don. Don managed to get close enough to shout, 'Eh Joe, do you think you'll make it t'Alps?' Ally chuckled with a self-effacing smile and at 56 revealed that same old spirit sustained by the redeemed joy of a Windgather victim: 'I'm hoping they make me redundant, then I could be leading E3s.' He was serious.

Beating the Boxing Day Blues: Nightwatch

It was the day after Boxing Day, a dead day in our climbing year – a day when we're usually on the road returning from relations or travelling to the crags, with no shortage of turkey sandwiches. I rang the Yorkshire Terrier at the crack of 10 o'clock. He lives a few streets away and we'd both Christmassed at home this year. We'd made the traditional ascent of Christmas Crack on Christmas morning with the other hangovers at Stanage.

'Open the curtains,' I shouted down the phone. 'The sun is shining. What about that route you've been mumbling about in North Yorkshire?'

'All right, all right,' submitted the Yorkshire Terrier. 'Pick me up.'

Forgetting the turkey sandwiches I'd made in anticipation, I raced round before he changed his mind. The Boxing Day Blues can be bad if you've made no plans to go climbing after Christmas. But they can really strike you on the day after Boxing Day if you're not on the road to a crag.

From time to time over Christmas the Yorkshire Terrier had been yapping through his whiskers about this classic Hard Severe somewhere north of York. He'd caught a sniff of it in some Crag Rag years ago and the scent had stuck, for future retrieval at this dead end of the year. 'Just outside Thirsk. I can get you there. The line's obvious.'

I trust the Yorkshire Terrier once he's on to a scent. He'll worry at a line with his little nuts until it submits out of sheer exhaustion.

I picked him up, returned home for the turkey sandwiches and two hours later he was shouting, 'There's the white horse.' I didn't look up from the road. He was hallucinating and I didn't need whisky. The sight of Jim Curran at the foot of Christmas Crack had been enough. Gill had confided in him that her son was suffering his first hangover at home. 'I'm suffering my thousand and first,' moped Jim, 'but don't tell Gifford. He'll put it in an article.' As if I would do such a thing.

Meanwhile the Yorkshire Terrier was barking away about Yorkshire. 'The White Horse of Kilburn. I think the crag's to the left of it. D'you know, youth, I came here on my first field trip from Batley Boys' Grammar School. We were about 13 and we tried to see how many we could get standing on its balls.' How to embarrass your trainer. They were a rough lot, those Batley Grammar pups.

We turned right just before Thirsk, excited by the one in four signs banning caravans from Sutton Bank after miles of fossil field systems with real hedgerows across the Vale of York. From the car-park at the top of the hill we slid along a mud path to what can only be called a belvedere. This, I knew, had to be a classic viewpoint down across a classic route. But instead I saw this yellow sandy crag with boulders arranged in it like fossils and a particularly green bulging crack which the Terrier identified as 'it'. We only had his nose in the absence of a guide so I abseiled the obvious descent gully and then called to him that it was dry, out of the wind and unoccupied. Strangely so was the rest of the crag. I unpacked the turkey sandwiches and the less important gear.

'Big nuts,' the Terrier solemnly said, looking up the wide crack reaching above us to the top. 'Middle-sized Friends,' he commanded noticing the way the crack narrowed back. 'The set of Rocks,' he artfully selected, spotting the narrow horizontal breaks. 'Big slings,' he finally surmised, backing a hunch that proved most cunning of all. After barking his orders for a pretty shrewd selection of gear to crack this particular crack, the Yorkshire Terrier set off, as usual, with everything we possessed. I pulled on a balaclava.

He took an hour. It's a long pitch. He ignored the bolt in the wall to the right. This is Yorkshire style, Batley Boys' style in fact – four nuts in the first four feet and just test them until they settle down from sheer embarrassment. It was winter, in North Yorkshire in late December. In Scotland they would be all fashionably photogenic, with élan, on winter ice. We were still climbing rock in Yorkshire.

And what rock it was. Having been to the library I can now reveal that the guidebook (Cleveland Mountaineering Club 1985) calls it 'cretaceous grit'. Think on. Are you any the wiser? Well, if you've not been, you'll not know. '1,000ft in length and 110ft in height'. Now there's a major Yorkshire crag. Neither limestone nor sandstone, it seemed to have the knobbliness of carboniferous limestone with the finish of sandstone, and bedding planes of boulders with the fragile feel of fossils in limestone. The result is small lumps for the feet and large lumps for the hands – if you can find them, reading the erosion at the back of the boulders.

The Terrier shouted three things: 'Watch your head,' as he stood on the small ones; 'It's covered in guano,' as he pulled over a big one; and 'This top bit seems to be wet,' as he left his last runner. But the Terrier always gets there in the end.

Tight rope. I removed my balaclava and popped the Terrier's ski hat down my shirt for him. It would be cold in the wind on top by the time I'd got up. The crack begins with encouragement, but if you get, like me, too far up inside the chimney at the first bulge you have to reach out, face the lake below, and the rest of Yorkshire, to go boldly up the amazing holds, hiding your inhibitions behind jugs and feeling freely over the rock for higher hidden comforts. This is a hand-searching route.

At the last of the three bulges, as you look for footholds on the face, the bottom of the climb has disappeared. You slap on to the guano-layered ledge and settle for the last steep lap, reading now, the pattern of erosion that makes this route unique in character and unusual in threads. It's simply the best Hard Severe in Yorkshire.

'You go down the gully,' insisted the shivering Yorkshire Terrier, 'and I'll belay you back up with the sacks.' I brought up the turkey sandwiches again, as it were. 'I know just the place to eat them,' said the Terrier and drove us round to the car-park right below his white horse. It's looking a little worn now with its chest-bones sticking out. It's obviously never recovered from that battering by the Batley Boys over 40 years ago. As I ate the turkey sandwiches at last, my fingers still stank of guano.

Driving west we watched the night flame yellow across blue, until back at the Old Grindstone in Sheffield we slipped into the empty snug (remember them?) to sort the gear. We were unclipping stuff from our harnesses and tossing krabs on to the floor, when the landlady appeared at the door with a broom shouting, 'Watch your fingers.'

We looked at her. She looked at us, and then she said with a smile, 'Oh, I thought you'd broken a glass. Well, that's all right. Do you want a turkey sandwich, love?'

Spinnaker

Sometimes it's hard to know how to start. This time it's no problem. The best Severe on Yorkshire gritstone – you've already done it?

I bet you've never even been to the crag. Too easy for you E-leaders to bother with?

Well, I happen to have heard of at least one E-leader with nearly 40 years of weekly experience of exploring Yorkshire gritstone who was baffled by the crux of this Severe (no – it's not even Hard Severe in the guidebook!). He was eventually saved from his embarrassment by the lucky arrival of the local 'curator' of the crags, Tony Barley, who pointed out the solution to the crux. But if you think I'll be doing the same, then, tough – after all, it's only a Severe isn't it?

And don't get the impression this route's just another one-move wonder. Every single delicate step is exposed, steep and thought-provoking. Of course, if that isn't enough for you there's also the two two-star HVSs, two two-star E1s, and a three-star E4 at the same crag. So, where is it?

Well, it's not at Rylstone where the Yorkshire New Testament (Desroy 1989) says of Dental Slab that it 'could be the best severe on Yorkshire grit.' Interesting and varied as that well-known 1930s classic is, it lacks the steep seriousness, curious rock quality and continuous challenge of Spinnaker. This gem is so hidden within its hidden valley that you can't even see it when you're on the path 30ft below. And this little lake-filled wooded valley is so silent that the calls of the coots echo eerily up to the crags.

All this, three miles away from the trippers and boulderers at Brimham Rock, known to climbers since prehistoric man, or Dennis Gray, which ever is the earlier.

It was W. P. Haskett Smith who tipped off the climbing world in 1894 to rocks hereabouts which, 'though very small, can only be climbed with considerable difficulty'. Even earlier, in 1870, one Edmund Bogg was surely dropping a big hint when he mentioned in his book, *From Eden Vale to the Plains of York*, that 'Ea'ston Beck murmurs through a charming woodland gorge' (cited in Desroy 1989).

But it would appear that right up to today, even some climbers who would have considered themselves Yorkshire aficionardos still have to discover the backwater charms of Eavestone Crags.

In fact, access could not be easier. The crag name is signposted on the B6265 from Pateley Bridge to Ripon, just past the turn off to Brimham. Two cars can be parked beside the footpath sign, on the right of the road past the farm. Slip down through the pine woods and you'll suddenly see the buttress called 'The Fort' rising out of the rhodydodies reflected in what is actually the little upper lake, but which the guidebook mysteriously calls 'the Lower Lake'.

To find Spinnaker, you will have to forego the temptation of ascending the two-star E1 (or the Severe) on The Fort.

Wade into the nettled path leading off right, just before the stream feeding from the upper lake into the lower lake. Then, while fighting through the jungle, do not miss the faint path up right through the pine needle loam. If you arrive below an undercut buttress and find yourself staring at three teabags circa 1947 on the sandy ledge at its base, then you've discovered Jib Sail Buttress—only ten minutes from the car.

The distinctive mark of this buttress is the semi-circle up on the left, which you traverse into above the roof of the sandy cave. What looks a pushover from the shelter of the trees below can be what used to be called 'a tightsqueezer' when you're above the wood, with the lake at your heels and the slightly friable steep gritstone under your fingertips.

Take a rag up to the start of the traverse in from the left because the scree of pine needles are loath to let go as you try to step from vegetable to mineral.

The sudden undercut of the cave you're crab-stepping over is likely to produce a yearning for an early runner. Resist it. Be a brave Severe leader and think of the rope drag when you're stretching for the final holds on the arête a world away around the buttress. Be assured that an early crux will offer plenty of in balance opportunities to place, adjust and place more runners, between attempts to get wind in your sail.

But to detail the moves of this crux would be to miss the whole point. Just let me say, there are times, very few times in my experience, when you can delight in not being able to flash 6c. Only a true Severe leader will understand that strange satisfaction in being deceived by the several polished red herrings, the perverse pleasure of stepping back down and being forced to think again, chuckling at the rock and chucking more chocks in. Then with a certain amount of surprise you'll find yourself full stretch hand-traversing the horizontal break and hoping it doesn't!

You need to be mentally prepared for sandy friable edges as you reach up from one break to another and swing boldly along them towards the far flying arête. This, too, is not a soft touch, so save some of that deep ecology and a certain amount of oneness with the rock for the steep long reaches for holds that shouldn't be swung on like jugs.

Finally, you won't regret taking a full rack of Friends on this route; it can get very lonely up there. The climbing turns through 180° across the pinnacle – for that's what you'll discover you're on when you look down the V Diff descent at the back.

It's worth spending some time on the pinnacle top, looking down on the flash of a trout leaping in the lake, or up left at the white horse on the crest of the hill, having climbed one of the hidden glories of grit.

It you don't, you can stick with a clean and polish on Dental Slab.

The Brain

'An ugly bit of rock,' said Dave Cook immediately I mentioned one of the most beautifully archetypal of gritstone VSs – delicate slabby wall, steep stepped crack, rough arête, even a final pinch-grip on a fluting. Could this connoisseur of grainy outcrops, author of `True Grit', really be telling the truth about this bit of Curbar Edge?

'Are you doing The Brain?' we called down to a sitting second.

'Yeh, what route have you just done?'

'We've been in bed.'

Well, there'd been so many wet weekends in succession we'd got out of the habit of early Sunday rising, and then finding this unique bit of rock from above takes time, because it's well below the top of the edge in the central section of Curbar. But once found, its name gives it away. Soft saucers of conglomerate lie in bulging lumps that turn a slab into what feels like a wall that just happens also to be undercut. Sitting uneasily on this crumbly base is a jutting tower with a corner in its right side. Above, today, all is ice-clear sky after the autumn's first frost.

'I'd like a runner here really, now I'm above that pit', the traversing leader says to his mate.

But of course there aren't any in the middle of that traverse across the lumpy slab. Time to turn and watch blue smoke rising from bonfires of leaves tidied from the lawns and tennis courts of the rich houses below. The air is so still that the birches hardly tinkle, their leaves of green turning yellow to orange here in the tumble of boulders. Curbar's speciality of steep heather, bracken and mosses are now brilliant in the still sunlight.

'There's just enough little rounded layaways as you move across,' he says as he seems to climb right into the rowan which fills the right angle of air at the end of the slab. It's thin on leaves but strong on singing red clusters of berries, thrown out like confetti from its fan of stems. Rising from this burning bush the crack of The Brain reaches up steep and straight. He's soon up it and releasing his mate from a belay bound in the roots of the tree.

So it's our turn, and it's one of those starts that tempts you off the ground with jugs and pulls you across, soloing perhaps, to this commitment and then to calling, on a damp day, for a top-rope. Where a lobe has come out, your fingers find sharp holds round its inside edges, then hands hold each side of a blob of brain and you're across on a foot traverse that you find it increasingly hard to look down at. On this pitch as on so many gritstone slabs, momentum is everything, protection unlikely, so don't stop or gritstone will find you out. I found that my fingers seemed to be climbing it backwards, pushing away rather than pulling across, until at the far end delicate steps up on big sloping footholds lead to fingers feeling falsely secure over the edges of more friable holes.

The only protection for the second is in a crack below the tower above the right end of the traverse, but it's worth using because a belay at the foot of the crack is still round the corner after passing delicately under the tower's projecting foot. In fact the pendulum made possible by this runner fits exactly the scoop of the pit below the slab. This useful discovery was made by a certain photographer's wife whom I would not be so indiscreet as to name. Normally. But many a now-confident second may wish to offer thanks to Viv Smith.

The second pitch is archetypal gritstone climbing of yet another kind. Square-edged side-teeth allow a lay-back start before a pull round gets the fingers locked in the crack, and just as it gets thin on the feet a secret side pull gets you up to a foot-flake leading out to the left edge. The reach across gives you a marvellous moment, pulling blind on to the arête with two points of contact, magnetic left fingers and left foot. Suddenly you know that you're on a wall of Curbar not a slab of Froggatt, and the fall of fell down to the river pulls at your heels as you look for suggestions of friction for your toes. In a move you find that the arête edge is a fluted shaft you can pinch, grasp and finally pull over on.

And back at the bottom, talking through the variety of beautiful gritstone moves, delighting in the day, the situation and the singing tree, could we have said this was an ugly bit of rock? On a damp day would that lumpy slab have been ugly, or would that be our own small-mindedness? Echoing the shape and texture of those rock lobes are circles of lichen, the basic brain cells of evolution, slowly growing and colonizing this fossil seabed that overlooks the River Derwent quietly grading gravel as it passes through the woods below. The circles of The Brain are the cycles of the past, present and future. They are beautiful, and so are the moves across them. The Brain is a beautiful route on uniquely beautiful rock.

CHAPTER 5 WALES

Obsession

It was the best of times, it was the worst of times, it was the age of wisdom, it was the age of foolishness, it was the season of Light, it was the season of Darkness, it was the spring of hope, it was the winter of despair, we had everything before us, we had nothing before us – in short, Mid-Wales, Michaelmas Term lately over and Lord Sumner sitting in Bryn Hafod Hall. Implacable January weather. Snow everywhere. Snow up the hill, where it drifts loosely across the moor towards Aran Fawddwy; snow down the gully descent to Creiglyn Dyfi, where it crunches promisingly underfoot. Bits of aircraft everywhere in Aero Gully, where we pull up on plane parts and suppress ghoulish stories. But no ice in the Left-Hand Branch where axes sing off-key and crampons stub the turf.

A fire in the hearth, Driskell's old jokes and Kevin's elderberry wine can transform the season of Darkness at Bryn Hafod into something approaching the hope of Spring. And hidden in the dusty attic is a hollow-cheeked presence making mountaineering dreams for the spring, lord of the turf, the wiley old bookmaker himself, Lord Sumner of Hafod Hall. His cunning gamble of placing three stars on Pencoed Pillar had given us a run for our money, and he freely admitted that by the form book of North Wales the route lacked the distance. But, with the straightening of a line on the Cyfrwy course in his guidebook (Sumner 1988) and the correction of a 16 to a 14 on his crag diagram, he offered us a hot tip for the new season, straight from the horse's mouth – in short, thus began our obsession With Obsession.

I've blown it. Layed away and stepped up – into a cul-de-sac. I eyeball slopers and slap at everything. A spike squats a mere universe away. I've been rumbled. Cranking down off one arm has it screaming objections. I fail to find the same foothold again and stem away on friction. Cruising. I thought I was cruising and stepped up without thinking.

'That must be the "awkward move to reach a spike".'

Some second I've got here. Norman. He sounds a lot like that guy in 'Paris Texas'.

Except he adds, 'Get some gear in youth'.

This is the big pitch. He wants me to lead it and he wants to lead it. Both. Above me stretches the smooth slab under the leftleaning corner. We've been glassing it from the tent. It soars 130ft to the top of the north face of Cader Idris. 4c is the limit of my leading and now I'm doing it wrong. My quivering calves tell me I've got to crack this fast.

Way left is a little triangular incut. I reach out a toe, slowly, like a prehensile thumb. It docks

TG on Obsession, Cyfrwy, Cader Idris, Wales.
Photo: Norman Elliott.

first time. Carefully I lean my body over towards it, towards the space falling free to the lake below. No-one is yawning. I span left, palming back right, and lock onto an edge. Gently I pull across, reach up for a ledge and swing back right onto the spike. It's a done thing!

I get cruising up the corner again, jimmy in a Friend and clip on a long, long sling for the commitment to the slab. Suddenly I'm singing across it. 'Reach up and it shall be given unto you'. Edges turn to ledges and there's the sweet jamming crack to lift you to heaven. Blues. Bottleneck. Open tuning. Perfect pitch.

It had nothing to do with where we came from. Certainly our warm weekends of working-class initiation above the city of our youth will have been an ingredient. But we could have lived in London or Llanberis, catching a May Day weekend on the empty rockspaces beside the queues on the Cwmfry Arête. It had everything to do with having somewhere to go and by this I mean having new ground to travel. The previous weekend we'd visited, for the first time, the bellicose charms of Den Lane Quarry. If this does not entirely define the nature of our obsession, it perhaps puts a finger on an essential element of our sport. Michael Tobias bases his book *After Eden* on the notion of aftermath: 'Aftermath is endowed with powerful emblems of heaven, as well as the gruelling and damnable crusades to get there – all that I longed and feared for.'

The propensity of every boulder in the scree below Obsession to trap an ankle at the slightest touch is a challenge to the existential experience of, not heaven itself (we accept the risk of failure) but the crusade to get there, the control of will, the joyous launch into the creative challenge the rock presents to the body and the mind. But the fired finding of a solution, whilst attaining the top, is not the only satisfaction. There is something beyond the exercise of the will. As Blake wrote of Swedenborg's road-widening near Dolwyddelan: 'Verbesserungen machen gerade Strassen, aber die krummen Strassen ohne Verbesserungen sind Strassen des Genies'. ('Improvements make straight roads, but the crooked roads without improvement are roads of Genius.' *The Marriage of Heaven and Hell*, Plate 10.)

But I deviate from my theme, which is of heaven's need of hell. We came home early from this weekend. 'What can follow that?' was Norman's response when I proposed doing another route to recover the slings I'd taken off in the heat at the top of the big pitch. (The age of wisdom is, indeed the age of foolishness.) One Obsession was enough. And you will believe me when I say that the water beside the way is also of the way. I make no apology for offending the miserable sham of decency that requires a costume.

Later that evening, in the broken way of friendship that is the Lebenslust of the sport, we fell in with two companions who shared with us the joys of their day on the Table Direct approach to the Cyfrwy Arête. I do not know their names. But as the soft evening light slowly faded and a large white moon lifted over the mountain, we knew that, whatever went on in the magazines, we had shared a sport with dignity, without rancour. We knew we had passed through the gates of Idris.

Angel Pavement

The place possesses a distinct allure: nowhere in Wales could a more confused and romantically sculptured disarray of rock be found; loose it may be, but like many a loose climber it scarcely lacks character or attraction.

Typical journey into Wales, away from the coastal sands towards the hills to the west of Snowdon and under threats of rain down the valley towards Nantlle, above which, on Craig y Bera, hangs a neglected gem of a route, Angel Pavement. It was 13 years since my only ascent of it. As the years have passed, that climb has glowed with memories of delicate moves, serious situations and of the old team I used to climb with.

Now, as I saw with relief that the heavy wet clouds seemed to rest just on the top of the route, I remembered that clear spring weather when we burst out of Sheffield on a day trip to do it. The chanting song on the car cassette seemed to have got it exactly right:

> The first thing I met was a fly with a buzz
> And the sky with no clouds
> The heat was hot and the ground was dry
> But the air was full of sounds.

We'd spent a weekend at Cwm Silyn and driving home up the valley from Nantlle we noticed this south-facing ramp of slab, nearly 500ft long, narrowing as it side-steps to the left of overhanging rock. Angel Pavement was in the new selected climbs guide (James 1970), where Ron James explained why we'd never heard of this long line of pinnacled rocks: 'This large cliff is composed (or decomposed!) of numerous totty ridges.' But here between them lay the irresistible line of Angel Pavement, the first of Tony Moulam's honourable list of new routes in Wales and graded by him Severe in nails. We had had to wait until the following Sunday to step on to that sunny pavement of slab.

Now, 13 years later, I was again driving from home to Craig y Bera, already late in the day and in the wettest August for years. 'It's going to rain, can't you feel it?' Mrs Evlyn Jones told me, painting her gate at the farm below the crag, duffle-coat hood over her head, on the last day of August. A peregrine was calling above us.

'It's only rained in the mornings in Sheffield'

'Do they grow bananas in Sheffield?'

The guide warns that access to the crag is not allowed by the farmer living below it and that the situation is delicate, so I asked this diminutive lady with the round smile and ready wit how I should approach the crag and where to park.

'You can leave your car here and tell my husband I told you so. He's gathering stones on the hill there.'

And he was, gathering stone into great molehills to make a scrap of cultivation on a level bit of hillside. 'In the villages that nestle on these slopes lived a special brand of people, little known to the brightly clad hordes that pour into Pen y Pass car park every weekend', wrote Dewi Jones. 'These are the Tyddynwyr (small-holders) and the quarry-men, an almost vanished race.' Gathering stones below this tottering mountain as we made our way up to the unstable scree was a tyddynwyr of the almost vanished race, straightening up to look at us as we passed above him. We didn't necessarily expect to be allowed these indulgences of access another time. But what indulgences? The direct approach to Angel Pavement is a moving pavement of scree on which you feel as if you're going up the down escalator. It's still best to do as Tony Moulam did a week after I was born and traverse into the crag from the head of the valley.

The route description of Angel Pavement is actually superfluous, such is the purity of its superb line. I had forgotten how easily it starts, scrambling up heathery rock ledges until a little route-finding linking the ledges is necessary. I found only one runner in a full rope run-out, but no move is more than Diff. The second guidebook pitch is harder and actually best taken as two 75ft pitches of good friction and square-cut little fingerholds. Whenever a straight-up approach meets steepening rock a solution is to be found on the left. The next stance is the crucial one, cramped under a dribbling roof in which you'll find two small chockstones, although nuts can be added easily to improve the confidence.

I remembered my former leader, John Driskell, disappearing left round the corner from here where the slab narrows and steepens to a little wall. The slab is undercut below and by this height has leaned a long way left. Now the evening light had shrunk to the bottom of the valley below the slab. John had had not one brain haemorrhage, but two since I watched him confidently step out on to the edge where the last light now gathered. He still comes camping up in the high cwms with us, watching his pulse-rate methodically, mocking our modern gear and our not climbing in 'a little light drizzle'. To him I owe a lot of my first VSs, as his enthusiasm pulled me upwards against my instinctive reluctance. And I owe to him my memory of this route and this little crux. It's certainly a Severe move on a route that is still graded V Diff, although from here you'd fall off the slab and hang in air. Angel Pavement has a deep gutter and if you step off the edge of the pavement you'll need the wings and luck of an angel.

Above this pitch the rock gives way to scrambling over grass and heather laced with gorse.

There is just one more move round a corner which causes you to work out how to finger the clean-cut angles of steep rock to the right. But the belays are big sociable eyries where, 13 years ago, I had chatted to Dave as he brought up Agnes behind John and I. It must have been one of Agnes' first climbs.

The rumour in the pub had been that Dave had met this girl at a campsite in the Alps. Since Dave was a confirmed, pipe-stinking bachelor, there was much doubt about the story. Then one Friday evening as we were all assembled in the back room of the Nursery Tavern as usual, Dave appeared in the doorway with a small, shy girl who didn't speak a word of English. Dave had just brought her from East Midlands Airport on the back of his motorbike. At that precise moment, as she was having her first taste of Mrs Jenkins' best bitter, her parents thought she was at the pictures in Paris. She climbed Angel Pavement without hesitation too.

Back to the present – the light had now almost gone and what I'd not remembered was how to get down. I kept leading left, avoiding loose rock and the abyss below as much as possible, until the neck behind the buttress dipped down the other side to a scree descent to end all scree descents, unless you're careful.

We got down to the farm in the dark. Mrs Jones was shutting up the hens with a torch. She had obviously been keeping an eye out for us.

'You should have been here in the earthquake,' she said. 'I thought the mountain was going to fall down on us.'

Local climbers we spoke to the next day thought it was falling down already. It's this reputation of Craig y Bera that keeps Angel Pavement fairly untrodden. Between threats of rain and nightfall I'd snatched another angelic walk, although in the pub I began to wonder if maybe my memories had made it glow just a little more than it really deserves.

Make the journey to the crag of pyramids and pinnacles yourself one day, when it's raining on the higher hills but the sun is playing on Angel Pavement. As we drove away, America began to retell a tale:

> On the first part of the journey
> I was looking at all the life
> There were plants and birds and rocks and things
> There was sand and hills and rain.
> The first thing I met was a fly with a buzz
> And the sky with no clouds
> The heat was hot and the ground was dry
> But the air was full of sounds.

The Three Sisters of Craig Pant Ifan: Scratch Arête, Helsinki Wall, Stromboli

We left the beach at midday. Driving through the lanes of the Lleyn Peninsula in the heat we sang with Dylan, tuned in with the gypsy violin of *Desire* ... 'I'd like to spend some time in Tremadog/The sea and sky are aqua blue ... What drives me to you is what drives me insane ...' What drove Norman towards those ever-dry cliffs, that popular wet-day-in-the-mountains idyll was a photograph from way back: a simple fall of steep slab, a little black roof, an elf in mid-move, one hand hooked under, one somewhere above, and a heel kicking at the café so way, way back it wasn't even a café then. John Cleare's image developed in the darkroom of Norman's mind to the point where he would actually step into the frame for the first of our meetings with the three sisters of Craig Pant Ifan, the three very different personalities to be encountered in those rocks above the woods.

Scratch Arête is definitely the elegant one, the photogenic one, stared at with awe from the café

Previous page: Evening soloing on Jitter Face, Stanage.
Photo: Norman Elliott

Opposite page: TG on Pencoed Pillar, Cader Idris, Wales.
Photo: Norman Elliott.

Left: TG, Daphne Pritchard and Tom Gifford at Ailefroide campsite after a drenching on Palavar les Flots.
Photo: Mark Croft

Below: Christmas morning below Christmas Crack, Stanage.
Photo: TG

Above: Joanna Newton, 'The Craggiggler', on the first pitch of Central Buttress by Readymix, Beinn Eighe, Scotland.
Photo: TG.

Opposite page: Norman Elliott and TG on the last pitch of Adam Rib.
Photo: Kevin Borman

Right: TG on Reign, Craig Rhiw Goch, Lledr Valley, Wales.
Photo: Gill Round.

Opposite page: Tom Gifford approaching Espero Sur Central,
Puig Campana, lit by the dawn light.
Photo: T.G.

Above: The author blows bubbles on the summit of Cathedral
Peak, Tuolumne Meadows, USA.
Photo: Ira

Right: Wet weather bouldering in the Peak on
New Mills railway arches.
Photo: Norman Elliott

Opposite page: Julian Cooper painting Wisdom Buttress, Beinn Lair, Scotland.
Photo: TG.

Above: TG on the first moves of Original Route, Carreg Alltrem, Wales.
Photo: Gill Round.

Right: Norman Elliott on Nightwatch, Whitestonecliffe, North Yorkshire.
Photo: TG.

Above: TG on Central Route, The Red Slab, Craig y Filiast, Wales.
Photo: Izabel Brandão.

Right: TG on Espero Sur Central, Puig Campana, Costa Blanca.
Photo: Norman Elliott.

Opposite page: *TG on Tophet Wall, Great Gable.*
Photo: *Gill Round.*

Left: *Jim Curran on the crux overhang of Fionn Buttress, Carnmore Crag, Scotland.*
Photo: *TG.*

Below: *TG sandbagged on Spinnaker, Eavestone, Yorkshire.*
Photo: *Ian Smith.*

*Opposite page: TG at Hohenstein,
North Germany.
Photo: Gill Round.*

*Top: Gill Round on The Arête,
Continuation Wall, Ogwen.
Photo: TG.*

*Right: David Craig and TG on Croton Oil,
Rivelin Needle, Sheffield.
Photo: Ian Smith.*

*Following page: Norman Elliott on The
Brain, Curbar Edge.
Photo: Ian Smith.*

Previous page: Larry Giacomino on Hobbit Book, Mariuolumne Dome, Tuolumne Meadows, USA.
Photo: TG.

Above: Gill Round on the first pitch of Central Arete, Glynder Fawr.
Photo: Jackie and Dave.

Left: TG abseiling down Durdle Door, Swanage.
Photo: Gill Round

Opposite page: Tim Noble on the top traverse of Great White Book, Stately Pleasure Dome, Tuolumne Meadows.
Photo: TG.

Following page: Gill Round on Curved Ridge, Llewedd
Photo: TG.

door by VS leaders seeking an experience. All her charm and challenge is clear-cut and undisguised. She is not the soft touch HVS, as some say – her crux peg shows her age and is placed to disappoint some young pendulant. A firm, cool, touch – she is, like her features, nothing but fair. And one of those routes on which the first pitch is wiped out of your mind by the second: where the lower slab sets the tone … delicate but positive up to the peg, and actually harder than the slab above. Then it's the old foot friction, the undercut, and a reach that my fingers hooked as my toes took to space. Under pressure I improvised a completely innovative semi-critical sub-pumped tension move to delay stepping up. That is, I put my knee on. The top slab I remember as pockets of relief. Scratch Arête is not so much a one move route as a route dominated by one move.

Two years later, the car still screaming *Desire*, we sought the second sister. Helsinki Wall hides shyly round the opposite end of the crag. She is the coy one, slinking her way up steep undercut walls and tempting commitment with a false crux low down ... 'Your heart is like an ocean/Mysterious and dark ...' Each pitch of this short climb seems bigger than it is, but the mysteries have to be fought for. The first moves ascend the yellowed leaves of a book to find a peg hidden in the binding. The pull across to the ramp on the right tempts you into the trap. The second pitch steps in big strides across gaps whilst squeezing you with overhangs, but it's seductively easy. The third pitch is the stiffener, beginning delicately up a groove to a peg, but turning you awkwardly left into a crack of steep breathless momentum which finally pushes you into a layback of effort to what the guidebooks call 'a sudden finish'.

Two years later again and we were questing for the best, the third sister, the joker, on a day trip from Sheffield to Stromboli, such was her fame and the February 1984 deadline for this chapter of *US Rock*, which never even apeared, to become the best-selling book it should have been. Everyone spoke of her secret surprises. The omens were good and the Dylan was different, a classic tribute to a joker: 'Lenny Bruce Is Dead' we sang through Wales. On Scratch Arête we were nervous; on Helsinki Wall we were absorbed; on Stromboli we sang – well, one of us did, for a while.

The first joke is the start; the sick joke is the last one. We were tricked by rock below the real start disguised as the description, and the assurances of this bloke just starting who thought I was singing a Leonard Cohen song ... 'He was an outlaw, that's for sure ...' We should have suspected as much, but we grooved and traversed to the right pitch for Stromboli's final three stanzas, the three riddles of the third sister of Pant Ifan.

As I sat below the three roofs whilst Norman laced her up, I realized what it is about stances on Craig Pant Ifan: the vertical is mirrored in the horizontal. Angles and edges, square blocks and clean corners are fielded below the crag. A tug on the rope turned me towards a field-system of roofs and slabs. My turn to solve the tangible riddles of the rock. The first is in fingers exchanged in the undercut. The second is inside the crack high up. But the third is an elbow, a little cheek, and an expectant reach for a jug. Like Lenny Bruce, she doesn't quite play by the rules with this final joke.

Strong female characters like this can be as distinctive as their holds: Scratch Arête, fair and open with her positive pockets; Helsinki Wall, the shy shocker with her flat layered ledges; Stromboli, the mischievous trickster, has slotted jugs that will make you sing too. Although each sister might shock a VS leader, the protection should ensure that not much more will be hurt than pride.

'... He fought a war on a battlefield
Where every victor lay hurt ...'

The Glorious Diffs of Gower

In the evening, the sun came out and lit up the Boiler Slab drying, as only laid back limestone can, above a twinkling sea on May Day weekend. The drive through rain had been depressing, the campsite above Pilton Green, bleak and boggy, but the Boiler Slab above its little terrace was brilliant with possibilities, a 70ft slice of something for everyone. The Nottingham woman was leading a Hard Severe through the bulges, whilst local lads were tackling an E1 overhang with cunning wires and coolness. No, it's not in the guide, they said, they'd seen it in the magazines.

Just the thing for the kids was a corner crack called Classic. Yes, another neglected Classic, that scramble to a sharp white layaway, a bridge, a pull right onto the slab and its hand-sized pockets awkwardly placed apart up the steepening slabs. Daniel's first climb had made him stop and think. He

TG on Main Wall, Cyrn Las, Wales.
Photo: Norman Elliott.

was 13 and not keen. Nikola had surprised herself by readily romping up it. She was a strapping 14-year-old and ready for anything. Then we stepped along to Pinnacle Crack at the right-hand end, with its interesting steep moves on jugs and friction at a firm V Diff standard. This one was just for Gill. She was the 40-year-old I'd just moved in with in 1986.

Short but memorable, the routes on the Boiler Slab were a good introduction to climbing in Gower. Every crag seems to be an ideal evening crag, which can take a day's pottering to fully explore. Each crag draws you to a wonderful picnic spot, perfect for a family weekend, especially a first camping weekend with a new family. Our evening closed with a westward walk above the cliffs from Mewslade Bay to discover the Worm's Head rising out of the sea at sunset, and the black ribs of a wreck in Rhossili Bay.

Next day we reached the beach as the rain fell. After an impromptu picnic in a kind of kiln at the top of the cliff, we made it again to the beach between Great Tor and Little Tor. Whilst the kids scrambled round the grassy slopes, Gill and I chose a route on Little Tor. Our choosing the Little Tor might seem to have been in tune with the easy-going spirit of this weekend, but in fact it looks the more challenging of the two Tors, a vertical wall that rises straight out of the sand. Or what was sand when we started. As I searched for a belay at the top of the first and only pitch, Gill jumped ahead of the incoming tide. When I looked down Gill had started climbing above solid sea, and I knew what she did not know. This was yet another case of the guidebook writer taking a glance and calling it Diff. The corner of the right of the central protruding slab of Little Tor is V Diff, if there's to be any distinction between the two grades at all. Ask Gill, she'll tell you. Sometimes it makes a difference. It might be short, but it can be memorable with the tide licking at your heels.

On the next day we were ready for a bold attempt on the longest climb of Gower, the 240ft. East Ridge of Great Tor Upper Tier (V Diff). It was bold only because we slipped and hopscotched over rocks round the front of it at almost high tide again. Apart from that it was a bit scrambly. I spotted this at the start, which is supposed to go up a scrambly crack in a wall when the arête to the left is clearly what a ridge climb is for. There is little memorable about the moves on the longest route in Gower, until, that is, the wall of the last pitch where, several moves up and committed, a layaway on the side of a crack enables a long, long reach for the top to be grasped. I'd call that a Severe move, even if you do get a Rock 1 to stay in. You can go round the side to the right if you're rigid about gradings but not about life in general. Gill did. She'll tell you. She's rigid about staying at V Diff sometimes.

Since the tide was in on the Three Cliffs across the bay to the west, we opted, for the last of our weekend's sampling of Gower, to drive across to the north-west point and search for North Hill Tor. We waited for the inevitable shower to pass, looking out over the saltmarsh below the wonderfully named village of Landimore. There was something going on amongst those wild horses as we walked along between the wooded rocky bank and water-channelled expanse of mud. Whinnying and setting off suddenly, nervous as birds, they'd race at full gallop to be stopped by some invisible wall and turn back at full speed again. By the time we reached the crag, it had become a strange grey sounding-board of a slab, having few features, but an undulating rippling surface like the wild rhythm of horses running.

So West Slab is a Diff of a unique kind, requiring the reading of surface without the usual hints of cracklines or polish. At 25ft we gathered at a ledge, all four of us tied to one spike on the right edge, and we listened to the wild horses going slaperty-clap, slaperty-clap, over the marsh for some mysterious reason that probably made more sense than us all huddled nervously here on this ledge. I don't want to lose the real quality of this climb in the atmosphere of its context, but sometimes the two are so fused that even Bill Birkett couldn't separate them. West Slab is a route you'd always climb differently, reading different stories in the rock, but always ending up as Diff. As Nikola tussled to untie herself at the top, I pointed out the circling buzzard. Daniel missed the peregrine floating over its allotment, awaiting the three rising shelduck that were black and white flags against the marsh. And for some strange reason I seemed to be the only one who heard the first cuckoo at the end of that first weekend camping together in Gower.

Down the Tube: Scratch, Jacob's Ladder

I was ready to go home. I'd locked up the caravan and left for the phone box. After a week of gales and showers on the Lleyn Peninsula, I couldn't believe that Norman would want to come, not with his back still not right and the long drive alone. Anyway, I needed to go home. I was watching myself go mad, slowly, writing myself into a corner and then not writing for day after day, getting guiltier and guiltier on this beautiful clifftop caravan site. Didn't romanticism send even the Romantics mad?

The wind whistled round the village phone box.

'I don't suppose you're coming over tonight?'

'Oh!' Norman was surprised. 'I was just about to leave. The forecast is good. Have you got any booze in?'

'Well this wind will have to drop if we're going to do anything decent.'

So he came, and in the still, bright sunshine at Tremadog the following morning, we discovered that neither of us had climbed Scratch.

While Norman was making his ritual rejection of the big hexes and old slings he still tips out of his sack at the start of every route, I led up the groove of a little wall to pull through roots and belay on a tree. This got us established ahead of the other team who had arrived. Anyway, watching Norman's antique roadshow seemed to keep them entertained.

Under the shade of the tree Norman felt his back was not too bad and the next pitch looked a benign ramble rightwards across slabs, so off he went. He soon slowed down, mumbling that the protection was rubbish, but inevitably finding some. Nearing the arête he was calling back that it was great. This was a relief. I must admit I found it quite technical in places and admired its route-finding quality (that is I found it hard and I'd have got lost!).

Joining Norman round the corner on a ledge big enough to lounge on, you can see what a convenience this is. Above it lies the famous and much forshortened layback pitch, which has the potential for epics, as I have twice witnessed since. Norman's only comment was the usual one: 'Get some gear in youth!'

So I did, finding a good nut in a parallel crack to the left, thus leaving the main crack occupied only by 'Lord Baker in Langstrath', my first Friend, I bought with the proceeds of an article of that name published in *Climber and Rambler* in 1984 (see Chapter 3).

Lord Baker is a life-saver. He was all I needed to get me going up what I could see was 'a bit of a goer'. So why did I wait so long? Well, it was clear there was nothing but friction for the feet, and don't you ever find it hard to leave a good jam?

But the edge was perfect for curled fingers, and as I shouted down once again to Norman, 'Watch me then!' I launched up it, prepared not to stop until the top of the crack. Hand over hand, the edge stays sharp, even where it widens unnervingly, and just before the top a single beautiful crystal is waiting for your toe so that you can finish the crack in balance. 'What a goer!' I exclaimed.

The delights have not finished, however. The traverse right is terrific and tricky. Stepping down from a horizontal slot, you friction up on to a nose and cross towards the fist- and foot-jamming crack that soars to the top of Scratch Arête. 'What a pitch!'

So down amongst the chocolate fudgecake so assiduously shunned by the beanpoles at Eric's café, we found it hard to think of what could follow that. But in an inspired attack of divergent thinking, Norman suggested something he'd spotted in the Paul Williams guide (Williams 1982) he'd persuaded me to buy. Neither of us had ever heard of Craig Aderyn. Later I found that some Climbers'

Club (CC) members even older than us (and that no longer seems to be most of them) know of Craig Aderyn as the Teryn Slab. Anyway, this is the hot tip and purpose of this. Sorry it has taken so long to get here, but I hope you'll agree that a route like Scratch can't just be forgotten, and you'll need that emotional high to sustain you because, to approach the three star, 160ft Severe of Jacob's Ladder/Via Media, you have to go down the tube. That is, of course, The Tube – the CEGB's contribution to the environment in that quiet, less important region that is the Snowdon Horseshoe.

To reach Craig Aderyn, which is only 25 minutes from Pen y Pass, you have to leave the Miners' Track and cut across towards The Tube. As you climb over the new gate in the fencing and crawl under the belly of the thing, note the glassy surface of where it rests on its supports. This is presumably to ease the movement of the beast as it expands and contracts. Clever stuff eh? Of course, it might strike you that this crassly simple feat of engineering is the monument to 1990s technology that the CEGB is happy to leave us to live with for several years to come.

Walking down beside its monstrous presence we tried to enjoy the rock structures of the little bluff on the left before exploring round to the right, where we found ourselves under the most beautifully striated orange slab – an aboriginal triangle of still slightly tufted rock. 'Look,' said Norman, 'grass at the foot of a climb!' We sat down on it to gear up and I thoughtfully reminded him that he ought not to bend down at awkward angles so I should lead this supposedly 160ft pitch of slab climbing.

It was full of surprises. Pockets toothed with crystals ate Friends, unseen brackets ate fingertips and classic slots ate my trusty Moacs. My calves ached as though this was a long ice pitch. It went on and on until a thin, diagonal crack pointed the way to the very apex of the slab. A long way up by now, my feet balanced along the edge of the crack and little holds kept greeting searching fingers. Still there was good protection, right up to the final pull over the top edge.

The ropes had just reached, with long slings having kept them parallel

When Norman reached the top we were both bubbling with amazement that we'd never heard of it before. I even went so far as to say that this discovery was worth the purchase of the fat little book. A modicum of euphoria can be good for you. At the top of the Teryn Slab I forgot that, like Snowdonia, I'd been going down the tube.

In Search of Elizabeth Coxhead

In his review of *One Step in the Clouds* (Salkeld and Smith 1990) in *High* 96, Harold Drasdo makes a telling comment on Elizabeth Coxhead's novel *One Green Bottle* (which is included in that bulging omnibus): 'Coxhead has that indulgent affection for her heroine that we sometimes see in the great novelists (especially perhaps in the women).' I hardly think you could call the ending of the novel indulgent, but the exciting, frustrating, moving thing about what Jack Longland called 'by far the best novel about climbing that I have read', is that Elizabeth Coxhead cares about her central character, Cathy Canning, the girl from the backstreets of Birkenhead who wants to break out of the demoralization of poverty and the sexual repression of both men and women. Elizabeth Coxhead, I have been discovering, was a person who cared, with enthusiasm and intelligence, in a remarkable range of dimensions and ultimately with her own life.

So who was Elizabeth Coxhead? Since she died in 1979 at the age of 70 I did not expect to get much impression of her early climbing. But I found that she had written a chapter called 'First Mountain' for a collection of essays edited by Max Robertson under the title *Mountain Panorama* published in 1955. In it she describes the difficulties of getting started in the early 1930s: 'The established climbing clubs froze the ill-connected female with a glance. Inquiring at Wasdale-head, I learned that if I made my way to the foot of Pillar Rock I might there fall in with a noted Lakeland guide. It was true. He already had five clients with him, and they were roping up for the Old North.

With real kindness they included me, but naturally they did not change their plan'.

In fact Elizabeth's younger sister Alison still remembers that day in 1934 when the two of them were staying at Burnthwaite in Wasdale on a walking holiday. It was actually both sisters, the 25- and the 20-year-old, who set out that day in search of their first rock climb. Alison says, 'I remember us going out rather laughing.' You can imagine what she means.

Elizabeth was hooked and started going regularly on Jerry Wright's weekend meets, 'more the working-class end of things' as Alison puts it, in contrast to the FRCC. 'Jerry very much believed that climbing was a sport for everybody.' When I put it to Alison that *One Green Bottle* is clearly a socialist novel, she confirmed that Elizabeth was a socialist who became firm friends with Tom and Madge Stevenson of The Workers' Travel Association, later the architects of The Pennine Way. Perhaps this rejection of exclusivity explains why Elizabeth never joined a club, although her niece, Miriam, is a member of the Alpine Club today. In fact Jerry Wright's Mountaineering Association provided a kind of club which was orientated towards introducing beginners into the sport and probably gave Elizabeth a source of contacts who, like Maud Godward of the Pinnacle Club, went on the annual trip to Glen Brittle which for many years took up two of Elizabeth's three weeks holiday a year. By 1938 she had published her second novel. It was called *June In Skye*.

It was Alison who gave me the key to understanding *One Green Bottle* when I suggested that the novelist seems to be saying firmly that there can be no easy happy endings in life. 'But that', she said, 'was the Zeitgeist of the 30s. And we had that war which you're too young to remember!' I was chastened and convinced. Although set in 1950, it makes sense to read this as a novel written in the spirit of 1930s socialism, with its vision of the freedom of the hills for working people, its pervasive disillusionment in the face of rising Fascism and its retreat into a commitment to domestic duty. What would also support this reading of the book is an observation by Elizabeth's niece, Miriam. Apparently Elizabeth was indignant when she heard that some readers were assuming that Cathy Canning was based on Gwen Moffat, saying that the character of Cathy was created before she had heard of Gwen Moffat. 'In any case', Miriam pointed out, 'Gwen Moffat was clearly of the next generation from Cathy since she was able to continue climbing and raise a family.'

But Cathy Canning's retreat to a life of compromise is seen more autobiographically by Miriam. She told me that Elizabeth's first love ('That's putting it rather strong – a friend', says Aunt Alison) was killed in a climbing accident on Skye. Elizabeth never married. Part of the reason for that seems to have been her commitment to caring, first for five nephews and nieces whose parents were working abroad, and later for her mother and other elderly relatives. 'She had a strong sense of duty and doing the honourable thing', said Miriam. Cathy is equally concerned about her own integrity when she asks herself at one point in the novel, 'How could a lass who was on top of the world be so unkind to a lad who was down?' Elizabeth Coxhead's nephew, the writer and journalist Robert Chessyre, who was first cared for by her when he was two, said at her funeral that she was 'a rare human being who combined the highest moral, personal and intellectual integrity with a loving concern for everyone with whom she came in contact.'

So who was Elizabeth Coxhead the writer and intellectual? Her father was headmaster of Hinkley Grammar School. At a time when few women went to Oxford, Elizabeth went to Somerville College and gained a first in French. (She was at Somerville after Janet Adam Smith had left and Janet tells me that they 'met only once, for lunch, in the 50s'.) She spent her working life as a journalist in London, first on the staff of *The Lady* and then as a freelance for the Fleet Street offices of *The Liverpool Daily Post* and *The Manchester Guardian*. Her grandparents lived in Birkenhead and were of Irish extraction. After her eight novels she turned to biography with a particular interest in Irish women. *Lady Gregory* (1961) has been her most important biographical work. She also served as film critic on the radio programme, 'The Critics'.

These are the barest of facts. What they do not indicate are the qualities that could 'make each of us children feel special' as Miriam puts it, or Alison's memory of her as 'a strong personality who was extremely generous and willing to do anything for family and friends.' That spirit seems to be what Maud Godward observed when she wrote that Elizabeth 'was a great one for encouraging young climbers'.

But how would Elizabeth Coxhead have described her own experience of climbing? Amongst her papers when she died, she left what appears to be an outline for a climbing autobiography. In the brief 'Foreword' she explains that she is 'a poor mountaineer. I can lead a Difficult in rubbers on a fine day. For these deficiences I do not even apologise. I started at twenty-five, have always lived in or near London, have never owned a car'.

In her notes for 'Section 1. North Wales' two paragraphs in particular speak volumes between their terse abbreviations:

'The war years. Disappearance of cars and leading friends. Snowdon for full holidays of a fortnight, having it to ourselves. No one to lead but me – I am forced to – ecstasy of no longer being 'a parcel'. Beginners' routes and by-passes. At last getting to know the country and appreciate its quality – gaunt, austere. Night mountaineering.

Start of the mass week-ending movement as the war ends. Genesis of *One Green Bottle*. Much haunted by Cathy Canning thereafter. Temporary abandonment – as of other scenes where I have laid novels'.

In her 'Foreword' to this proposed book Elizabeth Coxhead insists upon climbing as open to anyone of any age: 'It is not the perogative of the strong and the brave'. This may come as a surprise to many of today's young climbers. So here is Elizabeth Coxhead's rationale for climbing: 'A sport is

David Craig on Lighthouse Arete, Castell Helen,
Anglesey, Wales.

Libby Houston below The Red Slab, Carnedd y Filiast, Wales. Photo: Izabel Brandão.

advanced by the handful of people who do it brilliantly, but it is kept sweet and sane by the great numbers of the mediocre, who do it for fun. And this is especially so in the case of mountaineering, which is something more than a sport, being an atavistic hark-back to the original ape in us, or at any rate our nearest approximation to the way primitive man must have covered the ground. It is an urge, an instinct; there is nothing artificial about it; it is like discovering another dimension, like flying, like gliding; it brings one, with senses sharpened by physical effort, into the closest contact with natural beauty in the most dramatic form'.

In September 1979 Elizabeth Coxhead took her own life. She had recently had a fall, fracturing a femur, and at 70, realized that she was probably going to end her days as a burden to others. Having spent much of her own life looking after elderly relatives, and being the strongly independent, supremely generous person she was, she wanted, as she wrote in a letter to the family, 'to go out with a bang not a whimper'. It was a brave act of caring, in her own way, for those whose sensitive kindness has helped me try to give climbing readers a little more understanding of the creator of Cathy Canning.

Meeting John Taylor

John Taylor has died. Who was John Taylor? He was an ordinary unknown student climber, serious and ambitious about his climbing, but you won't have read his name in the magazines until his death was announced. He won't get an obituary and I can't write one. I know nothing about him, but for one wet weekend in a hut and one conversation beside the fire amongst the steaming socks. I knew John Taylor for one night and I liked him. I can't let his death pass without recalling that weekend and the quiet, friendly impression he made on me. Doesn't the death of an unknown also deserve a moment's pause, for aren't these fleeting moments in the hut also part of the sport?

John Taylor was killed when he and Andy Fanshawe were avalanched whilst descending from the summit of the Ben in the dark of New Year's Eve. They'd climbed Observatory Ridge, moving together most of the time, and reached the summit at 4.30 p.m. They then put into operation their descent plan. After taking 100 paces due south they walked on a bearing of 270° through a snowstorm. They found themselves contouring a slope after some time and were not unduly worried by the condition of the snow. They were still roped together, about 10 metres apart and with Andy carrying the coils when they simply started to slide.

'22 yrs old from Leicester and a student at Stirling University' read the newspaper report of his death. The Stirling University Mountaineering Club was a band of surprisingly jolly people considering they'd had three days of continuous rain when we arrived at the CC Hut in the Llanberis Pass on the Friday night. I remember it was raining so hard that night that Norman didn't bother to close the boot of the car after grabbing his gear and running into the hut. I was trying to dry out photographs I'd brought to show Tim in the pub later, grumbling at him yet again. Some students cleared three bunks for us and we opened a bottle of sherry to wash the drive and rain away. They must have thought this was a CC ritual that was obligatory after signing in. They were all very damp and very kind. John Taylor did not stand out. Their wild-haired leader was organizing their booze and when we got back from the pub a girl offered us a nightcap from their wine-box. How could we refuse? We went to bed with minds on Mousetrap. We weren't the only ones.

It was raining in the Pass. It rained over the Menai Bridge. It rained across Anglesey but at South Stack it stopped. As usual. But Mousetrap was wet with black streaks and Castell Helen eventually became a substitute after we were battered by indecision in the gale swirling around the abseil ring at the top. Whilst we played a Rap on an empty wall, John was also deciding not to do Mousetrap, although he gave it a long look, and retreated with his mates back to the hut.

When we came in he was chopping dozens of cloves of garlic for the lentil stew he was in charge of. After we'd wolfed our pathetic Vestas John offered us a taste of his vegetarian speciality and it was a gift of genius. For some reason not everyone agreed, but John took it all – the piss-takes and the hidden compliments – with a quiet smile.

We got into a long chat that night. He didn't look to be in the modern mould of climbers, physically. Rather than the long-boned trendies we've come to expect in the university clubs, John seemed, under his jumper full of holes, to have the compact, steely physique of the young Don Whillans. Under the gentle, unpretentious surface I sensed a tough determination. We talked about routes I wanted to do that he'd done and about his own climbing writing – he'd just offered his first piece to *High*. He calmed before the fire in a way that suggested deep inner resources. He took the jibes from the student gang with a kind of patient wisdom. And he gave what he had quietly and openly. I just liked the guy, the kind of mate you make in an evening in a hut. And I'd like to record the passing of an unknown person who I sensed could give and take in the best spirit of the sport.

The Botanist, the Poet and the Red Slab

'Oh look, a tiny stonecrop.'
The botanist was at the back.
'Where? Let me see. Hey! Slow down Tairy Geeford! You are missing some amazing things.'
The poet was in the middle.

Libby, the botanist, was from Bristol. Izabel, the poet, was from Brazil.

And I was in front, heading for the Red Slab at last. F. Graham's Central Route had been there since 1924, clearly visible from the road and only a 20 minute walk-in, a brilliant line of white, up a sweep of tufted slabs, overlooked all these years when I'd been flicking through the guidebooks in damp cafés and cold huts searching for exactly this kind of route. When fingers froze, when the clag was on the mountain, when it was pouring it down in the Pass again, this route would go on and on and on for two perfectly straight rope lengths of classic Severe slab-padding. And it had been here all the time. Today, in the clear light of late July, glistening like a glacier above the Bangor road from Ogwen Cottage, it was sparkling more than its two stars in the Paul Williams' (1982) *Selected Climbs*. It's another esoteric gem for a bad day that he's slipped into his last edition, like climbing below Betws y Coed in a suntrap beside a wooded river, but that's another story.

It being July, the heather was in full bloom all around us as we walked up the right-hand side of the stone wall that rose up behind Tai Newyddion on the former A5 road. The botanist was botanizing and the poet was poeticizing.

'The purple stuff is "bell heather".'

'The bells hang like little grapes.'

'And that paler heather is called "cross-leaved heath".'

'It has a misty look, doesn't it.'

The Red Slab was nowhere in sight and it might come on to rain later. But I took Izabel's advice and once I'd slowed down I soon joined in, bending down to let the small world at my feet come into focus.

Of course, Libby is not only a botanist, but a climber and a poet. We were on our way to run a course together on 'Writing in Mountains'. But she does earn part of her living each year doing a survey of flora on the walls of the Avon Gorge. She has found that the intermittent climbing bans there have been bad for some plants that actually like being trodden on at stances. 'Well, it's not so much that they're masochistic, but that old man's beard and ivy would take over if climbers didn't keep them down.' She smiled her soft smile behind her glasses and gently stepped on towards Red Slab.

Of course, Izabel is not only a poet, but an expert on *Women in Love*. She's over here doing research on women in the works of D. H. Lawrence. I was giving Izabel a lift to join our course and I'm not sure she knew why she was climbing up towards Red Slab in her white trainers, but she kept flashing her smile from behind her glasses and saying, 'Tairy Geeford, you are completely mad.'

And there it was, as we came over the lip of the cwm, on our right above a short tumble of boulders, an easy-angled slab that was distinctly tufted with interesting flora, but mostly sheer crystalline white up the centre, hardly showing a crack or a break in its 280ft length. But first we had to negotiate the boulders.

'Ah, now these lichens are in fruit.'

Libby had got her magnifying glass held on the end of her nose and was prostrate on the rocks before the marvels of the miniature world. She was inviting Izabel to look at an orchard of lichen.

'At the top of each stem you'll see a little bright red ball. That's the fruit. Here, take a look.'

She surfaced, refocused on us and passed the lens to Izabel. She rubbed her nose on the rock and began to let out South American cries of ecstasy:

'Ahee! But this is fantastic!'

And it was. When my turn came I was amazed at just how intense that minute redness of the tiny fruit could be. It was like looking at an underwater universe for the first time, everything clear, colourful and completely new. Then I turned the lens on to a different species, a grey one, then a luminous green one, then a rich ochre one. Izabel looked at them.

'It is like the cracked surface of the moon.'

'And those black craters are the fruiting bodies of the plant', Libby added.

We were all botanizing and poeticizing together on a wave of discovery. A short walk to a crag had never been quite like this before. Now it was the turn of Red Slab to enthuse us with its secrets.

Between the first and second overlaps from the left, orange patches are parted by what looks like a white watermark. Compact and unrelenting, the slab suddenly seemed to offer a long, lonely, unprotected journey. But first the angle made the initial invitation and then the friction felt good. I set out to link together those occasional triangular slots that lay ahead. These turned out to be flared so that they wouldn't take nuts. The texture of the rock was still encouraging, though, like a sandstone of granules which stayed together better than it seemed they might. Soon the first of the unseen holes appeared, toothed with large crystals which bit Friends. Breathing became easier.

Increasing confidence and momentum brought more triangles and mouths of crystals out of the white desert above. Occasionally a thin crack would bend away up right, but it was simply unnecessary to deviate from the line of the rope. Little islands of grass came and went in the flow of sun-reflecting stone. Just before the rope ran out, a block in a diagonal crack offered a creaky belay, but the nuts above it were sound.

Libby raced up, barely pausing to botanize. Izabel was working her way up through heathers on our right, pausing to photograph. Libby said, 'I should have worn colours if I'd known. I'm in my usual tatters from the jumble sale.' But nothing really mattered. We were high, and soaring on a thermal of enthusiasm.

Libby declined the lead, so it was more of the same, except that now Izabel's black hair flew out from the top, then her smile shared our thermal of fun. Finally she was clicking away as I tried to concentrate on the last moves.

Again Libby lapped it up. For some reason, as we gathered up gear at the top, we were all giggling in the wind. We even shook hands. Izabel wanted a picture taken of her, too, up here in the sky.

When we returned to the bottom of the route I happened to mention that not only had we seen no-one all day, but that the neglect of this route could be seen from the strong growth of grass at its base.

'Well actually, this isn't grass, it's a sedge.'

Pencoed Pillar

'What's this stuff? Rock? Not a pitch of rock?' Norman was midway up a climb in Mid-Wales which the 1988 guide declared to be 'a very good mountaineering route of considerable character' (Sumner 1988). It's a three star Hard VDiff that maintains its considerable mountaineering character for 740ft to reach the top of a massive projecting pillar that Haskett-Smith suggested in his 1895 guide (reprinted in 1986) 'looks quite inaccessible from the grassy buttress at its foot'. He knew what he was talking about because he had just climbed the gullies on each side of Pencoed Pillar with O. G. Jones. The East Gully is still graded Severe and Great Gully, which Jones raved about for years as 'scenically the most dramatic gully known in Britain', is graded Hard Severe today. Even the combined boldness of this formidable team stood in awe of Pencoed Pillar. They probably guessed that its exposed crux is in its last pitch from which retreat would be difficult.

I smiled at Norman's sweaty dust-streaked face, the grasses in what's left of his hair, the burrs on his vest, his muddy knees and his soaking lichen-licking sticky boots.

'What you've got to remember,' I said, 'is that this route was put up by a Professor of Adventure.'

In 1903 Millican Dalton had brought his brother to this southern cwm of Cader Idris to take up Haskett-Smith's deliberate twinkling-eyed challenge in his 1895 guidebook. We had been tempted here by the 1988 guidebook and its intriguing challenge which is equally twinkling-eyed: 'The initial vegetated slabs will deter the non-mountaineer.' Decoded, I found this means, 'You cannot even reach the initial wet slabs without first getting wet feet. And if you don't like the mossy unprotected moves on the bits of rock littering the lower half of the first 120ft pitch, you can always fall into the interesting jungle of grasses and woodrush which you will later traverse anyway (doubtful spike here) to belay on a dug-out thread.'

'There's nothing "doubtful" about this spike mentioned in the description,' muttered Norman as he waded through the woodrush jungle. 'No doubt at all,' he mumbled as he lifted it out to recover the sling I'd planted round its base, 'it's definitely loose.'

He took some Friends from me, more in hope than expectation and set off on a 200ft 'wander up vegetation' which was apparently the next pitch. When he hit rock he belayed on it. Bucket steps have helpfully been stamped up the mud of this pitch, although in summer they can be obscured by fascinating ferns which it is hard to avoid folding rather firmly aside. At one point on this pitch I found myself moving up the down escalator as I tried to step up on the edge of turf which unpeeled slowly to reveal something looking doubtfully like rock.

However, on the next pitch there was rock, or rather rocks, lying on ledges of mud up a chute that is called, in this part of Wales, a 'chimney'. Fortunately this soon led to a grass-pull on to a steep meadow where foxgloves and willowherbs tried to out-purple each other. But it was the little white star of the mossy saxifrage that charmed me on the belay. Beside the thread a single plant bloomed white out of its dark wet hole, despite the fibre fag-end flicked at it by a previous belayer, and my almost crushing it with the pouch in which I carried the guidebook.

It was here that Norman became sarcastic about encountering rock. But he spoke too soon and was disappointed by an easy scramble to a mockingly fine thread belay in a hole. The belays were becoming more interesting than the climbing. 'Zen and The Art of Belay Meditation' will probably be the title of my climbing memoirs after years of climbing with Norman, but I would like to touch a little rock in between trances – sorry, stances. My next pitch promised better: 'a rising traverse line on big holds'. But decoded this again meant 'a choice of big grassed ledges for the feet and no move harder than Diff.' Predictably now, an exposed mantleshelf revealed a wonderful eyrie of a stance on the arête of the buttress. It was an undercut and airy eyrie. Looking down from here you saw what the Welsh poet Gillian Clarke once described as, 'Llyn Cau like a secret cupped in hands'.

It was mid-June in Mid-Wales and Llyn Cau still seemed to be a secret. We were the only people in the cwm. We'd set off up the track from Idris Gates at 8 a.m. to beat the queues you might expect on a three star 740ft Hard V Diff in Mid-Wales after weeks without rain. We were beginning to wonder if everyone else knew something we didn't about this 'route of considerable character' in the absence, so far, of any three-star rock climbing. 'Position isn't everything', commented Norman as I invited him to look around when he joined me. Well, the sun was hot, I was climbing just in shorts, the cool lake promised a skinny-dip later, and there'd be queues on Cloggy.

But the best of our rock was to come. For 100ft Millican Dalton climbed just left of the arête of the Pillar, on rock which is characterized not so much by jugs as by brackets – flakes which fitted a fist clenched over them. We went too far left, belayed and traversed back to the arête, but this route is an adventure and a bold bit of route-finding by a man who didn't hold with belays any more than he'd contemplate wearing socks in his boots, if the photographs in *A Century On The Crags* (Hankinson 1988) are to be believed.

Above a long grassy ledge, at the very top of the Pillar, there awaits the crux of the climb. Out of the comfort of a short corner a ramp leads up to a wall where the holds get smaller as they keep rising towards the edge. I was belaying Norman who suddenly felt the steepness and uttered the familiar words 'Are you watching me here, youth?' But before I could utter a familiar reply he was running the rope out to the top. 'Good route finding for its day and a bold effort, but not a three star route,' was his judgement as we scrambled across the neck of the Pillar.

'Well it depends what you're expecting,' I argued, looking for the third gully left. 'Compared with rock climbing in North Wales it's not a classic, but this is mountaineering country.' I was descending the wide bilberry tunnel like the book said. 'It's a botanizing route, an adventure, an exploration.'

Three Tiers in Ogwen (*with Gill Round*):

Ordinary Route, The Arête, Central Arête

'Of course', I promised Gill, 'we'll be climbing in the sun all day and with an early start we'll have a picnic halfway up the mountain and you can sunbathe.' With a perfect forecast and unblemished blue skies, how could I get it so wrong? I sit in the hut the following morning, glancing guiltily at the goosepimples on Gill's legs as the sun clouds over and the weather is breaking all around us. For Gill's long-awaited return to sun-drenched rock I'd blown it. On all three routes we'd begun in the shade and I'd had to point out enthusiastically that we were climbing up to sun on the Idwal slabs, Continuation Wall and the brilliant Central Arête of Glyder Fawr.

Oh come on, how can you possibly not have realized that north facing crags wouldn't catch the sun? After the hottest ever working week in May, I'd been persuaded to come to Wales to catch the sun I'd been staring at all week out of the classroom window. On a day like yesterday I didn't mind getting up at 6.15a.m. to beat the hordes to the Slabs, but as we legged it past the lake I could see that he'd cocked it up. Only Gifford could bring me to a dark, cold crag on a glorious clear day in Wales.

As I hadn't climbed for over a year his plan had been to give me confidence on the Ordinary Route, but already I was feeling uneasy. We arrived just after another couple and while they hesitated over the guidebook (Williams 1982) for a couple of seconds, Gifford plonked his ropes at the foot of the Ordinary Route and said to them: 'What are you doing?' Surprise, surprise, they were doing the same route too. But they were happy to follow us, especially when they found that we were continuing up the tiers. 'We're only leading V Diff,' Jackie said, 'and didn't realize that you could bypass Holly Tree Wall.' It turned out Dave and Jackie lived down the road from us in Sheffield and were to save my day high on the mountain.

I shot off up the polished trench of the first of the day's 1,200ft of rock climbing, boots, picnic and lemon squash in the sac. Gill carried the sun-cream. Two rope lengths and Gill seemed to be motoring along so nicely that she'd enjoy upping the grade a little to the V Diff direct finish up the nose. A polished finger lock and long reaches suggested it was time to get some gear in – for myself. On a smooth scoop I put in more. A final steep pull and there was the belay boulder on a terrace promising sun on the ledges up to the left, thank goodness.

I was going well enough until I became aware that hot on my heels were three young men in big boots, bullying their way past Jackie and Dave towards me. Gifford called down to me crassly: 'I don't know what it is about your bum, but it seems to be attracting young men.' I fumed quietly and concentrated on this sudden steepening. Eighteen months after his gift I was beginning to appreciate Gifford's idea of a birthday present – sticky resoles on my old EBs. The final moves just flowed. I'd noticed sunshine ahead.

Moving together we zigzagged up left and on the flat terrace before the descent gully I was able to offer, at last, a sunspot. Gill promptly took everything off – rope, harness and boots and lay back on the soft turf. I discreetly went along a ledge right to find the start of The Arête on Continuation Wall. Yes, it was in the shade again, but at least the sun lit its left edge. This 80ft pitch is well worth seeking out, even as a final fling before descending from the slabs. It is just across to the right, level with the top of the sudden steep descent and is better value than ...

In other words it's hard to start, difficult to follow out of the sight of the belayer and really exposed on polished small footholds on the very edge of the arête. At one point I even had that 'Never again' thought. Then came the last move, Gifford's, 'high step and a long pull' that was supposed to be encouragement. I was getting tired, but with a bit of grunting I got it done.

It was boots off time again. I'd imagined lunch above the last of the rock here, before the walk over and up to Glyder Fawr. Here, another wall sat above us but Gill needed a sandwich so it was lunchtime. I noticed that the teams who were now steaming through soloed a groove to the right. One sandwich turned into three. Dave and Jackie made tea, and far up to the right climbers gave scale to our next route. I avoided mentioning that it was 650ft above the all too obvious scree. It was at this point that Gill first said that her legs were gone. Well, we'd plenty of time for recovery. It was only midday. Indeed after the scramble through the right groove we rested again on lush grass to coil ropes, change into boots and take in the soaring length of Central Arête across the loose mountain side. Here Gill asked if I could do it with Jackie and Dave, but I was gambling that her reluctance towards a lone descent of the mountain from here would keep our partnership intact for this final big one.

What I had in mind was simply walking down to the lake. No problem. But I sensed that Jackie and Dave were enjoying leading through. The longest Dave had led before was the height of Froggatt. So I struggled over the scree and, from underneath, the route didn't look so far to the top. In fact the first pitch was a scramble to something apparently called a 'pasture'. 'Easy stuff,' I was thinking until I looked up and saw sky between the legs of the leader on the third pitch. Overhanging rock was all I needed.

I started the second pitch up an open groove. Later I noticed that the book suggested traversing across to the start of the arête. But the rock improved with height. At 100ft a sudden steepening forced a step left towards the arête and long reaches for little flakes. Just at Gill's '10 feet of rope left' call a good ledge appeared, 'Sunshine in 40ft', I called down. 'Climbing' came the prompt reply.

Good ledge? When Gifford sat me down on it, feet dangling in space, I felt suspended in thin air. Then came his usual 'relaxing' line: 'If your Mum could see you now.'

Above, a spike pointed down providing a good grasp for a steep shuffle up and high left step. Gill would love this and the pull on to the arête again.

When will he learn that I'd do anything to avoid going out on to an arête? But try as I might it couldn't be avoided, and I had to admit that the thin edge was good to pull up on.

Only 300ft of pinnacles and flakes remained. I set off to the right of the first one, put in a runner, and ran the rope out over and down several others until it ran out. It really was a roller coaster climax to the day that maintained the interest and difficulty if you took the pinnacles direct. I called down to Gill, out of sight below, to follow this delightful pitch.

The left of the pinnacle looked the easier way but after a few feet the rope suddenly began pulling tight sideways. The rope seemed to be stuck. I seemed to be stuck. Gifford's only suggestion was that I had to sort myself out. Impasse. Dave appeared at the belay below, brought Jackie up who eventually released my rope. By now I was tired and emotional. One flake was as wobbly as I was. Past it I just put my head down and wept silent tears of exhaustion and frustration.

Oh dear, Gill was silent on arrival. I had realized that I shouldn't have clipped both ropes into the runner, nor have belayed out of sight so far away. Best to get up the last pitch and out on to the sunny summit where, as Jackie and Dave joined us, we rallied for a group photo and a happy end to a day of three tiers (at least) in Ogwen.

The Extraordinary Route (*with Gill Round*): Curving Ridge, Lliwedd

'Well, he's a man,' said Harold Drasdo enigmatically as I was fuming. I was standing shivering at the top of pitch 2 wearing every bit of clothing I could find in the sac. My finger ends were numb and the north wind threatened to rip the cap from under my cag hood. Looking out at that sparkling lake below and the cloudless blue sky above, I realized I'd been had. I was on a north-facing crag on May Day weekend, again.

'I don't know how he does it,' I'd just complained to Harold. 'He knows how much I love the sunshine and he brings me here.'

It was three years to the day since the 'Three Tiers in Ogwen' experience – (see the previous story). This year the forecast had again said, 'best in the west' and I'd thought it was safe to return to Wales for a tanning-while-climbing weekend. Having romped up Wrinkle (V Diff) in the sunny Pass yesterday, this Diff could only offer an enjoyable 700ft of sunbathing.

Harold didn't know I'd packed a big tube of sun-cream in my sac. He seemed amused at my annoyance. He'd packed a flask of coffee. As he offered me a sip he explained that after writing the last guidebook in 1972, he'd not been back much. In fact, he'd only been back two or three times in the last ten years, it was always so cold.

'Actually, I've only just recognized you under all those wrappings,' he said with a wry smile.

OK, there was a bit of a wind, but we roped up in bright sunshine, having followed a team of three up the scree. (Go high on the left before you cross it and you'll see the path.) We could let them get ahead on the easy first pitch because Harold had arranged to join us by traversing in at the top of the second pitch. Two women and a man, they'd had a brilliant day yesterday. While we were queuing in the Pass they were doing the three tiers of Ogwen finishing on the Central Arête of Glyder Fawr as we had done three years ago. 'Brilliant route', enthused Sue, the last one left at the start, as I kept warm by uncoiling ropes.

At the second stance Gill and I agreed that it had been scrappy so far and soloable anywhere. But we stood in the sun and Harold's white hair had appeared below, overtaking three more people who had come directly up the scree. To pass the time I wandered out right to drop him a rope into the stone shoot beside the buttress.

'I just passed three youths pulling hand over hand up a rope on the scree,' he said. 'They sent a leader ahead and then shouted "secure the rope"; extraordinary,' he mumbled to himself.

The sun had gone off Gill and he sent me back with his flask for her while he hid his rucksack. What a gentleman. As he was sorting himself out, I led into the left groove where a little wall suddenly steepened towards an awkward move into a V-slot that gave on to a large platform. Here I could belay and get Gill moving, now that Harold had joined her.

Well, that steep bit wasn't too bad. At least it was getting interesting, if not warmer. Soon the rope disappeared above and it was my turn to climb a short slab to a runner high on the right. I took it out and tried to move left across the bottom of a groove by straddling a knife-edge. I got a foot across, but there was nothing to pull up on. I realized I was stuck and in pain. (The bruises later would have made even Jim Curran blush.) I suppose I panicked a little bit. I was annoyed at the false pretences of a Diff that was doing this to me. This was supposed to be enjoyable.

Gifford's voice from above suggested I went down and entered the groove from the ledge at its foot. From there, with a foot jam and a haul on a jug I reached the polished main groove with a knee.

'Trust the friction of the slab on the left,' said the voice. But the drop on the left of this narrow slab made the polished groove preferable. There were only wrinkles on the slab for my stubby, frozen finger ends. I finally slumped on to the big ledge in silence.

I had chosen to belay on this big ledge because the sun was still on it. But by the time Gill arrived it had crept away into the void: failed again. Harold led through to the next little groove which proved to be the crux today, although all other guidebooks place it higher.

'He's placing a cunning nut out of sight above him,' I commentated to Gill.

'I'll need all kinds of cunning to get up this,' he declared.

His final solution of two high stepping layaways were impressive. In her turn, Gill needed to stand on my knee. (At this point I could make an epigram to the effect that combined tactics make a marriage, were it not for the fact that we're not and they probably don't and it would be an appalling sentence. Good job I decided against it.)

The next pitch led right on to an exposed, steep ridge stepped with chunks of quartz. Then came a series of vertical flakes before a horizontal knife-edge abutted the mountain.

'You've got an audience on your right,' announced Sue from the mountain. T-shirted walkers stood on a sunlit platform below the bulk of Snowdon's summit that bristled with figures. From Sue's stance I looked back as first Gill's cap and yellow hood came into sight, then later Harold flapped into view, balancing up with a wild wave of an arm. 'Would you like a sandwich?' he asked on arrival, producing a rather crumpled packet from a pocket in the flapping cag. I declined.

Terry led up another 'rib on the right'.

'You should see a scoop above,' called up the guidebook writer.

'I can,' the voice came back, 'and it's full of people.'

This was an enjoyable pitch to the foot of a corner where their boots had delayed the team ahead of us. When Harold arrived, a discussion of Boukreev v Krakauer's versions of the 1996 Everest disaster began as we waited for the boots to grunt and scrape out of sight. I think Boukreev won, but I couldn't care less. I huddled in a corner thinking 'What a place to start a literary debate'. At last Harold hinted: 'Hadn't you better get going?' I think he wanted us off the stance so he could have another fag.

This next supposed crux pitch started easily up a slab, but steepened into a corner as the holds ran out. A turn to the right revealed a big high foothold, a full reach and an overhanging pull to step, off balance, into a groove. Stepping right to descend to the belay ledge I could not do. By now I was really tired. I couldn't trust my legs to step up with no handholds. Another burst of frustration and annoyance brought me through.

When the guidebook writer flowed effortlessly up to join us, I let him have it.

'There's no way this is a Diff.'

'Well it was Moderately Difficult in Menlove Edwards's guide [Noyce and Edwards 1939] and I upgraded everything half a grade. In warmer conditions you'd just romp up it. But you might just be in time to suggest a revision at proof stage for the next one.'

Gifford's voice interrupted the passionate debate: 'Come on up into the sunshine.' I cringed.

But there was sunshine at the top. The ninth and final pitch pops you out suddenly into the flow of following Snowdon Horseshoe walkers. I didn't realize there'd be a welcoming committee from the gallery. 'Well done!' someone said.

'I'm knackered,' was all I could say to the assembled T-shirts. Swathed like a mummy, I sank into a grooved granite tomb facing the sunshine and thought horrible hieroglyphics about this Diff.

But this unusual day was not yet over. When Harold descended to the right of the buttress (a descent worth knowing about), he spent 20 minutes searching for his rucksack among the boulders. Suddenly he saw it descending towards him on someone else's back. A rope traversed out from the belay at the end of the horizontal ridge. 'Sorry mate,' said the youth, 'we thought it had been left behind. We were going to hand it in at the Pen y Gwryd and tell the police!'

'Well thanks,' said the crag guru. 'What's your plan?'

'We're heading for the ridge.'

'That's all he said,' Harold told us in the pub later, "We're going for the ridge". Extraordinary.'

Tremadog's Diffs (*with Gill Round*)

Not normally thought of as a suitable place for beginner leaders, the Tremadog guidebook (Ferguson etal. 2000) has three routes that are full of character, protection points, short pitches and unfrightening starting points that are perfect for those who have been persuaded that THE TIME HAS COME. Unnamed Slab, Bramble Buttress and Canyon Rib, will, if taken in that order, act as a dose of salts to the ordinary caterpillar crawling up Little Tryfan who has been convinced she can become a butterfly on Tremadog, winging it (or hopefully not) with the rest of those colourful leader types as Gill can tell you, because she's now one of THEM.

Cathy Woodhead's to blame. And she's still feeling guilty about it, as she told me below Tremadog. We bumped into her coincidentally, the same day that I had done my first lead there. I'd only met her once before and that was when she'd given me hell at the Climbers' Club dinner for only ever seconding. I was really put out. 'But I enjoy seconding', I'd told her. 'I'm quite happy following Gifford up various routes.' She'd been a guest at the dinner in her role as President of the Pinnacle Club, the female-only club. Her final retort was, 'If the next time we meet you're not leading, I won't speak to you.'

That was in February and by March it had been forgotten as we approached Little Tryfan to get Gill back into climbing after a winter lay-off. We needed somewhere without a tiring walk-in, at an easy, unstrenuous angle where sunshine and a following wind would produce those positive vibes without which Gill can be less than her smiling, sweet-tongued self. She seemed to be keen to make a climbing partnership of the upcoming season, so after an obvious romp behind me up the first Diff, I suggested that she lead the next one. After a quick reminder about belaying on two points and equalizing the tie-ins, Gill set off, probably offering too many concessions to gravity with the complete equipment store display on her harness. She belayed early and turned the rest of the route into a demonstration of just how short the pitches can actually be on this benign crag. When I suggested she run the rope out on the next route to get the real feel of leading, I found that I was seconding before the leading bit had stopped. It was time for Tremadog and a proper leader's crag.

Sure, we'd both forgotten about Cathy's tirade. However, something might have lingered because it was a surprise to me too that I was keen to give leading a go. After those two routes on Little Tryfan, which even I found easy, I was fired up to find a more difficult crag to lead on. Gifford said, 'The sun's always shining at Tremadog', and it was.

On the right of Oberon, across a vegetated gully, I had spotted a cleaned slab which seemed to have had a lot of use, despite not being in the 1989 guidebook (Pretty et al. 1989). I had soloed it some time ago and remembered that it was a perfect route for a new leader. Whilst the second belays in the roots of a sheltering tree and the leader gradually gets a feeling of exposure as she soars up those sharp-edged cracks. Whilst Oberon has queues of budding climbers, this unnamed slab has always been empty, although the V Diff Boo-Boo starts around the corner and pulls onto the slab higher up. I thought instructors must use it regularly, it's so clean and polished on its first moves. But it remains a little gem amongst the giants of Tremadog.

I remember thinking at the bottom, 'This is quite different from Little Tryfan. Can I really do this?' While I was tying in, Gifford went up and put in the first Moac, for some reason. 'What happens', I said, 'if I freeze half way up?' 'Put in a nut and I'll lower you off,' appeared plausible, so I set off and felt deprived of the pleasure of placing that first nut. I was really quite enjoying it, looking down on Gifford's bald pate instead of up his other end. 'This makes a change!' I shouted down. 'Are you bored yet?' The climbing was airy but exhilarating, and I felt in control. How much more satisfying it was to be putting in the nuts, rather than waiting at the bottom getting increasingly apprehensive about following and having to get them out. The top came quickly and with it an amazed feeling of achievement. The edge was taken off it slightly by Gifford calling up marks out of ten for each nut placement.

Bramble Buttress is surprisingly good value, given the way it barely seems to emerge from the encroaching triffids on either side. It's the ideal place to face the setting sun on a languid evening. But watch out for two new bits of information in the recent guidebook: a changed road system in the village necessitates a different approach up a new bit of road and the farmer now allows cars to park just inside his cattlegrid rather than blocking the narrow lane. Townies like us have only to run the gauntlet of the farm dogs and dying lambs to reach the pastoral greensward at the foot of the climb.

I was surprised to find that, after years of saying to myself 'I'll never be able to do that!' I was actually looking forward to leading again. It was a bit disconcerting, though, to find that the young lad leading in front of me was having problems. When I came to do the first pitch and solved his problem by a high step right, I felt doubly reassured. The second pitch, however, brought me up short. I really didn't fancy the strenuous pull out onto the arête on the left and instead followed Gifford's dictum of 'Take the way that seems easiest'.

This led Gill up right, steeply up the back of a pinnacle. She steadily climbed the third pitch up the arête to finally enter a green door in the brambles where they closed over the buttress. She emerged at a ledge below the final soaring of the buttress. The obvious groove was hard and the face to the right even harder.

Yes, it was, but when I looked down for a hint of encouragement, Gifford, instead of holding my ropes, was taking pictures! He paused to suggest the slab on the left. It was balancy but blessed with positive handholds that just seemed to go on until a little steep wall below the top of the crag. Here I ran out of steam and shouted 'Can I belay here?' I'm not sure why I needed to ask. I was going to let Gifford lead the last two moves to the top.

The previous Tremadog guidebooks contained some isolated routes at the back that tend to be climbed only by the cognoscenti. Christmas Climb (Severe), for example, is a most enjoyable route away from the crowds on a high heather moorland facing the sun. Canyon Rib is another improbably great adventure that most people just drive right past to get to the café society at Tremadog. For a beginning leader it's full of surprises, including its highly secret location. I was determined to crack this old mystery for the 2000 guidebook because the established description was clearly wrong, as I'd conclusively proved on my previous three attempts to locate it. On each occasion, when eventually I'd found it, I couldn't remember how next time. One day, trying to take Ken Wilson to it for his first time, he returned to the road, paced up and down shouting in frustration as the cars avoided him, but still couldn't spot the line. So, here's the simple secret: 170 paces from the gate. There's a dip between two trees and that's where you start crawling up through the rhodydodies. This time we found a sling knotted round a tree beside the start.

It was all sloping the wrong way and definitely damp enough to put you off the climb. But with irresistible encouragement from below I slowly stuttered upwards into the vegetation and a belay below jutting blocks. I started up the blocks but when I found I was leaning backwards I knew this wasn't my style of leading. Gifford was keen to grab the lead.

OK, it was strenuous and committing, requiring a belief that these flakes were solidly stacked as you step out on their points. Gill seemed pleased not to have lead this bit and didn't lack momentum for the next leaning wall.

Ah, this is the kind of climbing I like. It's just like going upstairs. And at the next belay there's a great view of the rushing river below and a rewarding feeling of being high in the gorge above the trees. The next pitch traversed out above all this up a sloping ramp. Surely I couldn't do this!

But she could. By this stage there was enough experience of leading in the battery to charge up to the 'Well, I'll just have a look at it' level.

Of course, handholds appear at full stretch when they are needed and the friction on the ramp is better than it looks. Now I was out on this soaring arête which had both jugs and protection. All too soon I arrived on the ledge below the final wall.

The old guidebooks suggested a frontal assault on this, but on all three previous occasions various partners had backed off it, mumbling something about 'Not at this grade!' and crossed to a groove on the right.

And this partner was no different from the others, although the entry to the groove took several goes. Higher up in the groove I came to a stop and suggested I belay.

The traverse left from here is exciting, although I couldn't make out at first at what level to go for it. When you pull onto the arête the exposure is always surprising. People come away from this route forgetting the vegetation between pitches and remembering those final peregrine-perch-holds suspended in the wild air of the gorge. This may not be the most suitable pitch for a new leader, but it is surely something to inspire a return.

As I said to Cathy Woodhead below Tremadog, 'You'll be pleased to know that you can speak to me today!' She was a mixture of apologies and delight.

Under Adam Rib

There's something disturbingly sinister and at the same time gigglingly innocent about standing for the first time in a huge empty cwm. In front of us the black curtain of Cwm Du was bristling with buttresses which were each lit at the top by the early evening light. The left-most of these is Eden Buttress and flaming like a candle was the crux top pitch of Adam Rib, a 400ft two-star Severe first climbed in 1911. But here was a whole cwm of delights, for up every buttress there led a starred Severe, sunlit, naked, and like Adam Rib, as dry as a bone. The cwm seemed newly created, an untouched Eden.

We searched quickly for a spot flat enough for the tent, not realising then how it would get in the way later on.

Of course, it came as no surprise to come over the lip of this cwm on the north side of Mynydd Mawr and find it deserted, even after weeks of dry weather. The previous week we had been the only climbers in the cwm when we climbed the Pencoed Pillar of Cader Idris.

In the Moelwyns this very morning there had been queues of climbers on Mean Feat, but no-one on the brilliant Hard Severe called The White Streak. These are the secrets really worth knowing: Adam Rib escaped the books and The White Streak escaped the stars. Both are full of surprises and routes of remarkable character. I don't mind sharing these secrets with you because Adam Rib in particular needs regular attention. One of its surprises is loose rock.

*Norman Elliott on Adam Rib,
Craig Cwm Du, Wales.*

'What about doing one of these other ribs tonight and Adam Rib in the morning? It'll probably get the sun early on', I suggested to Norman.

'No. If we're going to do it, we'll do it now. You don't know what the weather'll be like in the morning.'

All I could see was a blue sky and a wonderland of rock waiting to be climbed. It had not rained for three weeks and it was unlikely to rain in the morning. But Norman was already heading towards the scree.

'Well I'm not carrying a sac,' I called as I scurried after him, 'just trainers.'

At last I stood where I'd wanted to be ever since I discovered the quality of Angel Pavement on the other side of this hill – and that was under Adam Rib. The evening was young and the tents were below. There was no need to rush up the long reclining rib to the sunlight.

And this was just as well, really, because it quickly became clear that it was not the climbing that was going to give us innocent fun, but the situation beside an amazing emergence of minarets on the left, and the beautiful basalt-type columns of Fluted Buttress on the right. Similarly it was not the shadowed presence of the black crag that would be sinister, but the loose nature of the holds that would give an edge of seriousness to this climb. We would need the time.

The rock of the first pitch so disturbed Norman that he belayed at half height, reducing the potential rockfall by 50ft. Leading the second half of this easy pitch I found the holds to be flat-topped blocks which sometimes eased free of the face. Then, in his turn, moaning with unease and his rucksack, Norman faced the prospect of a groove to the left of the arête, a traverse further left on to a subsidiary rib followed by a traverse back right again. He insisted that I belayed him directly below the groove (and in the line of fire) the better to hold him should he fall. My survival was assumed. I shivered in shorts, helmetless again. The serpent was beginning to uncoil on Eden Buttress.

Fortunately, Norman threw down more curses than rock. When I followed, I found that at every touch of a suspect hold there was one that was sound within reach. It was a matter of listening to the rock. I remembered a recent rope advert: 'Just you and the rope against Nature'. Whoever wrote that has not been here, or on Cloggy, or in Chee Dale, or on Pillar, or in Scotland. In fact where have they been? Obviously only on the bolted sport climbers' crags. Perhaps this is the difference between the sport climbers and the rock climbers: the former have to fight against nature to win a hollow conquest, whilst the rock climber has to listen for hollow holds in order to tune in with nature, attentive rather than assertive, receiving rather than taking, reading what is given rather than problem solving with technology. This is why the art of placing runners is so integral to the rock climber's way of reading the rock.

Having said which, there now appears a peg in this story, at the start of the next pitch. It is ancient and unnecessary and I clipped it because it's there. On Eden Buttress this is not an original sin, merely an acknowledgment of the serpent's presence.

I found the moves past the peg quite testing, but belaying above, on the narrow spine of the arête, I thought this next pitch was going to be the crux. Herbert Carr's 1926 guidebook description conveys something of the Alpine atmosphere of this final pitch: 'The rib narrows to a knife-edge which curls over on the left in a cornice of rock, leaving the straightest of paths set at an uncomfortably steep angle.' Belaying in the sun now, I watched Norman cunningly protect the moves above the cornice and teeter up, left toe on the edge of the overhang, right fingertips locked in the crack above his wires. Suddenly the rope was running out fast and he was shouting about what a brilliant pitch it was, how you really felt the exposure and how well Mallory did to climb it in December. I'll simply say that when my turn came it made me think a bit.

On the top we sat awhile, looking east to Snowdon's summit, then turning to the west to see blinding sunlight on the sea. To the south Y Garn's ridge stood stark and green. On the north side below us the land lay open to the golden beaches of Anglesey. In Greek the word 'Adam' is made up of the four initial letters of the points of the compass, so Adam Rib can mean simply 'the rib leading to Adam – the viewpoint for everywhere'. But this is not the real significance of this route-name. That came to me only after a night under Adam Rib.

Camping is not allowed in Cwm Du. It is Crown Land to which the uncrowned may have access solely 'for air and exercise'. We'd fulfilled the exercise part of this requirement and, having unbuckled our harnesses, we lay where we fell, taking in air and alcohol. We got into our sleeping bags as the air chilled, and, one by one, we fell asleep beside our tents. We were therefore not actually camping, just taking maximum air after our exercise. I woke to find this tent pitched in the way of where my feet wanted to be.

To sleep out under Adam Rib after the experience of that climb is to rediscover an original state in which the world is whole. Adam Rib is an image that is both male and female. It is a climb from darkness into light that requires a certain fusion with nature to negotiate splintered rock. It is an experience of both the athletic and the aesthetic, just as it is an experience of both the sinister and the silly. This was the integrated art of rock climbing before the Fall.

And this is not a backward-looking nostalgic notion. Nor is it a flat-earth attitude to progress. It is simply to say to the sport climber, 'This is the way the rock is now. Before you bolt it, think about how you're going to take away the freedom of others to use and to see only what is given in this place. You don't have to be manipulated by the commercial interests into using equipment against nature. The alternative, more demanding discipline, of listening and learning is still available.'

In fact, the reintegrating art of rock climbing is available to anyone who stands under Adam Rib.

CHAPTER 6 SOUTH WEST ENGLAND

Diamond Solitaire, Lundy

It was in a cave at Burbage that we first heard its name mentioned. Squatting under a boulder during another Sunday afternoon shower we found ourselves wedged against this Old Man of the Crags, lean of look, thinning hair and yellowed gritstone fingers.

'Yeh, Ulysses Factor's good, and Albion is better than the Devil's Slide.'

But the only route he'd done twice in all the years he'd been going to Lundy was Diamond Solitaire.

'Today's the day for it. The tide'll be just right,' Norman said casually as Neil and I were standing in the shop, open only in the middle of the morning, which can take the motivation out of your day – that is if you've got any left in the middle of a wild week in October after blown rain, blown fog, blown squalls, and a damp lighthouse with free rat pellets in every room. The problem was I'd promised the farmer I'd help him take young stock down to the beach for a waiting landing-craft, made faintly hospitable with hay. He treated the calves like his own children, and the several other visitors, who'd apparently made the same promise, acted as sheep-dogs to cut off the gaps in the steep path off the plateau down to the bouldered beach.

So, just a little later I was stripping off the layers as I raced back up to the Old Light – cheapest rent, and highest point on the island – to find a note. They'd left already, keyed up by the lowering tide, and taken some of my protection. Checking that they'd actually left my EBs in my sac I stalked off, muttering, towards the Old Battery. It squats like a matchbox, below a bracken slope, on the neck of a rib. Hidden below it is the most beautiful route you've seen, a secret gem, Diamond Solitaire.

From the plateau I see that they're geared up and descending. Shouting to me to bring another rope they disappear down a path. When I try to follow it's more of Lundy's skidding down soft soil and white crumbling granite to a climb down sloping rock steps which lead to black bristled rock. Round the corner and there's the flying buttress, the white sea foaming through its ring, a great arching curve, vibrant in the wind.

A sloping platform at its base gathers us together. As Norman pulls into an open chimney in the black rock I look back and notice from the surge and suck of sea that retreat is awash already. Norman makes himself a chough's nest of rope in a dark cave at the top of the chimney. Neil leaves the sunlight of the arch's base, leads through and then bridging above the cave he commits himself to the wall of the arch. He tiptoes up beside a thin crack that leads onto the bridged back of the wind-strung structure, but at every touch he withdraws his fingers from the flared crack choosing the quartz crystals on the wall. Past the sloping block at half height he picks his way up on the 4c diamonds to perch finally on the spine of the soaring harp. Wind plucks at his belay.

To dare to step out from here above the strung rhythms is to find sharp-toothed slots across the flying wall. At each reach fingers are saved by the bite of a friendly 4a pitch in this position. And then another crystal crack steeply plucks you up to a land on a cushion of sea-pink thrift. Look down at sucking sea, crashing white and green where you have been. At the route's end Lundy's sea-change works on you again. You don't believe it, but pausing on the stile you see a rainbow arching over the sea to the east. On the sea to the west diamonds dance in pools from sun shafts. You don't believe it? But who'd have believed that you can live the tales told in a cave at Burbage by an Old Man of the crags raving about the magic of this crystal ring, the gem of Lundy, Diamond Solitaire?

Saxon

What makes a good route name? When you find it coming up from the depths of your memory like a fresh discovery as you stand confronted with the physical evidence of the line, the situation, or the atmosphere. No other name, somehow, could be more imaginatively appropriate. Pat Littlejohn is a well-known master of the art. I'd skidded over Saxon in the guidebook (Littlejohn 1979), not really expecting to be climbing a 140ft pitch of HVS 4c. That's a scary grading even before you go on to read that it's an intimidating line. But it was at Zennor that the word surfaced to explain what I was feeling.

As we walked down the lane towards Zennor Head a dour farmer was tangling barbed wire and brambles to fill a gap in the ancient walls of his horse's field. To our friendly 'Good morning' he did not reply. He was losing the battle. The granite-fringed field system was collapsing. The rough-hewn feel of those fields remained. Saxon was the word which came to mind to fit that landscape. Zennor village itself is a farmstead frozen in time, its church growing out of the granite and hiding in its cave of light the pagan image of the Saxon mermaid.

After we'd failed to contribute the name 'Zennorphobia' to the guidebook we sat on the cliff top exhausted from the defeat of jumaring back up two rope-lengths and refused to feel despondent. We were engulfed by gear and stoicism, eating fudge freshly brought from St Ives, when I suggested that we go and find a Gneiss Gnome.

Little did I realize at the time that on the cliff called Carn Kenidjack beside the steep corner of Gneiss Gnome (4a) lies the steep slab of Saxon (HVS 4c 'intimidating but nevertheless low in its grade'). So we came to be hunting the Kenidjack like characters out of a looking-glass. The sea cliff of Carn Kenidjack is attractive because it is found below the cliff top car-park. But it has to be said, I'm afraid, that the approach to Gneiss Gnome is not nice because it's not gneiss. It's mud and grass. We abseiled again.

It was hard to concentrate on the climbing in the corner because the eye was drawn further right to peruse the mysteries on the face of Saxon, capped by its hairline hand-traverse above which stands a further 20ft pitch of hairy 4c. John was talked into leading it.

Getting started is a strenuous problem in pulling over an undercut seeping bulge. Quartz jugs come in long pulls if you can get your left toe to stay on a wet little edge. John balanced along a left-leading ramp which curved up into a crack biting his fists as his feet found horizontal slots in the slate. As the crack closes and leads out at a steepening of the slab, the climb gets into gear and the full play of its varied holds exercises the arms in a rhythm of long reaches.

The next reach right for a finger ledge reveals a hole which as you rise turns into a side pull. These cindery holes and slots are made for Friends. It was above a small Friend that John placed a poor wire to protect a move over a slight overlap. A left toe-shaped little scoop has to be trusted for another long reach towards a side pull that's as sharp as all the holds on this wall. In its upper section indented triangles appear in just the right places as though cut for the purpose in the compact rock. So with

Opposite page: Tom Gifford on Right Angle, Gurnard's Head, Cornwall.

sustained steepness the route makes for the left end of the finger-wide hairline slot that opens and closes each time generously just short of full reach, although John seemed to be making very wide strides. When I did it, I found that what makes this possible is the ability to lock the fingers against the closed ends of the slots. Then as you pull downwards swinging across underneath them you find that inside they're not so much incut as upraised for fingertips to close over, gratefully.

The block belay at the niche in the middle of the great wall right of Saxon is supported by the two usual rusty pegs. The last 20ft pitch is serious and sustained. Getting started is again a problem as you step left on the thin edge of the hand-traverse crack and reach for a small incut triangle. This pitch acts as a kind of summary of the first, a rising leftwards linkage of pockets, slots and side pulls, all at full reach and of a distinguished kind. As I pulled on to the loose soil and steep grass at the top I knew I was going to rave about this route for some time. Very protectable and made for Friends, it is nevertheless steep, long and unrelenting in its technical demands. It has no tricks or spectacular features, but demands solid, steady workmanship. A unique route is produced by unique rock and unique holds. But to become a classic it really needs a name that is so imaginatively appropriate that it fuses with your memory of the moves: Saxon.

Right Angle

On the second day the caravan was still singing. Spring tides were boiling in the cold wet zawns and the gale blew right through Easter. The door ripped open and The Catcher filled the gap, shoulders broad as lintels and big fists anchoring the door. 'I just wondered' – a wry grin flickered under his beard – 'if you fancied Right Angle,' he said, pausing for the passing of stunned silence. 'It should be quite exciting in these big seas.' Behind him the sky grew darker. We vibrated with the van. I'd settled down to write a review of walks in sunny France and Gill was suffering *Storm and Sorrow In The High Pamirs*. Slowly we came back to Cornwall. 'OK, you're on!'

Really we'd come to Cornwall for The Catcher to snatch this new route on Zennor's bottom tier. He'd been obsessed with it since last Easter, anxiously scanning the mags each month and still finding it unreported. He'd even sent me three photos stuck together that were supposed to show the line. But his driving force was the name he'd got for it: 'Zennorphobia'. As we'd crawled through the gale out along the cliff for a look the previous evening, I, too, couldn't understand why it had not been done. A long clean crack right of the Eyass just waited to be entered by a traverse after a scramble from the boulders in the bottom of the zawn. All we gained that evening was a glimpse of the Zennor mermaid, carved in a wooden bench-end in the church. It was into this cove that she had eventually drawn the choirboy, Matthew Trewhella, whose singing she'd come regularly to listen to. It's a weird coastline this.

And nothing is stranger than the fact that the meeting of undercut walls at Gurnard's Head should hold a climb of only Hard Severe in its Right Angle. It's weird too, to be climbing on the black and slatey greenstone on this granite coast. Thomas Hardy might have been writing about Gurnard's Head in a gale when he wrote: 'In chasmal beauty looms that wild weird western shore' (Thomas 1970). The contemporary poet John Heath-Stubbs lived in the cottage on the cliffs at Gurnard's Head for a while and felt the darker side of that wild weirdness:

> This is a hideous and wicked country
> Sloping to hateful sunsets and the end of time.
> (Thomas 1970)

The start of Right Angle slopes down in a traverse that certainly feels like the end of something. When we got there the rock was wet and the air damp with both drizzle and spray. Perhaps this was close to what Matthew Trewhella felt.

The Catcher descended, disappeared then reappeared, out across a hidden gulf in which swung the odd dislodged runner on the looping rope. Behind him a black cave vomited white foam. That descending traverse, above the undercut cliff with a big sea running was, as The Catcher promised, exciting. A walk down turned into a scramble until a move round and down into the roof of a little cave demanded that you think ahead and get your feet sorted out, never mind the descending finger slots. Bridging too high across the sea-charged corner I banged my head under the roof. But jugs on the other side pull you out on to a big lichened ledge and a block belay solid enough to steady the pulsing of the heart, if not the sea.

Again The Catcher stepped down and along the ledges then up and out of sight. It may be a lonely lead, but that was certainly a lonely stance, as my eye followed the rope towards the gaping wet cave, waiting for the seventh wave. Suddenly, there was the mermaid curled on the cliff opposite, inviting action as she focused her glinting eye. Steep but sharp, the rock lost little in being wet. As I came round the bulging wall I saw that The Catcher had considerately not down-climbed the first vertical crack to belay on the pegs under the cave. So he'd saved me from seconding that dreaded downclimb. Instead he'd kept traversing into the bottom of the big corner and was hanging in a web of slings and ropes grinning like Holden Caulfield, The Catcher in the wry tangle.

On that final hand traverse I was glad he was there. Just enough holes for the fingers made up for lost foot friction. Then The Catcher pointed down. I slithered 20ft to a ledge below and clipped into two very rusty pegs. Here the sea was Extremely Exciting. I shouted to The Catcher to hurry up and haul me out of there. He shouted to me not to let the ropes drop and get sucked under and snagged. So between my legs and the rock I piled the ropes in a right tangle. And the mermaid smiled. And I got drenched.

But that last pitch has everything in 120ft of bridging, jamming, wall-climbing, layaways, overlaps and underclings. At the top the mermaid, like the Practical Princess, produced a flask, and then took us off for cream teas at Compass West. Whilst he was washing up our cups Rowland Edwards told The Catcher that seven years ago he'd cleaned and climbed that long crack in Zennor zawn, finding it only 4a. But the direct link up from the bottom went round a roof on loose rock and was going to be disproportionately harder. 'It didn't seem to fit, and you can get fed up with a zawn after a while, so we left it and went further down the coast.'

So next day we abseiled into the zawn well to the right of the long crack and placed a peg belay in the back of a little sentry box. From here The Catcher sneaked a delicate traverse across to the base of the crack where, leaning out from his cat's cradle, he called me across before romping up the Edwards' Crack to the top. The name 'Zennorphobia' is now not only in the guidebook (Hooper et al. 2000) but it carries a star for quality.

D. H. Lawrence and the Count House

At one point on the walk Lawrence's friend, Koteliansky, who was a Russian Jew, had leant back against a drystone wall and sung in Hebrew the 23rd Psalm. Half-remembering a word from that song, Lawrence took the name 'Rananim' for his colony of like-minded souls, with whom he would withdraw from a materialistic society destroying itself and create a new life which Lawrence described as 'communism'. Rananim became the cottages at High Tregerthen, midway between the Gurnard's Head and St Ives, until the Lawrences were expelled from Cornwall soon after a police raid on their night's singing in the Count House, now a Climbers' Club hut.

It was in the month of January in 1916 when Lawrence moved to Cornwall, a month when an increasing number of modern climbers are discovering there can be still, mild periods between wild winds: 'There have been great winds, and the sea has been smoking white above the cliffs. Now it is still again, and the evening is very yellow.' Climbs had already been recorded on the rocks below Lawrence's house by the father of Cornish sea cliff climbing, A. W. Andrews. Lawrence and Frieda swam in the cove below High Tregerthen called Wicca Pool.

In 1902 A. W. Andrews and his sister made a number of routes on Wicca Pillar, which is approached down the Lawrences' lane. It was here that in 1912 Professor Noel Odell was shown by Andrews the advantages of 'tennis shoe' climbing, which Odell was later to apply on the Idwal Slabs. Also in 1902 Andrews climbed Bosigran Ridge, which makes a 700ft Alpine ridge type challenge across the gully from the Count House. Just four years before Lawrence came to Cornwall, Geoffrey Winthrop Young with George Mallory had made the first ascent of the ridge of Carn Les Boel of which Young wrote: 'It was a rock surface of volatile changes, from chimney or column, crystallised, friable and prickly, to the sea and the time-smoothed perpendicular or overhang.'

Lawrence immediately found in North Cornwall what he needed: 'It has never taken the Anglo Saxon civilisation, the Anglo-Saxon sort of Christianity. One can feel free here, for that reason – feel the world as it was in that flicker of preChristian Celtic civilisation, when humanity was really young.' He drew this sense of Celtic life directly from the landscape. Writing of a cove near Padstow, Lawrence said: 'It is a cove like Tristan sailed into, from Lyonesse – just the same. It belongs to 2,000 years back – that pre-Arthurian Celtic flicker of being which disappeared so entirely. The landscape is bare, yellow-green and brown, dropping always down to black rocks.'

In fact, it is Bosigran Farm that W. G. Hoskins names in *The Making of the English Landscape* as the classic surviving example of a Celtic farmstead: 'the network of small, irregular fields bounded by miles of granite-boulder walls was almost impossible to change once the pattern was laid down.' Perhaps Lawrence was told later by local people that the name Bosigran means 'dwelling of Ygrain' who was, in legend, the mother of King Arthur. I can remember a fog-bound night in the Count House in 1968 when only the four of us were crouched round a huge fire listening to the Pendeen fog horn and the rats running round the skirting board, telling ourselves that the mother of giants was dead.

Lawrence embraced her spirit and despite the prosecution of *The Rainbow* for obscenity and the burning of remaining copies by the common hangman, Lawrence pressed on with the original core of the project of which *The Rainbow* was only the prelude. *Women in Love* was written at High Tregerthen and finished, but for the final chapter, by 30th June 1916. Meanwhile Rananim remained a lonely idea as Lawrence fell out with potential colonists, starting with Bertrand Russell and ending with Cecil Grey, the young musician who rented the Count House. Middleton Murry and Katherine Mansfield did move into High Tregerthen in April, but had left by June.

By November 1916 Lawrence was writing to Koteliansky that 'the people were wrong.' Those who visited High Tregerthen at this time tend to have been more or less struck by the pans flying between Lawrence and Frieda during their violent rows.

But another war was going on within their hearing. The next time you're looking out over the sea from the sentry box stance of Doorpost, imagine the view in August 1917 when destroyers and seaplanes accompanied by an airship were hunting a German submarine. The noise of exploding depth charges was terrific even at Tregerthen Farm, where Lawrence taught young Stanley Hocking how to play chess. In a BBC interview years later, Stanley remembered Frieda saying to him: 'What an awful thing war is. In that submarine may be some of the boys I went to school with.' Huge patches of oil remained on the sea for several days after that particular hunt.

Frieda was, in fact, a cousin of the Red Baron who was destroying British aircraft so famously; she was German and wrote to her relations regularly through Switzerland. One day Lawrence was walking home from Zennor when a policeman jumped out from behind a hedge and demanded to see the contents of Lawrence's rucksack. It contained nothing more incriminating than loaves of bread, but the suspicions were growing that Frieda was passing bread and information about British shipping movements to German submarines down at the coves at night.

The local people who held these suspicions knew the traditional uses of their coves for illicit activities. 'Owlers', as smugglers were known from medieval times, had been so active in these coves in the 18th century that Customs and Excise Preventative Boats were stationed at Sennen, Pendeen and St Ives. But everyone was at it, including the Mayor of St Ives in 1767, John Knill, who also happened to be Collector of Customs for the 20 years from 1762. He is said to have helpfully erected a steeple on Worras Hill as a landmark for smuggling craft. One such boat caught in a storm discharged its cargo of 'double-headed cod' (code-name for spirit kegs with handling loops at each end) which came ashore at night near St Ives. A crowd gathered and dispersed before the Excise men arrived. *The West Briton* of 25th November 1814 reported, 'Not a single ray of moonshine was to be seen. The boat reached shore safely, but the crew were in a dispirited state'.

In fact it was believed that Lawrence, Frieda and Cecil Gray at the Count House, were the ringleaders of an elaborate spy network. Local feeling ran so high that one day locals armed with scythes and pitchforks set out for the Count House to murder Gray and throw his body down Suicide Wall. In his autobiography Gray wrote: 'I was only saved, in fact, through the fortunate circumstance that the malevolence of the Cornish was only exceeded by their cowardice'.

The Cornish people might have been amused to know that Gray was himself being scared by the Count House 'Knocker' – Bosigran's poltergeist that emerges from the disused mine to plague the inhabitants of the Count House.

More serious was an event which Lawrence described in Chapter Ten of *Kangeroo*. After supper at the Count House, German folk-songs were in full swing when a hammering at the door was followed by the appearance of half-a-dozen men with loaded rifles who searched the house. Lights had been seen flashing out to sea from the windows. A drawing pin had worked loose from the black-out curtains in the westerly gale and allowed an insidious flickering which on this coast could only mean one thing: more nocturnal signals of 'owlers'. Gray received a heavy fine, but a few days later High Tregerthen was searched, papers taken and the Lawrences given three days to leave Cornwall. Gray had to give them the money to get to London where they were to report to the police.

Lawrence next settled at Mountain Cottage, Middleton, above Cromford in Derbyshire, and almost within sight of Black Rocks. Rananim died, although the house where Lawrence wrote *Women in Love* can still be seen with its square tower jutting above the bank of the lane. This tower where Lawrence worked had been built for a previous writer, the best selling novelist Guy Thorne, who had never occupied it. From it, Lawrence reported in a letter, the death of a local boy of 16 one May Sunday, whilst collecting gulls' eggs on the cliffs. These primeval origins of climbing were still alive in the Cornwall of 1917, as was much else that still appeals to the modern climber exploring its cliffs, coves and zawns.

'This Cornwall,' wrote Lawrence, 'is very primeval: great, black jutting cliffs and rocks, like the original darkness, and a pale sea breaking in, like dawn. It is like the beginning of the world, wonderful: and so free and strong'.

Kinkyboots

It went against the grain for a gritstone climber to approach a route with mud curling round the toes of the battered old EBs. But this was Baggy on a sea-misty morning and the top of a route called Ben, smiling Ben Wintringham's route. Marion is the name of a friendly crack in the same slab and named for his wife. But all this pleasantry from me is simply delaying my recalling the first fall of that Easter Day, backwards from the muddy slope over the edge of the slab towards white foam shifting uneasily round a wet platform 130ft below. What anchored me to earth seemed a chain of increasingly thin things: descendeur, rope, crab, sling, crab, stake in the sloping mud.

In pulling down the ropes it would have been impossible to have avoided them falling into the big sea-salty pool. Feet and hands on the first holds were wet too. Really, flippers seemed more suitable. An applause of spray agreed. But the clammy crack hid sharpnesses for fingers and pinched feet until friction even better than gritstone's emerged above the level of high-tide seaspray. Mist still hid Lundy and its familiar Old Light.

A hundred feet up I came to an impasse, thankful for a small Friend and a big one below. Big Tim, Noble by nature as well as by name, came up to solve the problem, laybacking past my ear up the parallel sides of a mud-smeared groove. Trying it Tim's way I had to agree with him that, yes, there were finger pockets, yes, in fact, the feet do stay put on the inside of the groove, and yes, I could see now that there were big holds to the top. This second fall of the day was a moral one. A bite of a Friend had offered a belay and I took the way out of the forbidden fruit – a climber who stopped climbing and belayed below the crux of a Hard Severe! The third fall of the day brought me even lower psychologically, but it also brought me onto a redeeming slab of brilliant white rock, the journey up which is paradise regained. What could be more kinky than the start of Kinkyboots: forcing yourself to fall, hands outstretched, across a black greasy pit where the sea at high tide surges slobbering, white and green? Everything tells you not to. Yet you have to make that fall to find the long exquisite slab of light.

'It's out of condition!' I had tried, whilst Tim made his unhesitating preparations. 'We're not going to do this route today, are we?' was my final attempt. Tim was so tall that he could make that fall, place a Friend up under a loose leaf of slate and push back upright again to walk down a few feet and lean across for The Move opposite The Hold. I watched him pull across and then up through the layers of little overhanging pieces of slatey blocks with the concentration of one about to pick his way through purgatory. When it came to my turn I studied the greasy sloping faces that were footholds on the other side. I seemed to have stood staring and muttering 'I hate this kind of thing,' for a long time. When eventually I fell across and took out the Friend I found that I couldn't push back. Now really on the rack I had to walk hands and feet down at full stretch to find The Hold to pull across on. When I moved I moved fast and picked the right slots over the blocks to rest in balance at the peg before the last test. Tim had left a long sling from a tiny brass nut in the crack round the overhang in which you're supposed to finger-jam. In the event I pulled on the jug on the lip, got a right knee in the sloping V-groove and, with great physical and moral effort, avoided touching the long sling. I grabbed the crab instead. Out of the darkness into the light! Only one or two stances on only the best of routes provide that equal balance between relief and anticipation. As you look up the slab you know it's going to be good.

In fact it is such a journey of discovery that it deserves not to be over-described. I'll only say that, in searching for the way, you find a fascinating variety of rock formations, textures and colours. It is a much more interesting pitch than anything on Pink Void, which in comparison seems over-rated.

Indeed if, after the fall, you ascend the gleaming slab of Kinkyboots in one pitch, you'll generate a relationship with rock forms and textures that is a re-affirmation of what rock climbing is about. But only after The Fall.

Durdle Door

Big guns were booming through the air above the sound of the sea, interrupted by the rattle of machine gun fire.

The sun shone at Swanage as if it were June, but this was April and the bird restrictions were in force. You know what they're like at the BMC about Swanage. They'll go to any lengths to enforce those restrictions – tanks, red flags everywhere, Mike Harding patrols and a cunning photo in the guidebook (Jenkin 1986) of an inviting, unrestricted, sea arch. Mike Harding patrols? Gill was supposed to be taking pictures, but there she was, chatting up two blokes sitting on the beach. When she got up to go and get dramatic photos of us on Durdle Door the small one with glasses said, 'Stay and talk to us. When they come back we'll say we're famous insect collectors.'

Big blocks fell through the air, booming into the sea, followed by the machine-gun rattle of stones. This was just my delicate abseil technique and Norman was already down there somewhere. When they say 'restricted' in this guide they mean it (the army still seemed to be giving hell to those guys who had sneaked on to Marmolata Buttress where the route names indicate the general attitude: Riff, Raff and Teenage Wasteland). When they say 'unrestricted', they're referring to the rock (nothing seems to hold it together). And when they say 'fairly serious and a fair amount of loose rock' they mean 'silly'.

But at Severe, Archway on Durdle Door looked a picture postcard route. That's because it is a picture postcard in Lulworth Cove shops. You know about seaside postcards – the thing is to be able to tell which are the funny ones. We really should have guessed when all those tourists were falling about round the postcard stand and saying in mock Dorset accents, 'Durdle Door! Durdle Door!' Climbers should realize that if in Dorset 'fairly serious' means 'silly', on Durdle Door 'a fair amount of loose rock' means nothing less than Fawlty Towers.

Anyway, I knew what Norman would be saying 90ft. below me somewhere (and in what accent), but all I could hear were the sea and the army, both battering the landscape. Unintentionally doing my bit to disintegrate the loose lip of a roof, I found myself suddenly hanging in the air like a seagull and inclined to match their mess on the rocks below. Then I saw Norman grinning coyly like a grizzled Merman on a platform round to the right. 'Glad you remembered to bring a rope this time', he quipped wittily. (The day before I'd arrived at the bottom of the Subliminal cliffs without one.) We were leaving the abseil rope hanging round its stake belay over the end of this long white stick of seaside rock with a giant Polo stuck sideways in its end.

And I sat and I sat, the rope going out slowly with long pauses and finally a very long pause. I could tell Norman had arrived because the abseil ropes started rising skywards as I was beginning to see a black intrusion of Mars Bars in the rock beside me.

The move off the platform round the corner was gobstopping – hard and solid – and there was Gill again, sunbathing in her undies with those two strange men taking the photographs instead of her. But a ramp leading left demanded concentration, as did the flake handholds. The trick was to press down so that the holds were literally held in place. The shadowed wall of Durdle Door steepened fairly seriously to a bulging shield. I pulled up, bridged a bit and reached round for a loose block that had to be held down until a higher crack could be gently pulled upon. Stepping rightwards off this block I must have murmured something like 'Durdle Door!' Norman grinned wickedly down and said 'See if you can trundle it'. Now I'm not a natural trundler, but this seemed a social service and there aren't many of them left, so away it went. It's trundle at Durdle or die. The relief nearing the top on a daft route like that can effect the brain in a mysterious biochemical process that Mike Harding was apparently studying through his zoom lens. For he it was, watching with Gill as I released the tension and a few more blocks.

Back at the beach we immediately saw through his 'famous insect collector' disguise.

'You were going a bit mad over there, lads,' came the voice of the Rochdale Cowboy. Caught red-handed by a BMC-funded Mike Harding Swanage Patrol! 'Well, it's a silly route', I explained. 'In fact, we've been doing weird things all week. You should have seen Norman yesterday up in the roof of this cave called Avernus. He was bridging facing the sea and trying to put a Friend in backwards, above his head, with his eyes closed against the sunlight.'

He could see straight away that we should be kept off the streets at night, so he left us four free tickets on the door of his show in Poole that evening.

CHAPTER 7 EURO ROCK

Les Calanques

I thought, as I watched Andy start the route as middle-man, that he was conspicuously English. In fact he was slightly over-dressed for an August midday in En Vau: my old maroon shorts, given to him when I got too fat for them, a best Marks and Spencer's shirt, and a white Bill and Ben sunhat. I had opted for swimming trunks, and that was more than most people were wearing at En Vau. Andy took a bit longer than Norman had done when he had led the first pitch. But Andy had been out of climbing for a time, and, whilst we were camping, he had been living it up along the coast in a luxury villa owned by a woman who had been his mother's lodger 20 years ago. Obviously Andy's style worked on women if not on rock.

This morning our three families had chartered a boat from Cassis for 24 francs return per adult, and approached En Vau in Andy's style whilst others walked across the desert from the town. En Vau feels like one kind of climbing paradise, a Cornish cove with walls four times as tall, until you walk off the path up its valley and the smell hits you in the heat. To enter En Vau is to enter a community of permanently temporary residents. Below each of its white arêtes studded with trees and thinly parted by tree-filled gullies is a scree of excrement. So it goes.

We had chosen a classic route of the Calanques, the second arête on the right up the valley with the romantique name of Sirene Liautard. It's a totally sexy place, except for the scree. In fact at the very moment Andy was lingering over the first pitch my wife was approached on the beach by a naked man who asked if he could borrow a snorkel. My son pointed out that her question 'What for?' was not really necessary. Anyway she said 'No' and Andy took a long time. Another Livesey 3c in the first English guide to French cragging (1980). Although Andy was being eccentrically English and not trusting the usual French polish. In fact whilst the holds always seemed to be sloping for the feet, they were finger-shaped up the front of the buttress, after we had got on to it from the right.

The first pitch had actually established that once again we were climbing at 4a on interesting square-cut features in the very front of a buttress that, to be honest, seemed from below to end in a grotty grotte. We couldn't have been more wrong. The spectacular finish from the tubular cave was out of sight, and this was as absorbing as climbing on limestone is from Cheedale to the Calanques. But it was the second pitch which made clear *la différence*.

Two big pegs in the shaded wall above the stance led up to a crack. The French expect you to pull on the pegs, that's why they're so big. If you don't step on them also you're miles away from 3c.

The Italians ahead of us had obviously read Livesey's guide and banged in another peg, after an epic, to get up the crack above the short wall. Norman found that if you pull right, with a finger-changing lay-away you could step into a groove on the wonderful Calanques arête so sun and sea come into view again at En Vau.

Which brings you up to another stance in the shade on the left of the arête with a poor tree. Not a Tremadoc poor tree, a last weak root, but a Provencal poor tree, spreading roots generously in thin soil to catch at ropes. Once again a step right on to the edge gains the sun, and rock fluted by a kind of Calanques caress. When I ventured to offer this observation I was met with 'Have you brought your dictaphone?' and 'Is this a recorded talking rope?' from the darkness of the cave above. Some philistines have never even heard of Ed Drummond, never mind experienced a climbing poem in their lives.

But that cave, a hole through the buttress – striped inside with chocolate ice-cream and growing a little leafy fig-tree on the outside with just one fig fruiting in the sun – that hole made, in effect, the final buttress fly. Norman, who had traversed out of the hole and round on to the front had unfortunately overheard these last observations. 'Stop eulogising you two!' he called down from somewhere. 'Take this slowly and savour it!' Ah well, there's hope for him after all. Certainly that final pitch must be one of the best at 4b anywhere: high steps into little squares with the full fall to the yellow beach and transparent green sea, make you pinch the ridge to stay real.

The summit of the buttress is a detached boulder which the BMC Peak Committee would have decided definitely ready for a trundle in the interests of safety. We abseiled off to the right behind the Italians actually using the Italian hitch. Andy pulled the ropes down at the bottom into the inevitable dried excrement, and began coiling, I thought, remarkably quickly. So it goes.

A few paces to the beach, after dropping harness and EBs and I was watching climbing without moving myself, bobbing on my back. Andy's hat swam towards me. Who needed a sirene liautard amongst those mermaids? Unromantically, our route, on the buttress called Sirene was first climbed by J. and P. Liautard in 1937. So it goes.

The Delectable Dentelles

'We've got to be off that ridge well before midday or we'll be sizzling like spitted oxen strung between those pinnacles.' In Britain the heat-wave burned on. It was probably the best August for climbing in Scotland for years. (I just noticed that in Richard Gilbert's recently published diaries of his ascents of all the *Memorable Munroes* (Gilbert 1983) there are very few entries for August – the month of highest rating on the McInnes Scale for Wet and Midges.) And we were sweating in Provence, drawn south by the cover photograph of Peter Livesey's (1980) *French Rock-climbs*.

The Dentelles de Montmirail do not disappoint. As Livesey hints, they stand out like a full set of his teeth above the plains of Provence about 30 km north-east of Avignon. Approached from any direction they are a sparkling limestone spine two kilometres long with pinnacles that are so fine that they actually appear more frail the closer you get. The word 'Dentelles' suggests the delicacy of lace with its pointed edges. It is only when you get really close that you realise the lace is full of holes. In fact, Livesey has noticed, with accuracy, that 'Dentelles' in the plural means 'small teeth', in this case with the fillings fallen out.

Looking north from our family base camp at Camping Bregous (clean and cheap) in the village of Aubignan we could actually make out the features of the ridge shown on Livesey's profile sketch. This helped give us our bearings. Further round to the north and east lay the long wooded slopes of Mount Ventoux leading up to its inevitable communications tower. Daily, cyclists seem keen to re-enact the death of Tommy Simpson, the English professional cyclist who died on a Tour de France ascent of the road that crosses this mountain. In the thick heat at our campsite we just had to increase our intake of Cote de Ventoux (buy it by the bucketful direct from the *caves*) and plan a dawn attack on the Dentelles ridge.

Driving up through the village of Gigondas in the dark there was little sign that its wine is, along with Chateauneuf-du-Pape, one of the most respected (i.e. expensive) of the Rhone wines. There were to be signs that its quality is apparently being threatened by the attempt to push the vines too high. The road from the village became a dust track leading to the Col du Cayron, really just a car parking pause as the track splits left and right in the face of this white spikey barrier. From here it became clear that the route Livesey describes is the right hand kilometre of the ridge starting from the Breche de la Pousterie, just left of the two most obvious holes.

As we stepped from the car the air was already warm and the ridge was a spectacular silhouette in a dawn which didn't so much break as creep under the night clouds that strangely stayed in the sky. The ten-minute scramble through the scrub was rather like approaching Ravensdale before the steps were made in the scree through the woods. Pausing after another backwards slide, I was struck by the variety in what had appeared to be a boring scrub of stunted trees. Oak and ash were mixed in with juniper and yew, tearing at the already sweating exposed skin and tuning us into the part that vegetation plays on a climb in Provence. Athletic rock moves are the least of the pleasures of a traverse of the Dentelles which is a total sensory experience reaffirming all the other things that climbing can be about, such as, in this case, herbs of Provence poking up your nostrils.

Yet we had to find some rock moves to get on to the ridge from the breche, or col, where we were looking at the smooth steep end of the spine. Livesey's book states 'avoid the first ridge by a couloir on the left to gain the ridge proper'. This took us round to the south side of the spine where a groove leading to a crack was the nearest we could find. The rock looked loose and brittle but was actually firm enough. Its unfriendly feature was its teeth. They pointed downwards to bite the flesh that wanted to move too fast up the groove to belay at a block, before scraping round a bulge rightwards in a delicate 4b move that allowed scrambling up on to the ridge. A glance back from here clears up a point of additional confusion at the breche. We really were supposed to turn our backs on the bit we recognized from the cover photograph of the guidebook and search in the opposite direction for the start of the route.

The French are so keen on permanent piton protection that limestone lines are often studded with cemented ring-pegs every few feet. But here at the top of the first abseil of the Dentelle traverse (and the only one in retrospect that we didn't fancy climbing down) there was no peg to be found. So a large sling left the blue mark of itself round a low shattered block and we abseiled from Pointe Lagarde on to a narrow neck of the bright white rock. It was only from the other side that we could see we'd balanced just across the top of a hole as perfect as a giant Polo. What added to the adventure was finding that the rope, pulled through the sling after the last man, had snagged on a tree on the south side. The feeling of exposure from the 200ft walls of the north face is rather spoiled by the scrub creeping closer up the south side of the ridge. And it was climbing upwards from the other side of the arch that brought our noses up against that characteristic smell of the Dentelle traverse for the first thyme. Even in its three foot wide sections, the rock is impregnated with the strong roots and scents of herbs.

The easy scrambling along the spine gave an airy sense of being above the patchwork plain of Provence. The mist still hung over Avignon, unbelievably the cloud cover had stayed – for the first time in two weeks we had a cloudy day and across the hills it even appeared to be raining. Before we reached the summit of this section of the ridge a loud tractor noise chugged through the high stillness. Below us on the south side of the ridge a bulldozer was levelling scrub for a new high vineyard for the apparently inferior Gigondas of the future.

A wander through a juniper brought us to the summit cross, marking the highest point of the entire ridge. Voices on the other side of the juniper turned out to be a French family party who had obviously scrambled up here because they'd heard that in *French Rock-climbs*, Livesey describes the descent as 'both intriguing and devious (paint marks).' So, of course, we missed the turn. But it was not too devious for them. When we looked back they'd all disappeared, as though down an invisible submarine chute. They had. We should have descended a few metres looking for a red splodge on the right marking the entrance to a polished chute through the ridge that deposits you in a sort of Knights Templar turret. Out of the bottom of this a loose handrail leads down into the trees of the south side. A scrappy scramble back up to a breche gives access to the final section of the ridge.

A rhythm of Mild Severe pitches, scrambles and abseils (two, with pegs, and handholds down grooves) now became routine. The alpine swifts were less numerous, sweeping into nests hanging on the north face. A rather dirty deviation on the south side took us under bushes to bridging moves through another hole. The ascent of Le Doigt du Gréponnet was our last real pitch, a final finger in the fine lace which can be climbed down airily on its south side. Beyond it the spine drops back into the hump of the hillside. It had been a sensuous experience of textures and smells, strange features and strange weather, exposed but relaxed climbing on this traverse of the delectable Dentelles.

From the Lip of Pic St. Loup

The view from the lip of Pic St-Loup must be the best in Langedoc, partly because it's the first uplift of land west of the Rhone Delta. It's a long wall of rock, or a tooth from the side, until turning round to the south you can see its rounded back, up which can be found a pleasant path.

But it's the view from its summit that deserves to be better known. To the south, 20 km away, Montpellier sprawls along the edge of a twinkling sea. The lakes flashing to the east signal the Camargue. Between industry and étangs a distant aircraft ceaselessly trawls an advert above the miles of sordid sultry beaches. Better to be up here in the cool air in August, gazing across the slopes of steep scrub that levels to the bright green squares of vineyards nestling the orange roofs of sleepy villages.

It's not an arduous or especially interesting walk following the usual red splodges on rocks. But be warned that paths marked on the map as providing ascents to this south side have all been fenced off so that a start must be made from the village of Cazevieille. It's better for business that way, and the little bar by the car-park does seem to come in handy later in the day.

The broad path lifts above the plain to the right whilst the great summit cross hangs over you on your left. Shelter from the sun is soon provided by groves of thick-leaved scrub that increase in density with height. We lingered to look at a purple-backed beetle fully two inches long. It reared on its back legs and pointed its pincers at us. 'The ant's a centaur in its dragon world.' Ezra Pound must have met some invertebrates like this in his time.

The first plane to fight its way suddenly over the summit ridge was a shock. Its noise burst upon us for a moment before it turned away down the other side trailing a line in an apparent attempt to hook the great cross off the top of the mountain. Then the glider it had been towing rose silently above us like a harvest moon over a hilltop. When we got to the summit we realized why.

The north face of Pic St-Loup is a 1,000ft sheer limestone escarpment up which a hurricane races with such force it is difficult to stick your head over the edge. The rock-climbs on this face are described as 'vegetated and suitable for beginners'. That they are serious undertakings might be indicated by the plaque on the summit commemorating the deaths of two members of the same club in separate rock-climbing accidents. The seriousness with which the Face Nord of Pic St-Loup should be treated should not be scoffed at simply because the club these two unfortunates belonged to was actually that of the Cyclotourists de Montpellier.

For serious rock climbers the view to the north across the Fametou Pass will reveal, below and opposite, an unrelentingly vertical clean sweep of rock called Hortus, hard and only recently developed. For us the discovery, on our return to road, of the 20m wall north-west of the village gave us a lot of fun on middle-grade routes. But Hortus remains little-known by British climbers. We gazed beyond it across rolling vineyards to the distant higher hills of the Cevennes. There is no other high point between Pic St-Loup and the popular walking area of the Cevennes. This view from the lip of Pic St-Loup lifts you to longer walks, or is a gulp of air before returning to the sea.

A Tempest on the Mer des Rochers

The thunder started as soon as we arrived up on the plateau above the Languedoc village of Sauve. But we hardly noticed the distant rumblings as we tried to distinguish the crag from the scrub. Here we were again, Norman and I, adventuring boldly to the minor crags of France in the season of summer storms. Not quite as quick as lightning we realized that La Mer des Rochers is several little crags, white waves rising with the rhythm of frozen movement just above the hot green skin-tearing scrub. The thunder rolled away for a while leaving just the heavy black sky closed down on the layers of rolling horizons on which the odd castle appeared as an island of ancient civilization and feuds.

We fought our way towards the highest wave of limestone that was fisting its knuckles above the troughs of juniper. Was there really any cragging that had been worth including in the book that brought us here, Jean-Pierre Bouvier's (1984) *Rock-Climbing in France*? Was this the sort of inclusion the English re-publisher Wilson was hedging his bets about in his Introduction? Quite by chance we found an open crack that launched us on the undulating journey that is the boulder circuit of La Mer des Rochers. Norman bridged up, saying that the jams were sheer hell, the rock was so sharp and unpolished for a change.

On the top of this pinnacle we saw the nature of the voyage round this uplifted sea. The yellow C at the bottom of the crack now matched the yellow arrow pointing down the other side and another pointing up the next boulder. Never more than 30ft high, these boulders made a circle of water-shaped stones. Their texture seemed the result of wiping wet fingers down each white fist, giving sharp vertical edges crossed by lines of finger-shaped jugs. To reach up was to fit the fingers into a waiting mould.

We were drawn round the circuit by the rock. Despite the fact that we were in this dark sauna of a day, we warmed to the game, making steep moves relieved by sharp little finger moves, or finding that a yellow star meant 'jump from this spot' to the next pinnacle, or making a traverse of toe friction on the edges of the grooves, or descending an undercut wave on its horizontal slots. At one point the journey went under La Mer des Rochers through a tunnel equipped with a spade in case of total immersion. It got to be fun. The thunder rumbled off elsewhere.

We were caught up in the spirit of the thing as we went surfing the white sentinels. We balanced above the green wind-shifted scrub where only the white crests kept still. We nearly took a header on the second half of the circuit, not expecting the delicate 4b move up a pillar without finger flutings to pull on. We were tuned into the rock but were definitely flagging. The roller-coaster continued to run its course, until on the final, most difficult descent from a crest, the lightning started. The thunder followed fast behind like a late lizard across hot rock. Raindrops began falling as wet cowpats on the rock. We tumbled into a cave, crouched like Calibans, moaning about this intrusion, this possession of our isle. The tempest changed La Mer des Rochers to a slippery exposed circuit of electricity. We were drowned running back to our sacs. But back at the car we started laughing, we were so wet, and the spell was broken.

As for La Mer des Rochers, it is not comparable with the variety of moves possible at Fontenbleau as Bouvier suggests. Bad landings are not the point. The rock does not offer bouldering traverses or alternative combinations of moves. But if you're passing and want to risk a tempest on La Mer des Rochers take Rue du Parc out under the arch in the corner of the square with the église in Sauve, Languedoc. And take a mac, or a towel.

Anne Sauvy

Anne Sauvy specialized in ice climbing, ticking off, since the age of 17, the north faces above her beloved Chamonix, together with some of the classic north faces of Switzerland – the Argentière, the Chardonnet, the Verte twice, the Courtes, the Bionassay, two routes on the Brenva Face of Mont Blanc, the Monch, the Aletschorn – her list of 170 ascents would be the envy of any Alpinist. But it was when, after a five-year period of miscarriages, she found that she was not strong enough to perform at the same level, Anne Sauvy's imagination turned to writing short stories set in the mountains she knows so well.

On the occasion of the publication of her second collection of short stories in English, *The Game of Mountain and Chance* (1995), I took a detour in my summer journey to Languedoc rock to interview her at the Passy Mountain Book Festival, just outside Chamonix. As we sat under the sunshades of the 'authors' salon', Anne revealed, in answer to my comment on the amazingly lively translation of the book, that Anthea Bell, its main translator, is also the translator of Asterix into English. In the opening story, 'The Bronze Mountaineers', the translator has great fun contrasting the West Country peasant voice of Balmat with the 18th century aristocratic sentences of Saussure as the Chamonix statues reascend Mont Blanc.

'Actually, I put in a real sentence from Saussure, and also one from Jean Jaques Rousseau, but now I can't remember which they are.' Her eyes sparkle at having caught herself out, but her brow suggests a strong determination behind the responsive sensitivity of her facial expressions. She speaks quietly and thoughtfully in a lilting English carrying a French subtlety of expressiveness that we lack.

Anne has had a studio in Chamonix for 25 years, and she remembers her first visit at the age of two because she was annoyed at not being allowed to go on the Mer de Glace. Her father had a passion for skiing (and rugby). When he took Anne to Zermatt at the age of 13, she says, 'I was so impressed by the Matterhorn and the other mountains that I decided I should climb.'

By 17, as a pretty girl who climbed well, she found herself in groups which included the most famous French Alpinists of her day – Terray, Desmaison, Herzog – and she has continued to keep in touch with the French élite. Michel Piola actually named a route after one of the stories in *The Game of Mountain and Chance*, the cover of which, incidentally, is a forceful painting by Marcel Wibault capturing the soaring Chamonix Aiguilles assailed by ice from below and storm from above. She is herself now one of the respected figures of Chamonix, the city erecting a statue of Paccard because another of the stories in this book called for it. It's an indication of her popularity that in the first four hours of book signing at Passy she had sold 36 books. Her new novel, *Nadir*, was being lapped up by the locals, perhaps because it is based on one summer's research with the local guides' helicopter rescue service.

One Chamonix guide, Claude Jaccoux, knows Anne from their student days in Paris when a group of 15 students and workers who called themselves 'Les Serrures' (The Locks) would catch the Saturday morning train out to Fontainebleau. Usually they would catch a glimpse of their heroes who at this time, in the mid-50s, were developing the bouldering in the woods there – Robert Paragon, later famous for first ascents of Mustang Tower and Makalu, along with Lucien Beradini who later achieved fame on the West Face of the Dru. After a day's climbing and a big meal each person dug a bivy spot out of the sand under a boulder. They bivvied all year round and on one January night, after a particularly convivial meal, they heard singing drifting over the snow towards them. Through the trees three of their friends who had missed the early train appeared dressed as the three kings bearing gifts. From the beginning, Anne's apprenticeship was based on the characters and folklore that became the focus of her fiction. And, of course, for more than 20 years she has been able to observe the diversity of characters attracted into the Chamonix goldfish bowl. Indeed, one is tempted to wonder if Anne's is especially a woman's view of the sport, focusing on the quirks of personality and motivation.

It was brave of her father, she points out, to encourage his only child to get into climbing.

'Perhaps he feared, but he did not show it. He did not try to stop me from climbing. He was very proud when I did even dangerous things, but well. I am very grateful for his attitude.' When I was writing to Anne in 1991 to persuade her to come to our fifth Festival of Mountaineering Literature, she wrote to me one day with moving simplicity, 'My father has died. I loved him'. Anne speaks of her father with that love and respect alive today.

'His father was killed in 1918 when he was 19 and already in the war himself. So my grandmother was a widow with five children and no money. But she made sure that all the children studied hard and they all did well. One of my aunts was an explorer and there has just been a book written about her. My father became a statistical researcher for the French government, eventually founded the world's first Institute of Demography and was awarded, by the UN, the equivalent of a Nobel prize for his life's work. But more important,' she added, 'he was a very interesting man, very good, very generous, very funny and he skied until he was 80.'

So, Anne Sauvy was brought up in the intellectual environment where she has established her working life, researching and teaching the history of publishing and censorship at the Sorbonne. Her life has been split between the Left Bank and the mountains, between the intellectual and the physical, between Paris and Chamonix, but in her climbing stories this double life is unified through the medium of her creative energy. Her stories sparkle with the fun thats in her broad grin. The marvel is that her wit and word-play and spot-on-satire (read 'The London Dinner') have been so spectacularly celebrated by this new translation. Of course, she says, her professional research has contributed to her sense of storytelling, and originally she was very much influenced by the little known French novelist, Evenne Bruhl. But basically, she says with simplicity, 'I dislike boring books, and try not to write them.'

Some reviewers have argued that her stories do not take narrative risks, although Robin Campbell recognized the 'inner tension' of her kind of fiction. It may be that the 1995 Boardman Tasker judges, who failed to shortlist the new book of stories, considered them as limited narratives. In fact, reviewers' comparisons with Maupassant, by tending to emphasize the elegance of her stories, really miss the point. *The Game of Mountain* and *Chance* shows again and again that her narratives are driven by the emotional twists, ironies and conundrums that her ideas make possible. I ask if she was aware of this.

'No,' she says, 'that comes by instinct, but it shows that to write good stories you must not have too much technique, because that is rather dry. You have to have what is in the heart of all the different people, the mothers or wives of climbers, the people on the rope. That is what interests me most, together with mountains, of course, and the atmosphere of mountains.'

This is perhaps the secret of the compassion that underlies Anne Sauvy's work. To understand where that comes from one might reflect upon the fact that her creative energies were released after an agonizing five years during which she had a baby that died. Behind the playfulness of her stories there lies a deep comprehension of sadness. And part of the humanity of her work is the moral justice of her final twists – the hotelier who thinks a death would bring attention to his village finds, when it happens, that it is his only son.

'I like stories when – ah! – something at the end lands you somewhere else, sometimes changing what you have read.' Robin Campbell makes the point that in her work 'a tragic outcome is always on the cards'. I ask if she has had any epics herself.

'I was in an avalanche, but I had the luck to be dug out. I had been married to John one month.' John Wilkinson is an English climber and Oxford University expert on the Middle East. 'We have made a marriage between Oxford and Paris,' Anne says. I was ski touring in January. We were eight people. Suddenly there was a big avalanche to our right. By chance we were carried not too deeply and the two guides with spades got free and managed to find everybody. I put this experience into a story in *Flammes de Pierre*. Sometimes I use my own experiences.'

I told her I could see that her memory of the climbs is very detailed. 'When I did them I wrote lists of notes, and when I have not done them I talk to people who have. To write credible stories you must have a very strong base.' Once again the value of the writer's notebook is endorsed, together with a professional approach to research.

But will Anne now be writing mountaineering novels after her first experience with *Nadir* (the cover of which has been painted by Andy Parkin). Was the novel a form she enjoyed working in?

'I loved it, I was completely involved in the long story and the way people were developing. I had all my ideas at the beginning, but writing it was extremely interesting. It is one imaginary day for the rescue service and I invented the 12 rescues on this day, which I researched all last summer with special permission from the helicopter zone. I think I shall go on with novels.'

Whether we shall see an English translation will depend inevitably upon the success of *The Game of Mountain and Chance*. So let's hope that more readers discover the variety of witty entertainment and the dimensions of deep understanding that Anne Sauvy reveals in this book.

Hohenstein and Hönnetal

I have a hunch that wherever you are in Europe, you're within reach of a crag. But I thought my theory would be severely tested by two weekends based in Bielefeld, midway along the autobahn between Hanover and Dortmund, on the edge of the North German Plain. As Gill was driving us through Bielefeld my eye was caught by a likely-looking shop which said it sold 'Nichts für Stubenhocker!' As she reversed out of a tramlane we seemed to be driving along, Gill translated, 'Nothing for housemice!' Well, were we housemice, or were we cragrats, snarling for rock and Eurodiffs? Bursting through the door we fell upon the bookshelves. Sure enough, there were individual guidebooks to a crag in each direction on the autobahn, and even more whisker-twitching, the new German directory of information and topos for 51 climbing areas in every part of the country, *Deutschland Vertikal* (1988). The price threatened to turn us back into housemice, but only for a moment. We were on our way.

What we found were two friendly limestone outcrops hidden amongst trees, but catching the September sunshine. In contrast to French limestone crags, these two German crags had a variety of natural features and a variety of types of holds, plus good routes at a range of grades. Of course, both crags are protected by bombproof bolts in the European style of sports climbing. It's odd for a British cragrat placing a Friend on a V Diff crack-climb to realize that you've not seen the bolt cemented into the face outside the crack! Is this the face of things to come for British limestone?

So, for the benefit of those housemice who find themselves adrift on the autobahn and turning into Eurocragrats, here's how to find the German versions of Willersley and Wildcat – with bolts.

Hohenstein is 45km south-west of Hanover, on the edge of the Süntel mountains, between Hameln (of Pied Piper fame) and Bückeburg. This dry south-facing crag is 40m high and about 200m long. Chimneys, cracks and roofs offer climbs from V Diff to 6a, but the rock needs some care. In Hessisch-Oldendorf you leave the B83 in the direction of Zersen/Pappmühle. From the car-park at Gastof Pappmühle, where the guide is on sale, a path leads to the crag in half an hour, finally following signs to Hohenstein Klippenweg.

Hönnetal is a river valley 10km south-east of Dortmund in which several crags are hidden in the trees very close to the 515 going south out of Menden towards Balve. Five kilometres out of Menden a road turns left to Eisborn. Locals park on the triangle of this turning, but there's a layby 150m south. Crossing the road opposite the turning, a track leads into a field beside the railway. Across a dry (in August) riverbed there are two crags. Binoler Wand is on the left of the railway bridge and on its right is Feldhofstein where we climbed five routes between V Diff and MVS on varied forms of over-bolted solid limestone 35m high. This is the forcing ground for Dortmund sport climbers, so be prepared for lots of brightly coloured cragrats falling off the crag all around you.

Mentioning to Bonington the following weekend that I'd discovered some little gems in

Germany suddenly brought a light to his eyes and a whirring of the famous computer behind them. 'I climbed in north Germany, when I was in the army, at a place called the Hönnetal,' he said. This was no reason why I should have felt strangely like a Stubenhocker. But I did.

The Healing Mirror: Miroir Slab

We all have our differences from time to time. It's normal. Misunderstandings between climbing partners must be more normal than most, if that's possible. I remember someone telling me that when he'd got to the Alps he'd turned to his partner and said, 'Right, get the rope out.' His partner had turned indignantly back to him and said, 'I thought you were bringing it!'

Well, I'd thought I was going to do the Miroir each summer for three summers running. Pat Littlejohn wrote of it as 'the best Hard Severe in Switzerland', 2,000ft of slabs near Leysin. That's when he was advertising Leysin and the International School of Mountaineering in his early days as Director. 'Call in at Club Vagabond', he'd said more recently, 'and I'll give you a topo. It's quite tricky route finding. And avoid it on a Monday because we use it then.'

This year I'd planned to do it with Tim, but, as I say, differences can intervene, and it looked to be off. Until, at the last minute, after frank phone calls, long distance, we agreed to meet in Switzerland on the first of August for this one route. Up to that point it could have been any one of you out there I'd have paired up with if you'd been in Club Vagabond in early August: the blind leading the blind up a cracked mirror.

So driving into the Les Frassettes campsite in the remote Solalex valley to find Tim unpacking his car was a warm moment. They're always uneasily hypothetical, these planned meetings abroad, until that exaggerated relief of actually seeing each other and finding out whether you were right in assuming which route was the real priority, that you weren't going to carry bivi gear, and who was going to lead the crux. It's normal. But not for us this time. We were sharing the leading, wearing helmets, carrying boots, water and sandwiches only. Tim had done this route twice before and had come over from France simply to do the Miroir with me, the healing mirror.

Except that at the foot of the route I found I'd arrived 20 minutes ahead of Tim and forgotten my sandwiches. 'I've plenty', he said. Feeling I'd made a bad start I tried a hunch.

'What was your tune on the way up?'

' "Willkommen, bienvenue, welcome" ', he said.

'I find a tune always takes over an empty-minded plod. I kept singing "The morning sun when it's in your eyes really shows your age"!' (I'd just had my fortieth birthday.)

In fact I was now feeling zapped by the plod and the huge expanse of white shining rock above us. Fourteen pitches and this complex crag were a bit more than Derbyshire limestone, yet the Miroir is like a giant Beeston Tor, an inset convex shield, but with the headwall curving over from the right as well as the left. To settle my head I resolved to treat each pitch as if it were a Derbyshire one.

Tim had clipped into the two bolts that mark each stance and offered me the first lead. I appreciated that and raced up the blocky scramble of a left-leaning gangway. I paused to savour a single fistful of pink trumpets and further up to breathe into the last hanging harebell 'in which', I reminded Tim, 'sleeps, recovering, the maker of the sea'. Tim apologized for his delay in leading the next pitch. It wasn't necessary.

Steep steps in a wet crack led to a polished wall, in the middle of which, just where your foot wanted to go, there's a peg sticking out of the smooth rock. So what can you do? Step up and right with the route, up a ramp heading for a pyramidal pinnacle with an iron rung above it.

The step from the pinnacle top is the crux, the man said, pulling strongly through an overhanging crack with a dramatically high foot on its right edge. I preferred to watch the mist shifting about in white clouds below us. Tim didn't take long. I found I could swing onto the edge of the crack

119

and climb up it delicately to meet a peg and above that the iron rung. I tried to go above them both for the exposed steps left, but realized that staying anywhere near the grade you were expected to change hands on the rung and feet on the peg. I'm a purist in sticking to the grade and the rock. Tim grinned. It hadn't taken me long to find that it's wrong to miss a rung.

The mists were clearing.

If that was the crux, the next pitch was the best. I peered into cracks on the left edge of the mirror as they got steeper and thinner. When the friction became crucial the fingertip cracks curved inside comfortingly. Pegs seemed to appear just above the cruxes, but nuts fitted nicely inbetween. The shortest pitch so far was 120ft but it seemed the longest. Here I must confess to doing some 'whooping for fun' as Tim has put it, even to 'gabbling with glee' again.

Then these two sweating Frenchmen raced past us. Although they were faster, we were certainly having the better time. Until I was sent right too early and had to down-climb a pitch. The thing is to stay in the broken groove until two bolts are found below an overhang of flakes. It's above here that the groove forks and two crack-lines splinter right across the mirror all the way to its overhanging frame. The upper crack is the one to take, narrowing into an overlap that runs for four athletic pitches of feet on the slab, hands in the crack and some real Derbyshire handjams along the way.

At a peg below a transecting overlap we gathered for the final pitches. We'd been going well together, sealing up the cracks, enjoying the reflections we gave each other and were now moving towards the overhanging pitch to break out of the frame. Following Tim on the traverse below the headwall I heard the electric cry of an Alpine chough, then found its black feather on the white glass I was crossing. I accepted the gift and its message. Wearing the sign of the chuff in my helmet I launched into the layaways up the final wall. I pulled out into the sun and it was done.

'We did the Miroir,' I said to the campsite patron in French. My French isn't too good.

'That's normal' he said. 'I do it every day for washing and shaving.' He was going round each tent trying to persuade people to part with 13 francs for a big open-air meal at the campsite that night. He had a dramatically persuasive line of patter. This meal, he said, would change a 'ligne' like my Gill into a 'virage' like his tum which he carried undeniably curved between his red embroidered braces. We ate at home.

But they did light bonfires for us that night. Flames glowed in the dark from every summit. Even the Dent du Midi was alight. Then the fireworks started. Rockets were still falling on our tents as we went to bed. Firecrackers hardly disturbed our sleep, such is the healing power of the Miroir.

'Stay off the Pop, Lad': Sa Gubia, Majorca

'Those were Don's last words to me as we saw him off at the airport. "Stay off the pop, lad", he said. Of course he'd done nothing of the sort while he was here in Majorca. That's the great danger in Deià – for a small village there's an amazing number of bars. Within two months Don was dead. This was probably his last climb.'

Ronnie Wathen, smiled his quizzical smile. Behind his specs there was that characteristic mixture of mystery and mischief. He and I were waiting on the second stance while Norman searched for the line of what must be the best VS in Majorca – 800ft of varied, sustained climbing spiced by the need for good old-fashioned route-finding, if you get up early enough to beat the queue.

The soaring ridge of Sa Gubia can be seen from Palma airport. It's the left-hand skyline of a vertical scoop out of the nearest hills. Ronnie told me that Sa Gubia means in Majorquin, which he had learned fluently, 'the woodworker's gouge'.

It's a route of continuing interest whose secrets aren't given away by lines of bolts, or by my hinting that descents over the back of the mountain are usually made in the dark, finally passing the famous 'three-headed dog' to reach the road.

The late, lamented, Ronnie Wathen on Mountain Man, Majorca.

It was our third alpine start for this route from the mountain village of Deià where Ronnie had built a house for his family in 1968. We'd flown in on Boxing Day and on the first morning, as we were leaving for the crag with Ronnie, the first person we met in the main street was the widow of Robert Graves.

'Morning Beryl!' said Ronnie to his sprightly grey-haired neighbour who paused with her shopping basket to say, 'Terrible storm last night wasn't it, but just what we needed.'

It was Robert Graves who provided the focus for those poets and artists who, like Ronnie himself, have homed in on Deià. Where else would you find two poetry readings in one week? And one of them was Ronnie's reading that night, so we decided we'd better not hang about on Sa Gubia.

Ronnie took us, for our first route, to a pinnacle said to be associated with a pre-Christian phallic cult. Mountain Man was the ambiguous name of our route in Majorquin, a four pitch Grade IV up the side, and then the back, of an obvious tower on the road down to the bottom of the famous gorge walk, the Torrente del Pareis. It was a great introduction to the quiet wildness of the Majorquin mountains and their layers of history. We abseiled down to an ancient charcoal burner's circle of stones behind the pinnacle.

Next morning we watched it get light as we sat in the car at Gubia. A brilliantly striped hoopoe foraged in front of us while the rain started. We headed for the south coast and found the little sea cliff of Cala Santiyana, bolted and bathed in sunshine.

The second early start resulted in us watching more black rain clouds rolling over Gubia, so we turned north to find the austere quiet of the Boquer Valley. Tom and Simon got off the ground on the steep fingery holds of the 'shark's fin' left-hand route, while the rest of us got cold and hankered after the long Cavall Bernat Ridge across the valley that hid the sea from us.

Here we all eventually headed, panting up to the obvious col in the ridge from the end of the valley and then peering over the edge like kids. Ronnie produced some huge oranges. We turned towards the sea-sliced summit on our left to find that, while we were getting our breath, Norman was already scrambling upwards and getting smaller. The four of us followed. It's a unique experience, this ridge, with a sheer 1,000ft drop to the sea on the right and little walls on the left, sharp, fluted rock and a window that you suddenly find you've crossed when you descend to stare through it.

At the col after the window Simon spotted a possible escape off the ridge which led to a worn scramble and scree before a wall led back down to the Boquer boulders. Norman ploughed on to the end of the ridge, enthusing about it afterwards as an essential experience of Majorca.

So, third time lucky, we reached the foot of Sa Gubia in the cool of a New Year's Eve morning under a cloudless sky. Tom and Simon opted for the bolted right-hand start up a leaning crack-line, while Norman led off from the red-painted foot of the ridge. It's a scrambly, slightly loose first pitch to a belay in bushes where Ronnie, with his flare for the unpredictable, found behind a bush a gift of a bottle of water. We accepted it. The second pitch passes two pegs and begins to get into 4b mode.

Each belay has double pegs or bolts and is painted with a number. From R2 we should have

The Sa Gubia buttress, Majorca.

traversed right beneath a scoop to gain the crest of the ridge, but Norman's instincts led left and back right to a double peg belay on the right of a cave where a large ledge would detain Ronnie and I, plus the next team, for an increasingly tense impasse.

Norman looked round to the right and returned. Not likely. He looked left and returned. A long way left a line of bolts above and below indicated what he took to be the Super Nova. Norman tried the cave roof. Ronnie tried teaching me my cue for coming in with a poem of my own in the middle of his reading of his long poem in which he shows Lord Byron around Deià and its inhabitants. It's written in ottova rima, the form perfected by Byron, and Ronnie started quoting, but was stopped abruptly by Norman shouting down rather rudely, 'For goodness sake shut up! I'm trying to get us out of here and you're reciting poetry!'

He returned to our ledge which was getting crowded. Friendly, but crowded. Another leader had belayed beside us and his second, perhaps motivated by Ron's Byron, looked round to the right and returned. Not likely.

'Well, I've run out of ideas!' Norman declared.

So, having given up on this route the only alternative was any route. Norman crossed the cave to the left again and this time the rope kept moving. A steep bolted wall that Norman ascended out of our sight proved to be the delightful 4c crux of our version of this route. At the top a delicate traverse right brought a painted belay and a helpful red arrow pointing up right, as if by now we might be feeling a little lost. This was Ronnie's fourth ascent and he found that it had mysteriously got harder each time he did it.

'It's amazing,' he said. 'You don't need to work at raising your grade. You just do the same route every five years!'

Norman attacked the crack, indicated by the arrow, that slanted up a steep wall. He popped in hexes and Friends, swung out off the crack's edge and disappeared again. Ronnie took off his slippers, which he called his 'Chinese torture socks', and aired his horrible toes. His Majorquin shepherd's shoes were clipped to his faded Whillans harness. He wore out a pair of these shoes each year by walking everywhere in them, including the Boquer Valley ridge the previous day. From deep in his sac he offered me olives. I declined. He offered me garlic. I declined. So he popped the clove into his mouth and chewed on it.

'Just like Don used to say, "Don't put any of them olives or garlic in the cooking!"'

He offered me a satsuma.

'Thanks.'

'That's all right,' he said, 'they grow on trees round here!'

I tried to peel it whilst belaying. He popped an unpeeled orange into his mouth and chewed on it.

At the top of this pitch Norman hailed Tom, asking him to wait so that we could speed up the route finding. At R5 Tom's route joined ours. From here the route looked slightly easier and broken by the odd bush above. It's deceptive. Tom and Simon swung the leads away above us – and searching for the line remained an open question as to where to go at recurring exposed verticalities. Norman was beginning to feel the strain of holding up the accumulating queue behind us.

'Do you want to take over the route finding?' he asked me when I reached him. I had struggled, after the slanting crack, at an overhanging pull into a groove, not noticing the key pocket on the left, feeling the weight of the rucksack and the heat of the midday sun. I was sweating in my thermals on our first day without wind. Sweat ran from under my helmet and into my eyes. I declined. Norman sighed and pushed on up a slightly easier crack.

A German appeared suddenly from the left and joined the belay, asking me about the descent. When I told him 'over the mountain', he said he'd wondered why all the English were carrying rucksacks! Ronnie arrived, then the next two lads, then an English girl who was leading and had to wait at the top holds of her pitch.

'Are you happy?' one of the lads asked.

'I'm ecstatically happy!' she replied, relaxing on her small holds. Fair enough. We all believed her. For the rest of the route Ronnie kept reminding us that people in the queue behind us were 'ecstatically happy.'

Above the next belay, R6, a steep wall demanded strenuous pull ups, then a stretch left where a manky peg offered a dubious quick clip, before jugs tempted sweaty grasps in a groove. To say it's 4b is to convey nothing of the way it reminds you that there's going to be no let up high on this pillar above the plain. The following easier slabs might tease you, but at R7, another wall asks the old question, 'Which way?'

Norman took an airy ramp to the left, then came back right warning about loose blocks. A rightwards slanting groove led up to a tree in a recess at R8. When Ronnie joined us here, his tale this time was about the amazing etiquette on the stances of this climb. A German had arrived on a stance and asked Ronnie 'Do you mind if I smoke?'

'Here we were, 700ft up in the air, and he asked my permission to smoke! What did he expect me to say? "I'm sorry, this a non-smoking stance?"'

'So what did you say, Ronnie?'

'I said, "It's all right, if you give me one."'

The final pitch of this magnificent climb sustains its interest and quality right up to the unnecessary 'fin' painted on the rock at R9. A step right from the alcove reveals sharp fluted rock that tears at the fingertips. Above, pinnacles finally bring into sight the 400ft ridge-walk to gain the summit. The sun may be about to set, but the day is not over yet!

We relaxed as we walked down the long winding roadway off the summit through the olive groves. The sky paled from orange to yellow to green as the moon came up. Talk turned to Cerberus, the three-headed dog that guards the farm before the road. Dave Gregory had warned us about this dog. 'It rushes at you suddenly at full pelt, but its chain is just long enough for it to be pulled up with enough room for you to squeeze past with your back to the wall. That's when its neck is jerked back and its back legs swing round to kick you.'

Ronnie also vividly remembered this dog and he had plenty of time to give us the gruesome details as the moon rose higher. One by one, as we got closer to the farm, we each picked up an olive branch. It wasn't for peace. We were approaching some outbuildings. A vicious barking started up. Norman shouted back and amazingly the barking stopped. But that was the puppy. Cerberus was round the corner. And here was the owner, standing by a gate across the track through his farm.

Ronnie greeted him in Majorquin and asked if we might pass through. Somehow none of us appeared to be gripping sticks any more. The owner was charming and kindly told us to keep to the wall. We didn't need telling as the huge black dog came racing out of the darkness snarling at us and doing the business.

Later that night Ronnie gave a hilarious reading which poked fun at several members of the audience as Lord Byron was introduced to Ronnie's version of the recent history of Deià. To illustrate his poem he continued what he'd begun on the climb, producing props out of a suitcase and flinging them aside. Here he was doing what he loved best, giving his friends fun out of his magical capacity for the unexpected. That it was kindly and intelligent fun, often at his own expense, is what made him so widely loved by all sorts of people.

It was New Year's Eve. Ronnie took his Irish pipes to the bar and told me that once Mo Anthoine had heard him playing in a Llanberis pub and had said to him, 'Is it dead yet? I should get it by the throat!' It seemed impossible that Ronnie would be struck down by the same fatal illness as Mo and that I would never see him again after that precious week in Ronnie's company.

I like to remember him playing his pipes that night when, after the grapes had been eaten on each stroke of midnight, after the firework display over the mountain, the dog's three heads became six in the retelling and Don's advice was toasted again and again: 'Stay off the pop, lad!'

Malta: A Hot Tip

29TH DECEMBER 1993, GHAR LAPSI, SOUTH COAST, MALTA

Blue sky, sparkling sea and wonderfully rough rock at our first crag on our first visit to Malta – yet something is not right. Not sure what it is yet. Anyway, Norman's given me first lead of a route recommended to me for its peculiar interest, Commando Ratlines (HS). How delightful it is to actually be here, escaping the British blizzards, alone beyond the end of the road.

I romp up the lovely limestone slab to the roof where a crack rises leftwards under the bulge. Good thread in a big hole. I jam blindly left into a fist-tearing crack.

'Remember the rats that live in those holes and run down your arms,' shouts Norman encouragingly. Belaying, for Norman, is one of the creative opportunities of the sport.

Now I'm staring up a corner with the slabby left wall steepening up in occasional steps. It's wild and pure – no bolts, just rock, sea and sun over my shoulder. I keep going up the corner, hesitating at the final 4c step (not realizing that here I should have swung on to the front of the buttress).

'Good route for starters,' says Norman. 'It's a great line, better than pocket-pulling, and full of character. But take a look at this.'

He's unroping, standing a bit above me. When I pass him I look down at a huge dump of spent cartridges. We'd noticed one or two on the way up past those stone shelters, and here, on the level top of the cliff, are hundreds more of these iron rods with little flat platforms.

We've been climbing out of, and into, the killing fields. We step over wire leads and rusty bolts with chains attached. Some memory from Scotland says 'pole traps'. Suddenly I imagine the sky wild with birds migrating from North Africa, grateful for a first landfall on Malta's south coast. They are flying straight into the guns pointing from these stone hides and the traps closed by these wire leads – live trapped song birds for shops and cafés, 'pole trapped' birds that are caught by the legs and die unmarked for taxidermy. Norman starts 'monkey wrenching' poles as we pass them on the way down.

As we set off to explore the slabs further east we see a guy with a gun rising from behind a boulder wearing a camouflage jacket. We hope he's seen us. Hamrifi Tower Sea Slabs Crack (90ft) is the most obvious line in the marble slabs of that name (they are not above the sea at all). It looks friable, but is surprisingly sound and at VS 4c gives interesting moves using delicate flakes, pockets and finger locks towards a vertical juggy finish. Only half an hour's walk away from Ghar Lapsi this smooth rock is quite different.

30TH DECEMBER 1993, WEID BABU

Tiny yellow flowers, broken glass, old fires, rusty pram frames: this morning's crag environment. We go across to the sunny west side, Warm Up Climb, 60ft, is Norman's lead. Vegetated start, steep rough rock for a couple of moves, then a scrappy finish at Severe.

A boat trip into the Blue Grotto caves reveals impressive arches and walls about which we are bound to hear more; all still one pitch. Caged song-bird in café. Stuffed big birds in bar.

So to Ix-Xagga (Shakka) and the longest climbs we saw, 300ft of south facing slabs rising from the sea. First we descend through the washing machines, fridges and domestic rubbish that fills the upper gully. Here we meet four young locals who have tied a rope to their jeep on the road. They have been sharing one harness to abseil down the 40ft upper slabs. 'Climb safely,' they say, going up as we go down.

Lowering himself over a chockstone, Norman continues down the rubbish until he says: 'God, there's a dead dog here, and another!' They are young, smooth brown dogs – not puppies – and they've not begun to smell yet. We step down past them.

Norman starts up the 170ft Breezy Rib (MVS) but complains about the looseness of the rock. Then the first stone comes down from the top. Then another. I shout up. Norman shouts, the heads of the four lads appear above us, then disappear. Another stone, closer. By now Norman is down-climbing.

'We've got to get out of here or we're gonna die!'

I'm the only one wearing a helmet. At the chockstone we meet a photographer who witnessed the stone throwing and saw the youths drive off.

'Well, I'm not going down past those dogs again,' declares Norman and starts up a short slab of marble flakes.

NEW YEAR'S EVE 1993, FOMM IR-RIH.

A blue, bright, breezeless morning. Norman is ahead, finding a way down to the top of a sea cave. I notice a man on his terraced plot carrying a long box in one hand, going along the rows of iron rods. Hanging from the top of each one is a wire cage. In every cage is a fluttering small bird. He is harvesting last night's catch. I photograph him and he calls down to his mate on the plot below. I hurry after Norman.

This place is amazing. A wide shelf extends southwards above the cave, giving views back into it and the wall beyond. It's my lead and I'm humble enough to settle for Egomaniac, a 100ft V Diff up the slab above the left corner of the sea cave. It turns out to be a terrific route, steep, on interesting holds, to approach a curving layback flake leading to a delicate crux finish. As I bring Norman up, the inevitable hunter wanders across the hillside above the shelf, gun flashing in the sun.

This evening I read in *Discover Malta* 'Malta is sadly short of wildlife due to the Maltese man's love of shooting and trapping birds.'

I needn't have brought my binoculars.

NEW YEAR'S DAY 1994, THE INLAND SEA, GOZO

Over the sea to the smaller, less-populated island of Gozo and to the unique cirque where the sea enters through a tunnel in the 180ft walls. Up on the right wall I pick Virgin Soldiers (80ft VS 4c) which turns out to be the best route of our trip. It takes a straight black crack that has weird holds needing a feel to find their best use. By the time the crack runs out I feel that my feet can stay on anything, so I push on rightwards over a bulge. It seems longer than it is – a sign of an absorbing route.

We walk across to Dwajra Bay where the three star Little Gem (70ft) promises the best VS on offer so far. But the weather is breaking and the rising gale carries rain. We walk back past the poles and shooting hides we've got used to everywhere.

We drive east to look down on the 'Mgarr Ix-Xini' valley from the old waterworks tower. It's not yet raining here, but I fail to persuade Norman to abseil into the dense undergrowth opposite. Guns are being fired over the clifftop there in what sounds like a clay migrating-bird shoot.

2ND JANUARY 1994, THE OLD MAN OF MIXTA

We search for this 135ft pinnacle with a V Diff route that sounds interesting. We look down on the fisherman's steps leading to its base. In a few minutes we're glad we didn't find a way straight down those steps as a lorry backs into the rubbish-filled quarry we've just walked through and tips its load over the edge directly above those steps. Further exploration is cut short by the discovery that on Sundays all petrol stations close at midday.

3RD JANUARY 1994, WIED IL QIRDA

There's a road up this inland valley, with more rotting rubbish piled on each side. Watched through binoculars by a hunter in his hide above us, we walk to the Three Buttresses. Short and broken rocks lie under a terraced slope, across which walks another gunman.

'What happens when you stick your head up over the top?' asks Norman.

'It pays for climbers to wear bright clothes on Malta,' I muse as we return to the car and head for Ghar Lapsi again.

Amongst the broken glass I uncoil the ropes for Twin Caves Pillar (60ft VS 4c) which Norman now races up before revealing, 'It's not worth two stars. The interesting bit is too short and that peg's in a crack that would take nuts.'

When we look around we see two bolts in the pillar on the right. So here is the final desecration, climbers dumping on their own environment.

4TH JANUARY 1994, VICTORIA LINES.

Last day and our last dead dog, thrown off the car-park at Wied Fahan West Side and passed in descent. When I first looked over the edge I saw a white rabbit. It had a lump on its back and hid under a

The Inland Sea on Gozo, Malta. Photo: TG

TG pinches a cactus on Valencianos, Calpe, Costa Blanca, Spain.
Photo: Norman Elliott.

washing machine. Probably an escapee from the 'farmed' domestic rabbits now necessary for the traditional rabbit dishes of Malta. The climbing here consists of short problems.

Norman's verdict is, 'Malta's a rubbish tip and the climbing's overrated compared with other sun rock we've been to.'

My question is, 'Why have we been avoiding climbing on certain crags to protect birds at home, then come here and supporting this bird killing culture?'

Two Calpe Classics

'Below! Below! Below!'

Shouts echo off the walls of the south face of the Peñon de Ifach, above Calpe on the Costa Blanca. I'm sharing a belay bolt with a German whose son is sport climbing, bolt to bolt, on the slab to our right. Directly above us the last of three Spaniards, in trainers, has struggled up a thin crack-line. Somewhere further up left the bushes are quivering. I keep paying out rope in their direction. 'It is a trick,' says the German. 'It is Norman,' I reply. 'That's where our route goes. Valencianos.' Norman reads topos in the loo. He's an intellectual. He knows where everything goes.

Up right, beyond the dogging German youth, Rod (who is male) has just brought Andy (who is female) up the corner crack where the slab meets the huge expanse of the main wall of the south face. Andy has found the corner technical and sustained. So would I. And 5a laybacking isn't my favourite position for taking out runners either. But just as Andy is pulling on to the belay ledge, a boulder leaps over her shoulder and into the air.

'Below!' shouts Rod.

'Below!' shouts Norman.

'Below!' I shout to the young British couple who had followed us up the first pitch. He has belayed where I first did, at the bottom of the corner. He leans back and the boulder, still in slow motion somehow, having bounced once on the slab, drops towards his partner somewhere on the steep first pitch.

Our voices are willing that boulder to swerve in mid-air and magically miss anyone below.

There is a long silence.

Then Norman shouts down, 'That was a close thing. It bounced above her head and split into pieces going either side of her.'

Simultaneously we all curse in different languages and turn back to business.

Since our route went left from where I'd originally belayed at the bottom of the corner, Norman had insisted that, to prevent the ropes running over loose stones, I should belay over at the German's bolt. So it was that we came to be looking on at what might have killed us, and regretting, not for the last time on this winter sunshine holiday, that we'd left our helmets at home.

Tom Gifford on Espero Sur Central,
Puig Campana, Costa Blanca, Spain.

129

I lead past Norman along the ledge at the top of this slab. It is cluttered with people belaying, so I thread their belay bolts and climb round them as, er, 'unobtrusively' as possible. Then I tread carefully up the shoot of rubble down which the boulder had rolled. At a chimney I belay, watching Rod swarm up the crux above my head.

It really isn't as easy as he makes it look. Who would have expected the crux of a 'Hard Severe' to be a 5a layback? Norman gets a high side-runner, a low Friend and finds time to thread a chockstone. I find polished footholds and a lot of grunting coming from somewhere. It must have been me.

But this surprising thrutch of a crux gives access to the best climbing of the route, for which it deserves its stars and its lasting impression on Chris Craggs' mind as a 'Hard Severe'. The sweep of slab above felt a lot steeper and cleaner than the photographs suggest. The climbing is so sustained and varied that I certainly didn't notice the amount of vegetation that appears to carpet the slab in a view up or down it. The camera lies.

I shared a bolt and a perch with Andy. Rod was enjoying the slab so much that he obviously didn't want to stop – Andy had to take his rope out of the belay plate to let him reach the top. Norman, you will remember, is an intellectual. He sensibly belayed on the first bolt up the big slab, thus giving me the best lead of the route. Whilst he was tying in up there, the girl with the charmed life was approaching my perch and I saw immediately why she had escaped death. She had the eyes of a gompa (temple in Nepal – which I did apologise for photographing) on her T-shirt.

It's the route-finding as much as anything, that gives this long pitch its interest. You know it has to go left and up, but when do you go left? And when do you go up? At one moment you're frictioning across crystals shaped like little logs, the next you're tempted upwards by a pocket. There are pegs in place, plenty of Friendly holes, and even a fragile thread or two. Towards the top the slab steepens up, until the final pull and you're looking down at Calpe's harbour directly below. Even in December you can smell the sage and lavender growing here. I shoved some down my sweaty vest. It came in handy after I'd battled with the 4b overhang that playfully provides the last moves.

That was our introduction to the easiest climbing around Calpe. On our last day we did a route on the shaded side of the Peñon, which really was Hard Severe. There's no doubt that Via Pany is not as distinctive as Valencianos, but if the latter is too crowded or too hot, remember that this route also has some classic climbing on interesting rock.

Not that you'd think so from the polished chimney of the first pitch, but with height comes quality. The corner of the fourth pitch is undercut and exciting. I paused only to slip slings round the threads until the crack suddenly narrowed and cut up left. I hesitated. To the right a bolt winked. Pulling steeply on to the right wall I found amazing holes with crystal bridges between them. Above the bolt it was the delicate flutings that provided delightful holds. This is a pitch not to be missed. If you go left to belay as the guidebook (Craggs 1988) suggests, you've missed this pitch. The belay's on your right.

It is obvious that Chris Craggs can climb any of the rock hereabouts with such ease that the actual line of this route in his guidebook has been a theme for improvisation. The last pitch is an example about which Norman has strong opinions. Chris wrote that he should follow the obvious crack which Norman did, expecting 'awkward 3c'. After the overhang ('It can't go up here') and a few feet of the uncleaned crack above ('It doesn't go up here') Norman traversed left with delicate pinch-grips and balancy steps downwards ('I wish Chris Craggs was up here'). As I followed I noticed a tell-tale bolt on the buttress to the left where the Spanish Via Pany clearly goes on its last pitch. (A recent rockfall may have changed all this.)

On Via Pany, our last route of the week, we'd climbed 710ft and on Valencianos, our first, we'd climbed 820ft. In between we'd done harder things on the single pitch, bolt-to-bolt routes at Toix East and Toix West, but it was the long classic climbs of Calpe that have somehow lasted in our memories through the snows of winter.

Bonfire above Benidorm: Espero sur Central

'Look Tom, there's the ridge we climbed.' Norman was pointing out of the aircraft window, leaning back so that Tom could see. We were flying home after our first New Year holiday on sun rock, within reach of Calpe on the Spanish Costa Blanca. For 14 year old Tom it was his first climbing trip outside Britain and there, clearly visible below, was the best route of the week, Espero Sur Central, a 1,200ft long Severe which took an isolated ridge reaching down from the summit, left of the south face, of Puig Campana, the mountain behind our 21 storey tower block in Benidorm.

For this long ridge we'd made an Alpine start down the lift of our tower block and out into the mild January night air. As we parked the car it was getting light. A half moon hung over the massif of empty hills around us. We sent Tom off to find the start of the trail towards the dark Puig Campana. The air was perfectly still. A dog barked in the village below.

When Tom returned we loaded him up. Strangely, both Norman and I had developed bad backs before we came away and the hour's walk in did become a little awkward, beating through the bush and climbing over old terrace walls, even before we lost the regular path. But the best of it was the bonfire. As we got closer the rays of the dawn sun broke through the towers of Benidorm to set alight the huge limestone face above us in a bonfire of orange and red cracks and ribs. The black edge on the left marked the perfect arête of our route.

It is approached by a basin further left, round the back of the ridge. Hidden from the sun, this was a chilly place to rope up. But having Tom there, with the promise of a long day's adventure together, generated a warm glow of expectation. Dads (and mums) will know what I mean. Climbing in the middle, Tom was busy tying four knots whilst Norman headed up the first groove towards a tree. Following Norman on the first pitch, Tom got the sac caught as he traversed right from the tree. It was going to be a long day's test of patience, but the first belay brought us back to the sun.

I was supposed to walk 100ft along the broad ledge, but less than half that distance brought me to another tree at its end. In fact, every pitch on this climb was actually shorter than suggested in Chris Craggs's (1988) guide. Tom was about to follow when Norman shouted to me that one of Tom's knots had come undone. This is enough to send a shiver down the spine of any climber, but a father has to shoulder a bigger burden, especially on the second of 12 pitches. I suddenly felt queasy with guilt and quietly hoped that Chris had got the grade of Severe right. He hadn't for the supposed 'Hard Severe', Via Valencianos at Calpe, the polished crux of which is 5a. We'd not taken Tom on this. It was our first afternoon and we had wanted to get a feel of the grades. But Tom has learned from his father a devious line in cheating – only, you understand, if absolutely necessary, when time is short, if the survival (or sanity) of others is at stake.

Two pitches of fluid movement up open grooves brought us on to the arête itself. From an airy belay we watched Norman climb a crack on the left side of the arête leading up to a peg at a bulge. He was raving about the rock, about the situation, about the climbing even, but here he paused, made some of his 'watch me!' moves juddering left, then resumed his ravings again. Tom climbed smoothly past the bulge on its right face. Things seemed to be back to normal. When I joined them at their spacious belay ledge Norman broke open a can of tonic water, the first that week that he had actually drunk neat, undiluted by gin.

It is a measure of the pleasure we derived from this route that Norman thought, in retrospect, that he had led the best pitches, and I was equally sure that two of the pitches I led were the best. The next was one of them. I stepped left into the bottom of the hanging chimney which provided steep bridging with plenty of protection. In the still sunshine, high above cowboy country, it was my turn to rave about the flutings of the rock, the beauty of the moves. If only it had lasted for 150ft as the guidebook promised. I'd run out 90ft when I came to the break on the ridge that was the belay.

A scrappy groove led to the crux pitch where the guide offered a choice of lines. The arrows at the start of the leftmost groove (found only after a scramble up a ramp from the ridge) left no doubt about the classic line, with perhaps a move of 4c. The layback start and delicate bridging were somewhat marred by the big block at the top of the line, waiting to tumble on to the belayer below. I forget how many times Norman kept saying 'When you follow, watch that block, Tom,' before he finally reached a belay, out of our hearing. Tom stormed up the layback and again outflanked the crux moves on the right face.

According to Chris Craggs, two pitches now led to the top of the route. One was 'easier angled', and on the other 'the climbing now eases'. So I thought I must be off route – although on the ridge it was difficult to quite see how – when I found the next corner blocked by overhangs. Never mind, there were jugs underneath and an exciting swing right for a high step round the arête. A rare peg hinted at the exposure of the steep steps on the crest of the ridge. Tom would love this spectacular 'easier angled' stuff.

When his rucksack came into view, a grinning face turned upwards. When he arrived at the belay he coolly sat down and tied on. 'Look at that Tom,' I enthused needlessly, 'feel the sun. What marvellous situations climbing gets you into. This will last you through the winter, eh? When you're in school on a manky day in February, remember this view.'

He looked out from our perch. 'OK, Dad, OK,' he said, 'just don't start singing.'

But Norman was getting ratty instead of inspired. 'I thought it was supposed to get easier' he complained. When his next pitch was up the steep ridge in serious situations leading to a single ancient peg belay he was positively alarmed. We still had to find a way off a mountain, not a crag, and the sun was now getting low. It was January after all. He rushed off into the lead again, running out nearly a rope length. When I joined him and Tom, having climbed an overhanging little diagonal crack protected by a peg, I knew he would be fuming. Sure enough. He shot off up slabby rock that thankfully took him quickly to a red dot on the path that traverses the upper part of the mountain.

We stayed roped up, for it was clear when we looked round the corner that the red-dotted path would cross several ribs, down-climbing the far side of each of them and in between traverse the loose ground of the upper bowl of the south face. Only after the final steep down-climb into the big scree gully could we relax. Crossing towards a patch of the dying sun we sat down, changed into trainers and finished the water.

'You've done well Tom,' pronounced Norman, 'and you haven't complained once.'

As we kept looking back at the mountain a mist drifted across its face, which suddenly cleared and Puig Campana was a bonfire again. Now it glowed only with the last embers of the day, a warm pink bonfire in the sky, rising above us like the final flame of a memory that would warm us all through many a manky day in school that winter.

Mascarat Gorge, Calpe: Via UBSA

When, at the Alpine Club Millennium Symposium in Sheffield, Reinhold Messner said that climbing should be about risk, exposure and responsibility at your limit, he didn't mention anything about grades. He didn't even say it had to be uphill. His solo desert and arctic trips filled the same criteria, he said. He is now working on 'the horizontal walls' of the world with the same approach as he had to mountaineering. His key phrases were 'danger', 'going where others don't go' and 'going up to your limit – not over it, but not below it'. I suspect that the standing ovation given to Messner came from the surprising fact that Messner – the extraordinary mountaineer of our age – was speaking of the same activity undertaken each weekend by the majority of ordinary climbers in the room.

Few of the other speakers were doing things even remotely attainable by most of the audience. The gulf was impressively huge. It was clear that the current front runners are now in a different technical, physical and mental world from the rest of us. What was heartening was that their spirits weren't. The jokiness, absurdity and openness, of the British youngsters especially, was out of the same stable of madness as the legends of Wales in the 1960s, Wall End Barn in the 1950s and the Leeds Wall of the 1970s. But, as Paul Pritchard's (1997) book and subsequent accident remind us, this is *Deep Play*. British front runners are back in the business of neck, making the bolt-protected athletics of the others look like Shallow Play.

So it came as a surprise to me that I was thinking of a bolt-belayed long climb in the Costa Blanca not only as possibly the best vertical experience I had last year, but as a quintessential climb of the Messner criteria as far as I'm concerned. Climbed three days before the new year, Via UBSA rises for seven majestic pitches right above the road and railway of the Mascarat Gorge. Because only its belays remain bolted (or sometimes more dubiously pegged) it offers some necky positions, route-finding challenges and a crux pitch to push VS leaders to their limits. It is also an amazingly deserted buttress of rock, considering that many climbers cruising Costa Blanca rock, staying between Benidorm and Calpe, will have passed underneath it several times in a week.

But this is the way sun-rock climbing has gone – the outdoor climbing wall for safe sunny training at the start of the year. Many talented climbers I know do not climb anything longer than one pitch in two or three weeks amongst much more varied opportunities for adventurous climbs: sea cliffs, outcrops, gorges, buttresses, plus mountain ridges and walls. Well, the bolts are there and what's wrong with pushing your grade on real rock and training in the sun? Absolutely nothing. Just don't come home secretly yearning for the same thing here. That way leads to the end of climbing as Messner defined it to a standing ovation from an audience, where the battle for the soul of British climbing is being fought. An ominous sign for the home scene was Rick from Kendal, who was with us in Spain, saying that it's difficult to get people to go to the mountain crags when they're in condition. They'd rather avoid all that uphill walking when the same challenging grade of route is more predictably dry lower down.

So, on Via UBSA you're likely to be going where others aren't. So for those seeking a little adventure above the sports climbing, using your head as well as your strength, leading to as fine a place to be at sunset as you'll find all week, here's another hot tip.

Uncoiling on the old road bridge, relaxed in the morning sun, it seemed unlikely that I'd be leaving a sling behind in retreat from an excursion off route, or be battling with vegetated gullies in descent at dusk. This is, after all, a well-travelled 'long and interesting route at an amenable grade', as that well-named man Craggs says. Certainly the first pitch was a good warm up, feeling its way past rusty ironworks and cables to the top of the first pillar. Obviously this can be a draughty spot where the wind is funnelled through the gorge, but today I could feel more sun than breeze at the peg belay.

Norman led off up a balancy wall of interesting rock with plenty of natural protection. I found him belayed on a knife-edge ridge directly above the road.

'Don't knock anything down,' he said needlessly, as hundreds of British climbers drove beneath us flexing their clipping fingers round their steering wheels between their one pitch climbs.

I glanced down at the shimmering sea and led along the ridge, over blocky ground, to a terrace below the impressive upper buttress. The key here is a corner which Norman approached by climbing big ledges first left and then right towards the open corner and a belay at its foot. I bridged up it before pulling round right onto a steep wall with two parallel cracks. This lead felt increasingly testing, although the nuts were brilliant. I remember finding that a steep high step right off a little pinnacle gave pause for thought. At the top of this exposed pitch I was glad to meet the belay bolts.

Actually a short traverse along a ledge is needed to reach the official belay for the crux groove, which is out of sight to the belayer. So I believe Norman when he said he led this without pulling on the pegs. Dave Gregory had told me this pitch was probably British 5b. When I got to it I believed him, too. Thin laybacking off a finger crack and few small footholds out left did not leave much time for working it all out. Norman talked about facing left and stepping with one leg backwards blindly to the wall behind him. Quickly I knew I was beyond the limit of my January finger strength and actually enjoyed the alpinist's approach.

It was a mistake to think that the adventure was now all over. I was surprised by the uphill nature of the next pitch. I spent so much time trying to fiddle gear into threads and flared cracks that rather insistantly Norman drew my attention to the advanced time of the day. In passing, I clipped some single pegs above each other and rushed off towards an obvious exit chimney up left. This required pulling past a very loose block, protected by a peg below it. But having survived this danger, the belay tapes around a block and a flake encouraged deep breathing.

When Norman came to the rattling block he became rattled himself. Looking down at the road now way below us, he exclaimed rather forcefully that he was 'not going to pull on that'. I checked the description of his next pitch, which I had not done before setting off on mine. I had a confession to make.

'I think I should have belayed on that sloping ledge tied to that peg back there,' I concluded. 'You see that ring-peg on the arête? Well, I bet that's where you're supposed to swing round off that diagonal crack.'

So he did. With a grunt and a cry of, 'It's not too bad!'

Thus I came to leave a sling and crab on the flake as my back-rope covered my descent past the notorious rattler and a delicate traverse across the sloping ledge (which I assume I should have belayed on) brought the ring-peg's crack into reach. After some hesitation in order to register that there were no little footholds, a footless swing above the gorge and a change of hands brought a high right foot onto a welcomed slab and perfect balance.

Norman had belayed below a corner, splitting the final pitch. In this way the climax fell to my lead. Delightful bridging eased back before a final spectacular high swing of the left foot onto a hanging arête revealed the flat top of the buttress within sight.

The candle of Toix West was aglow and beyond it the Peñon was a rosy nipple in the sea.

Now came the concentration on a tired descent. The long traverse of the mountain was fine, bringing us to a rounded spine above the railway tunnel and the road. But to go straight over to the west, or back into a gully to the east? Rick and our friends were waving us down above the roaring traffic, but towards them, or behind us into the gully? We opted for the gully and pathless bushwhacking over loose stones.

Messner says that the climax of a trip is not the summit, but the moment when basecamp is within reach and one is poised between the safe return and arrival, between wilderness and civilization, between the inner and the outer. Only when we'd found we could step onto the railway line without sliding over the edge of the cutting did we relax, start shouting to our friends, and look forward to a beer or three.

The Fissure d'Ailefroide

You get out of the car, the kids make for the shops (where you should have bought the guidebook in the first place) and you look around. So this is Ailefroide, the end of the valley in the SW French Alps and famous base for ascents in the Massif des Ecrins. Norman said it would be good for a day trip with the kids. 'Look' he said suddenly, pointing. Figures were moving very slowly up rocks behind the village. 'What about a picnic over there?' We went across the meadow, settled the children below the boulders and found a familiar scene a little way above, where a bulging shield of rock confirmed a hint from the Bouvier (1984) guide. 'Bouldering possibilities' meant bolts, shorts, lots of people, many of them women geared only with quickdraws. Nuts are unnecessary. This was climbing in France again.

And here was the French granite, a herringbone texture of granules providing plenty of friction. And, like a flash, we happened to be wearing our quickdraws too. We found an unoccupied line up the boulder that looked about 4b. At the second bolt Norman felt pushed and he was only 10ft off the ground. I helpfully advised left, then right, as usual, but the fact was that this was really a soloing boulder, with no natural features, that had been turned into a guide's training ground by the European application of Le Bolt. We were facing the future of British rock, as a certain current logic might have it.

This being France we could enjoy it with a degree of hypocritical smugness, a good 150ft of 5a moves, trusting the texture that told the tale of all the other bolt ladders either side of it. Up the left end I found a crack with a layback round a little roof. I set off, on perfect jams, then underclings, to clip the bolt on the end of the bulge. Such sharp edges made it only 4a and after two pitches, a raving whoop or two and a song, the descent terrace led below a steep wall. Here a lady was valiantly attempting some 6b moves whilst her boyfriend wooed her up towards him with soft French love charms through the warm air. We averted our eyes in the direction of our sacs and there paused to look out from the crag.

Across the valley-head big peaks rose with armfuls of snow and sun: the Massif des Ecrins. We'd given up all that, Norman and I – the crevasses, the stonefall, the frustrating queues and the pervading sense of rush – for the intimacy, ease and athletics (in that order) of the roadside crags in France and anywhere else we could find them.

Time for a picnic in the meadow. 'There are climbers moving in that crack over there, aren't there?' Norman was pointing this time to a dark long wall that hung above the wide campsite beyond the village. He was right. 'That must be the Fissure d'Ailefroide that Bouvier refers to in passing.' Norman had been doing his homework in between canoeing the Durance and having beach parties at his wooded lakeside campsite.

Actually, I hadn't really expected to meet up with Norman this holiday. I'd given up trying to get him to go for the Miroir each year, so I'd met Tim and Sal in Switzerland and actually climbed it at last, whilst Norman canoed French rivers. Then Gill and I, with Nikola and Daniel, had headed for the Italian Riviera and Finale's fabled limestone crags 'with routes of all grades'. High prices mid-season soon forced us out, but not before we'd discovered the amazing holes of Monte Cucco, sometimes so big that Daniel and Nikola climbed the first pitch of Miguel in trainers. The verticality of the two Severes, Miguel and Luc, is eased by the way wafer-thin edges of holes, which turn jugs into undercuts, perfectly rippled to fit the fingers. Gill was slightly distressed to see that the local method of descent was to remove rock boots, hang them from the neck and then down-climb, barefoot, a gully so steep it seemed to end before the treetops. Two ropes, we found, just reached the ground and took us past a memorial plaque to an Italian climber killed on this descent only two months before.

Camping at Finale is delightful, the freshwater spring is wonderful and we knew it was Stoney-By-The-Sea when we met Graham Hoey from Sheffield, the way you always do of a weekend. But, because we were family camping, we hit the Mediterranean motorway and drove to a cool pool just below Mont St Victoire at Camping Chantecler, Aix-en-Provence.

In August, St Victoire is a white-hot solar reflector, touchable only after 6 p.m. when the semi-naked locals come scurrying out of the shady bushes to move up the walls like lizards. Here the pockets are fingery and predictable, and rather boring to be honest. Well, rather hard anyway. But up the left end again there's a remarkable Severe that climbs, for a full rope-length, a water-worn pipe that's been sliced in half. Mr Livesey (1980) gave it 3c, but of course the crux involves a 4b foot jam across the smooth opening and a pulling apart of both its sides before going for a fist-jam across a narrowing of the edges. A glance over the shoulder from this point, incidentally, can reveal a marvellous sunset through the haze of Marseilles miles away. The abseil off the springy bent peg at the top led to a phone call to England, to discover where Norman was camping in the Alps and this led to finding myself at the foot of the 250m Very Severe Fissure d'Ailfroide wearing shorts, vest and a heavy old Joe Brown helmet.

Norman was anxious to be off, grumbling and chafing at the bit whilst two teams of English climbers got stuck into the open chimney above us. 'It's harder than the guidebook says,' came helpfully from a youth beside is, who was seeing off his mates. 'And you need plenty of big nuts.' We would have

TG on The Miroir,
Switzerland.
Photo: Tim Noble.

been nuts if we'd taken any. As usual, Norman set off before I'd finished uncoiling the rope. Far from the crinolated holes of Finale or the fingerpockets of St Victoire, here were the granite holds of a French fissure par excellence. Climbing and route-finding were more like that in Scotland, but without the heather. Always at a steady Severe, the route never stayed for very long inside the shaft of darkness. A cave-roofed closure of the chimney would produce a teetering out towards exposure and a traverse back in again.

Norman was nervous. It wasn't just this unsettling sudden shift from strenuous chimneying to delicate face-climbing. My lead always seemed to take the rope over little ledges of gravel and the occasional shower of stones turned his grumbling into shouts. One 'little boulder' as he put it, caught

Tom Gifford and Daphne Pritchard on the summit of Montagne des Angneaux, Dauphiné Alps.

him on the helmet, scoring '180'. When he reached me after the sixth pitch I enthused about the moves, trying to relax the atmosphere. 'This is no time for poetry,' he declared. Later he admitted that he'd found that delicate traverse back into the fissure as hard as anything on the route. And the crux was still to come. And more stones.

From a distance, without scale, it had looked like a very long gritstone fist-jamming crack. But here was Norman, back-and footing it out, across a dark doorway that fell plumb to the campsite. Unprotected, he felt a little insecure in these chimney leads. The one that began like that, when it came to my lead, actually led up behind a chockstone and through a hole at the back out into the light again. But I did get the crux which looked easy enough and was looped with chains of little tapes and tat like a curtain rail at Christmas.

The trouble was, you had to hang on to the roof awkwardly with ascending undercuts out right to pull round on to the face again where the usual change of technique was demanded. At the turning point I must admit to holding tat in order to clip into the peg after the strenuous 4c moves under the roof. I don't think Norman noticed. He was impressed with the moves, the lead and the fact that I'd clipped the peg not the tat. He had another narrow struggle upwards before he was actually smiling on the top stance, and telling me to stop for a fantastic picture on the final slab.

Montagne des Agneaux, Ecrin

I'd stopped going to the Alps. Once was enough. A crocodile up the Wildspitze and a beautiful, but scary, morning on the Zinal Rothorn watching the team ahead fall off the crux concluded my apprenticeship in one season. Alpinists will say I'd hardly got started, and they'd be right. But I decided I could live longer and better without the hut walks, the hurry, the competition, the crowds and the stonefall. I saw too many accidents waiting to happen that were outside my control. OK, call it fear. So when the kids came along, I had great summers family camping around the crags of France – wine and warm limestone between games of boule.

But kids grow up and it all comes around again. Tom had visited Chamonix with his French exchange family at 14 and by 18 wanted axes and plastic boots for his birthday. It could be put off no longer. It was time for a return match. The joint annual Climbers' Club/Alpine Club alpine meet was at Ailefroide and the Dauphiné seemed a suitable place for a second look. We arrived early and went up on the Glacier Blanc, just an hour from the car-park, for Tom to try out his new tools and for me to brush up on technique. If you've never practised ice-axe arrests on glacier ice with your banana pick the mountain will make a monkey out of you sooner or later.

When the meet assembled, nine of us went up to the Pelvoux hut for the Pelvoux traverse by the Coolidge Couloir. At 3.30 the next morning Tom and I found that we had gone too high, too early, too fast. Going slowly and with lots of rests we were nevertheless a quarter of an hour ahead of the recommended time. Paradoxically, this was a measure of our unfitness for alpine walking. We hadn't found our rhythm yet. But this trip also showed us that Daphne was going at about our pace – and she completed the route – so we invited her to join us on our trip to Montagne des Agneaux. This had been recommended by Wil Hurford as a good acclimatization route of snow and rock. It turned out to be much more than that.

Daphne hesitated.

'I'm not sure if I should do this. Look what happened the last time I accepted an invitation from you!'

As the last person on the rope she'd finished in the dark at North Stack, Anglesey on Britomartis (HVS 5a) in January after Norman had been washed by a wave whilst leading the initial crux traverse. He had led the route valiantly in a slow state of increasing hypothermia, so spaced out he'd not stopped at the end of the first pitch but stretched the ropes to the cliff top. (His account of this in the 1989/90 *Climber's Club Journal* is called 'A Wet Weekend in Wales'.)

'But we are a long way from the sea', I persuaded, 'and Norman.' I'm not sure which point won.

'So what do you think of bivying above the hut and leaving at, say, 6.30 tonight?'

'Mmm. You know, I think I can manage without a sleeping bag.'

Daphne was upping the stakes.

'OK. I'll try it myself.' Well, it worked, almost.

The hour and a half walk up the zigzags to the Glacier Blanc was pleasant in the last light of day. There was someone new to talk to – or listen to, in Daphne's case – and there were no crowds charging up to one of the most popular huts in France. Above it there were several tents and the boulder bivy sites were occupied by sleeping bodies. But we found a flat patch with a low wall built to keep out the chill breeze off the glacier. By ten o'clock we'd built it up a bit and settled down. I was cold on my upper hip, probably because I had my thermarest mat inside my bivy bag. During the night Tom turned a lot in his plastic survival bag and I assumed, wrongly, that he was cold too. Daphne just snored, as experienced alpinists should. Somehow I'd got to sleep by the time the alarm went off at 3.30 a.m. Breakfast was bread, cheese and water, eaten whilst lacing boots by headtorch. All around us lights in the darkness indicated others doing the same. It was as if some ancient army had arisen from the earth at a silent signal. We appeared to be the first on the trail up the moonlit moraine. No torch was needed. It was windless and I was sweating already, still wearing all the clothes I'd slept in. At the snow we were overtaken by the first silent shadows. At the last boulder in the snowfield we paused to put on crampons, not a good place to do so because things can fall down the melted gap between rock and snow. Tom gave me chocolate. Daphne was still eating dry muesli. So we set off to plod up the snowfield, going as slowly as possible, happy in the knowledge that Daphne would be slower and still get to the top. A glance at the guidebook (Brailsford 1987) might suggest that this south-west face route to the south ridge is a boringly easy snow-plod to a worthless rock scramble up an insignificant summit. If W. A. B. Coolidge first climbed it in 1873, it is graded Facile and is only four hours from the hut, it's hardly a great achievement. But this is to miss the point. It is continually interesting, changing direction four times, linking three glaciers, climaxing in exposed rock climbing, and at 3,662m giving the best views of the entire Ecrins massif from the Pelvoux to the Meije, not to mention Mont Blanc beyond.

Fit people went in a straight line up the Glacier Jean Gauthier, head down, full throttle. They should have looked up. High on the left the route goes over loose rock which makes a line of stonefall down to those greyhounds cutting the corner below – lambs to the slaughter again. I spotted a guide taking his party on a long zig to the right, to zag back left higher up. I pointed this out to Tom and we did the same. When I came to cross those rocks, clumsily in crampons, I knocked one down and stood dumb for the word 'Below!' in French as it rolled silently, the word and the rock, down the snow towards a couple who were eventually alerted by the cry of the Frenchman beside me. They dodged it.

'Dad, you should have called', Tom said, embarrassed.

At the next rest, where these rocks meet the next glacier, the Frenchman gave me a long look. I accepted it, guiltily.

Now, as dawn was lighting up the Pelvoux and the Ecrins behind us, we turned right. Snow again led up to rock and a little narrow ledge that gave access to the knife-edge snow of the Col du Monêtier. As I waited for Tom and Daphne, a Frenchman told me my 'family' were not far behind. I smiled at my unexpected marriage to Daphne. (Sorry, Daphne, I know this is not the place for you to find this out. I have somehow forgotten to mention it before.) Here the sun hit us too and gleaming snow swept away below us towards the Briançon valley. A left turn, down, then up the snow brought the summit rock pyramid in sight for the first time. As we got closer it was clear that there was a certain amount of Gallic concern about the first steep rocks. The short, horizontal rock ridge of Col Tuckett was a consternation of crampons and axes abandoned, ropes and belays, climbers wanting to overtake each other and guides shouting at their clients. Daphne arrived and suggested we solo it. So we did. It was steep, exposed, Diff and delightful. We were on our home ground. Luckily no-one fell on us. From here on it was our turn to quietly overtake a few roped up scramblers on the loose, open but easy south-east face. When the next hold appeared to be a cairn, the summit came as a surprise.

And what a summit view! To our left the multi-headed Pelvoux, to its right the squat Ecrins, far right again the mighty Meije was outlined in all its length. For Tom's first alpine peak the weather, the view, the company and the climb could not have been bettered. He pulled out a hip-flask and offered me a dram, surprising me with the quality of his upbringing. Daphne ate some more dry muesli and posed patiently for photos. I looked around at my fellow summiteers. Mostly they were male and female pairs, all eccentrically dressed, but all roped together. On the descent over that loose easy-angled rock they were going to be lethal. So when a guide set off with his five-client-rope, I suggested that we followed. Actually I had difficulty keeping up with them. It was amazing. They all moved together, he shouting encouragingly at the woman in front to go left or right, whilst he belayed them over a spike before racing down to the next spike. He knew the route upside down and every belay spike along the way. Eventually I lost them and waited for Tom and Daphne at the bottom of a tricky bit. By the time I got to the initial rock step again his 'bonne corde' were sliding down the snow below. As I rigged the rappel ropes more consternation broke out from the French teams queueing up behind. They'd passed the bolts on the way up presumably, but did not realize that a rappel was the norm. Their single ropes, halved, might not reach, they now realized, and they began making friends with other ropes in order to join together, in that French sort of way. Tom had forgotten his belay plate so he had to learn the three twists round a krab method that is not in the manuals. Daphne helpfully suggested the hot seat method, but Tom's smile and 'No thanks' implied that, except for the French, contraception of a permanent nature was not required here. I also had a sentimental attachment to the possibility of the continuation of the 'corde de famille'.

By now we were so late that the soft snow allowed for a fast descent: Tom discovered the sitting glissade and I discovered that I had a hole in the outer layer of my trousers' seat that turned into an ice pack. By the bottom of the route, this had cooled my bottom into a dangerous state of frost-bite which I would have had difficulty explaining to Gill when I got home.

'Montagne des Agneaux' means 'The Mountain of the Lambs'. This time we had been the lambs of innocence, easily given a wonderful first, second and latest alpine experience on the continuously interesting Montagne des Agneaux. Perhaps, after all, you don't have to be lambs to the slaughter if you pick your routes, conditions and partners in the Alps.

Ailefroide Rock: Palavar les Flots

It was the Alpinists who suggested it in the end. They were twitching at the prospect of inactivity during the two days of storms that were forecast. We'd chatted the morning away under a continuing blue sky and by midday there was still no sign of the day's predicted 'orages forts' (strong storms). It was young Mark Croft, an Aspirant Member of the Alpine Club, who broached a little rock climbing: 'I think we should have a mass ascent of that ridge over there.'

That was it. Tom, my 18-year-old son, and I had been eyeing it up all week as it had had continuous ascents and epic rappels down the open face to its right, often well into the darkness of evening. We'd been looking across at it from the classic 250m VS Fissure d'Ailefroide that dominates one side of the campsite, noticing how much bigger it was and how the queues slowed people down on it.

Then John Brailsford, writer of the *Ecrins Massif* guidebook (1987), had turned up and raved about it. In annotating the new rock-climbing guide to Ailefroide for us he wrote against the route name Palavar les Flots 'VS recommended, not strenuous, seven raps, 50m ropes'.

'From the top, rap down the last two pitches of the route before rapping into the face,' he said. 'Those top rap points in the face are in the middle of nowhere, hanging belays that can be hard to find, and you'll need 50m ropes too.'

It sounded exciting. We had to do it. But Tom and I were on the Alpine Club meet to learn from the Alpinists who, when in the Alps, understandably didn't give rock climbing a priority. So when the best forecast had come, Tom and I had headed towards the snow too. Now we were feeling better after our 3,662m peak, Des Agneaux, but sat facing two days of storms. Then Mark flicked the switch that had us sorting gear fast. Daphne Pritchard had been with us on the big peak, so we asked her to join us on 11 pitches of VS followed by seven rappels – with electrical storms forecast – and already it was close to midday.

As we were gearing up, some lanky, wizened Alpinists drifted over, already made restless and slightly bitter by the bad forecast.

'What's all this then? Going low level mountaineering?'

I looked up at the blue sky and said, in my best imitation of an apologetic peak-bagger, 'Well, you've got to be doing something haven't you?' Actually, we were in for one of our more memorable adventures again.

The route, when we reached it after half an hour's walk from the tents, was awash with people on every visible pitch. A Frenchman was taking his two very young kids up it. A Newcastle University team were starting the first pitch, whilst Mark's senior Alpine Club partner, John Temple, was ticking them off for not being on a glacier somewhere higher.

'You should be preparing your bivy about now,' he was chiding, as he gulped down water in preparation for his own hot rock route. He and Mark were not carrying rucksacks, despite the forecast, because this was, after all, only a little rock climb of 1,200ft. Mark's two mates, Luke Clifton and John Chambers, went next, giving me plenty of time to photograph a butterfly attracted to the smell of Daphne's feet, or something. So we were the last in this long and varied queue of climbers who did not believe in 'strong storms'. And still the sun shone.

I set off fully convinced that we'd be rappelling well before the top, but the first pitch was sharp-edged Severe slab climbing, regularly bolt protected, as was the whole route. Tom and Daphne seconded simultaneously, then Daphne led through up a blocky flake and crack system that felt even more like Lakes granite than the first pitch, except for the intensity of the sun. On the third pitch I realized, once again, that linking bolt after bolt simply stops you thinking. That's why they will be the death of British climbing. Here, for example, the climbing line tended to go right of the bolts and I remembered seeing John Temple lead past the two kids on this pitch whilst they struggled to climb, one on the heels of the other, in a straight line between bolts. In true Alpinist mode he said nothing to them about the correct line as he pulled ahead of them. This third pitch steepened up and got interesting before ending at a queue sitting astride a knife-edge.

Above, the smallest of the two boys had fallen, pulled off by the rope probably, whilst hand-traversing down into a bottomless V. He couldn't unclip from the bolt above him to climb the slab opposite. I suggested that his brother descended to him to help him out. Out of sight of their father, all they needed was a bit of verbal encouragement. Their dad had left long slings on the bolts in the slab for this first crux pitch. The makeshift quality of my French soon had them scrabbling upwards, with Luke and John quickly on their heels. We put Tom in the lead for this one, which he cruised by going out to the right edge for holds. It was fine climbing on delicate edges in a spectacular position. And still the sun shone.

Two more delightful slab pitches followed at Severe until, with some surprise, I realized how good a little shade could be at a belay beside a small tree. There was even a slight breeze. A sip of water was allowed. Tom went into the lead again for the second crux which, this time, I found hard. It was smooth herringbone granite on which I lost momentum unclipping the bolt that, ultimately, expediently, became first a finger – then a foothold. As Tom pointed out later, if it had not been there I'd have had to climb the rock. My excuse was that time was becoming crucial. The breeze was now a wind.

I'd got Tom out of his pit to do this route, so he'd eaten nothing but a bit of bread and cheese on the walk across the camping field. I could see he was flagging in the continuing heat so, as Daphne led up continuing slabs, I allowed him (and me) half a Mars bar, with the minimum of water. It was getting tough. And still the sun shone.

My pitch followed a line of closed cracks at an easing angle and gave me the chance to overtake the kids. At the belay I found that their dad had not done this route before, that they lived in Briançon and had visited Scotland. In my rather gestural French we discussed the Scottish midge, whilst Daphne and Tom came up complaining about my rope management. Perhaps I got a gesture wrong, because now the Frenchman was preparing to jump over the edge.

As the wind got up, Daphne insisted, quite properly, that we completed the route's last two pitches. She led off fast. They are indeed interesting pitches, characterized by projecting 'chicken

THE JOY OF CLIMBING

heads' reminiscent of Tuolumne Meadows, but by the time we turned round to face the gale at the top, a black wall filled the valley beyond the camp-site. Here was the predicted monster and its breath was so powerful that it was difficult to throw down the ropes.

When you're rappelling in a hurry the ropes snag on everything, especially down slabs that suddenly sprout little twigs when you look downwards. It was obvious that we were going to get very wet. At the end of the first rap down the face, the rain started. As Daphne went down, Tom and I put on cags. When I arrived she'd got hers on but, clipping the next double bolt belay at a ledge, she'd missed the crucial rappel chains which were, indeed, in the middle of nowhere, below and left of her comfortable ledge. I clipped the ropes through her belay sling and continued tensioning across to make a long reach for the hanging belay on the chains.

The rain was torrential. Thunder broke over our heads and the lightning just had to be ignored. By now the face was a waterfall and I led down over a roof where water fell away in waves. I jumped into them and searched for the next chains below. Silver chains on silver granite could not be seen in the sudden darkness. I settled for a tree in a corner, put a sling on it and clipped in. As I pulled the remaining two feet of wet rope from my belay plate I watched myself drop it. I trapped it with my foot, bent down very slowly to pick it up, then breathed again. This time Daphne found what I had missed, so as Tom came down, I had to solo nervously up soft pine needles in a corner, then traverse to rejoin them. One more rappel took us to the ground and a soggy sigh of relief.

We arrived back at the camp-site looking as though we'd just been for a swim in full climbing gear. And of course the Alpinists hadn't even got wet. I had to admit to John Temple that the score was Alpinists 2, Rock climbers 1. 'Shouldn't it be 3:1?' he said, still trying to pull even further ahead.

Well, now that I've found out the meaning of the route's name he'll claim another point scored. Palavar is the name of the mountain ridge above the route. 'Les flots' are waves. But Palavar les Flots is a pun on Palavas-les-Flots, a popular swimming place in Hérault. God, can you hear that? It's the sound of him laughing as he is reading this.

Gorgeous Crete

On the day Gill, Tom and I walked down the Samaria Gorge last August, so did two and a half thousand other people. Since most of them reached the sea, like us, by the end of a long morning, you can understand a bit what it felt like being in a film by Cecil B. DeMille. If you stopped to take a picture you were in danger of being literally overrun by the hordes of Europe descending upon you. But in three other gorge walks close by we met a total of three people. There is more to gorgeous Crete than the Samaria Gorge and if you want a little adventure to liven up a family holiday that's beachbound, planning a couple of Alpine starts for the White Mountains could get you exploring some spectacular corners of Crete alone, even in August.

Firstly, it has to be said that as the longest gorge in Europe, the 11 miles of the Samaria Gorge are incomparable. These three alternatives would make good preparatory walks, although each of them does have its own distinctive character: the sudden narrowing of the walls in the Imbros; the pinnacles of the upper Samaria; and the Alpine path of the Agia Irini. The latter path has only recently been opened up so it won't be found in some walking guides. For that reason I'll let you in on the secret with more detail when I come to it.

The Imbros Gorge is short and will only take about two hours 20 minutes. But it is surprisingly varied, opening and closing, winding and echoing, before suddenly spewing you out at the sea. Away to the left on the coastal plane, shimmering in the haze, is the square castle of Frangokastello. From here, in the last century, the Turks tried to control the defiant Cretans of this rugged area. When my son Tom and I walked down the old supply route through the gorge, which is still cobbled in places, we met no one but the ghosts of travellers, bending in the shadows to smell the Jerusalem sage.

As the thousands went through the turnstiles to descend the Samaria Gorge (to be counted in and counted out), Gill and I turned uphill on one cloudless morning to explore the upper part of the Gorge. We were to meet only one person, an early bird from London who was on his way down as we zigzagged up the open bowl at the head of the gorge. I'd read about this walk in *High* 94 (Fell 1990) when the cover showed the path leading out of the bowl to the summit of Gingilos, the impressive mountain that the gorge spirals round. But I was still unprepared for the cool clarity of the air, the lifting views of the huge dried-up lake bed below to the right, the fall away to the left where a Bonelli's eagle soared above the ravine, and the intricacy of the path through an archway and pinnacles to a perfectly placed spring.

The delicious water here lulled me into complacency. I thought I knew where the path must go, through boulders steeply up towards the col. 'It can't go up here,' Gill said, as we pulled over razor-sharp boulders. Then, 'if there's much more of this I'm turning back.' I knew what was coming next, we were getting to the famous stage of, 'Terry, I don't need to be doing this.' I couldn't bluff any longer. I had to be off-route. Walks in Crete are always on paths suitable for trainers and you rarely have to use your hands. From the spring we should have gone horizontally right where an even path has been made across the scree. Fortunately I caught sight of it and crossed to it just in time to prevent mutiny.

It was cold at the col and blowing a gale, but a cloud of bees somehow maintained residence. Gill decided to take a slow return from here and I decided to take a fast scramble for the summit. The bees were a great help in carrying out this plan. There's nothing like walking in shorts over slabs crawling with dozy bees. I came close to stepping over the edge of two vertical sinkholes in the limestone slopes because I wasn't looking ahead. From the first summit you have to cross a weird lunar landscape of swallowholes and pinnacles to reach the true summit. For a walk of only five hours total, this really is full of surprises, and if you followed this with a descent of the Samaria Gorge the next day, you'd have made the complete descent from 2,080m to the sea down one of the most beautiful landforms in Europe.

But there is more to come. Looking for a way to relieve the pressure on this most famous gorge, the Greek government has constructed a path down a parallel gorge to the west. But fearing that it will go the same way as coach-fed Samaria, they now appear to be reluctant to let the cat out of the bag. I have every confidence readers visiting Crete will respect this beautiful environment. It is the tour operators who will be the key to the future of the Agia Irini Gorge. The government will have to control them if it really has had a change of heart. Meanwhile, for discreet readers, here's how to find a wild and interesting gorge in which we met only a local farmer and his son who were equally surprised to find us descending towards them near the end of our journey.

The road to Ornalos out of Chania is signed 'Samaria'. The turn off right for Agia Irini is at a sign marked 'Alikianos 1km'. Just after the sign leaving Agia Irini, three tracks go down to the left and there's parking space, but no indication that a superb walk starts from here. Pop down to the left and the usual red dots will confirm that, although largely unknown, this path is official.

Pink bougainvillaea flowers line a stream bed that quickly opens out under great white pillars. A wall for water control inscribed '1966' provides a check that you're in the right ravine. As the gorge suddenly plunges down ahead, a newly cut path slices across left in the first of several deviations from the stream bed. Clearly the authorities want to avoid a repetition here of the drownings in Samaria when people going down too early in the season cannot escape the flash floods from unexpected rainstorms. The path becomes distinctly Alpine in atmosphere as it hangs on the side of the walls before zigzagging steeply down to the foot of a waterfall of house-size boulders. Traces of blue paint up through the boulders show where the trail used to go.

There is still some scrambling down them to step through the arms of a zebra-skinned plane tree. In the walls above, caves hang like the high windows of a cathedral. Along to the right a nasty new scar of path leaves the dry river bed, but we preferred to flow like the water over the smaller boulders of the natural line. And so we journeyed into the depths of this secret ravine, over a bleak pile of grey scree, through a beautiful grove of peeling plane trees, past a graveyard of bleached flood-torn trees, under a family of five crag martins taking it in turns to fish the air for flies, and always these pine-studded buttresses snaked up to more complex canyons above. In places we were actually walking on grass and pushing through vegetation, showing how little this path is used.

Low down in the length of the gorge it narrows, like the others, into a sudden bottleneck before opening out as a river of pebbles leading into a now visible landscape of hills and olive groves. We hit a dirt road running beside the river bed. Was this the road marked on the map? A small bridge, nearly buried with river gravel, led to a white church beside our track. But it was still further down the opening valley that we hit the tarmac road.

It had only taken us three hours, almost all of it in the shade. We now stood in the full heat of the midday sun. Rather than follow the rubble down to the sea for the next couple of miles, we opted to hitch back up for the car to drive down for a swim. Gill hadn't hitched since 1965. She hadn't lost her touch. Two Greek family vans completed the circle of our journey. In the mountains of Crete people still help out other travellers. Hitching is not a problem, even for the middle-aged English.

Well, that accounts for three gorges cutting south through the White Mountains to the sea. I've just read that there are actually five. Watch this space.

Carrion Crete

The dead sing from the empty eye sockets high in the walls of the gorge. It is not much of a song now, for they have been dead a long time. Their song is reduced to the voice of a raven croaking from the edge of an eye hole, watching us descend the Valley of the Dead in the purgatorial heat of summer.

But Gill and I are descending towards the sea, gorge walking in Crete again, this time exploring away from the well-known gorges of the south coast that flank the incomparable Samaria Gorge. Gill wants to show me a gorge she ascended two years ago on the north coast near Rethimnon.

But first we have come to the far east of the island, to the upland village of Zakros, where an impressive board in the village square advertises a path down the ominously named 'Dead Gorge'.

The Minoans who beached their beautiful boats down at Kato Zakros in the 17th century BC built their villas above the little bay that faced out towards the Nile delta, the centre of civilization, trade and the green plenty of the then-known world. It was not until the turn of the 20th century that the British archaeologist, David Hogarth, discovered these pillared Minoan villas. Incredibly, only 41 years ago a Greek archaeologist, digging a few metres away, found the remains of a huge three-storey palace with all its treasures unplundered.

And in the gorge that brings fresh water to this bay of barren slopes, the Minoans found natural burial chambers in the hundreds of caves in the burnished orange walls of this limestone ravine that falls from the hinterland. Water is the source of life on Crete and to the valley of the source they returned their dead.

But this is not a dead valley. The raven's is not the only voice here. Gill pointed out the pale patterning of the soaring honey buzzard's wings as it turned and dived at the raven. Exploding into view a peregrine flashed across the narrow sky. Then there were bells, one high, one low, echoing from the opposite cliff. Two Andoran goats, on a ledge half way up, had their front hooves on juniper branches to reach the lowest leaves. Even in August, pink and white flowers were still springing from the bushes of wild oleander we pushed through. The taps of the sources of 'potable water' marked on the display board in Zakros had been removed to prevent frustration, but we paddled through seepages sufficient to bring blossoms flowing down the Valley of the Dead.

This descent only takes an hour and 45 minutes to the sea, but the return, by a slightly different route, will take three hours. We parked our hire car under a fig tree in the Zakros car-park and started walking on the road out of town towards Kato Zakros, passing the walls and central pillar of a Minoan villa. After 20 minutes a shepherd's corral on the left marks the point of departure for the ravine now seen below. Contouring round right, the indistinct path meets a rough track descending to a gate. Three languages ask you to close it behind you before you drop down into the bottom of the ravine. The first caves stare out above. A sign indicates a right turn along the stream bed. The path actually manages to stay on the (true) left of the bouldered stream bed most of the way. After an hour and a half a bamboo grove on the right announces a concrete road crossing at which a left turn brings you past banana trees to the Minoan palace ruins. While its ground plan is being picked over by tourists delivered by coach, a beer and a swim might be a priority. History, after all, can wait.

The variation on the return journey is delicious. Instead of climbing back up steeply to the road from the sign, the ravine is followed round right to a water tap that is still working, offering refreshment just when it's needed. Then a narrow aqueduct, gurgling with life, becomes the key to the return to the village. It's hard to spot when the path climbs up right and over the aqueduct to avoid big boulders under trees: it's after a dam marks a left turn in the stream. Later, at a sudden fence, the aqueduct descends from a side valley and the path takes the right side of this towards open views of the village. The key now is a gate, marked with a faded red triangular flag. From the house above this, a track leads back into the heart of the village. The intriguing route finding of this game of spot-the-red dots is much preferable to flogging back up the tarmac road into Zakros as an end to this remarkable walk through history.

The second gorge, the Prassanos, is a surprising contrast, unseen by the sun-worshippers on the Platanes beach strip east of Rethimnon where it emerges at a cement factory. We made a rather challenging eight hour round walk of this gorge descent from the house of Malcolm and Evie Watson where we were staying in the quiet village of Agia Paraskevi. The Sunflower guide (Godfrey and Karslake 1994) recommends catching the Amari bus up to the Mirithos turn to begin the four hour descent, but we wanted an adventure with our new German hiking map. We certainly got one.

Walking up through the sleepy Venetian village of Maroulas, a left turn into an orange cutting lifted us steeply above the coastal plain until on our right we could peep over into the bottom section of the gorge we would be descending. A golden eagle contoured round the side of the gorge to look us over. Perched at the top of this steep hill is a most impressively sited restaurant – Fantastica – which certainly has spectacular views of the coastal strip at night.

Continuing up this surfaced road across the high plateau to the south, we wondered why the only traffic was the regular passing of refuse lorries. The obvious answer was to hit us on the nose a little later. In a broad hollow on the right was a large covered cistern from which a shepherd was watering a flock of sheep. A mile beyond, a circling of corvids haloed the Rethimnon Rubbish Tip. Here the tarmac finished and we hurried on, holding our noses, down the broad dirt track to search for the European Trekkingroute marked in red on our 1997 German map. We found the E4 signpost where it came in from the east, although both directional fingers were bent back the way it had come. But there was no sign of the westward path that should have taken us down to the start of the gorge.

In fact, there was no corresponding roadside sign indicating the E4 path descending to the head of the gorge. Returning by car to check later, we found a sign, bent backwards again but riddled by bullets, some 50m from the road, down a track that went off right (south-west) after the cistern. Paint-marked rocks led in the direction of the gorge until we lost them in untracked, very prickly ground. This European Trekkingroute seems more a good plan than a reality. Malcolm told us the local shepherds were probably as pleased to have a trekkingroute signposted through their territory as they were to have the recent rubbish tip dumped on their wild hills.

So we continued down the broad dirt track, not unpleasantly, with wide views of the flat fertile valley from which the river drops into its deep and dramatic ravine on the right. Cloud cover and a breeze made this a perfect day for a mid-August day's walking.

It was feeling like lunchtime as we reached the main road to which Gill had ascended from the Prassanos Gorge two years ago. An isolated taverna had provided herself, Malcolm and Georgos with refreshment and a lift back home. This house now loomed in front of us. We sat at the only table and demanded of the two girls who appeared, a Greek salad and beers. But it was the olives we really appreciated and when we came to go they gave us a bagful to take home. Not only that, but they would only let us pay for the beers.

Eulogizing Greek hospitality, we descended from the road through fields and wire fences, making our way down to the river bed and its thin braiding of water. The arms announcing the start of the gorge were rising towards us. The plain in the bottom of this bowl of hills narrowed from fields of tall dry grasses into a wood-shaded snake of dappled boulders. At the last open moment before the walls closed, an E4 sign showed where the lower part of the trekkingroute we had failed to follow crossed the river to continue traversing the length of the island. Very soon it became clear that Gill's faith in her beloved Teva sandals was vindicated as she walked through water at a narrowing, while I scrambled through bushes up the rock walls and dangerously down again.

But from then on it was all delight – crag martins nesting on eye-level shelves, vultures soaring optimistically above us, amazing examples of vegetation clinging on in unlikely spots – and only one German couple with a small child seen in the gorge during the whole, long boulder-hopping afternoon. At one point, while Gill found the high level alternative, I down-climbed, on hidden holds, a corner where water, in spring, poured between two big boulders. Water had disappeared early in our descent, but in spring this must be a dangerous place to get caught after heavy rain inland.

As we began to emerge from confining walls to a field and then an olive grove beside the river bed, we were entering a favourite haunt of bird watchers on Crete. Straining for a glimpse of a hoopoe, all we saw were straggly chickens, plenty of rubbish and then a strangely medieval sight. Beside a circle of low ovens, a man covered from head to foot in soot was stacking coarse sacks of charcoal beside a track. Up on the back of a lorry another sooty man was loading the sacks for distribution around the villages for tourists' barbecues. At the end of a charcoal burner's day, two people walking out of the gorge provided a distraction not to be ignored. In broken Greek and English an apparently friendly conversation could not appease Gill's unease and desire to reach the cement factory, the main coast road and a taxi back up to Malcolm and Evie's house. It was Malcolm who broke the news to us. That house he and Gill had lunched at after their ascent of the gorge had stopped being a taverna a year ago. We had behaved like English pirates to the two girls left at home. No wonder they'd giggled so much. All we could do was to offer him their excellent family olives and giggle a little ourselves.

Four Canyons in Crete

Its name was a joke. A roadside sign pointed to 'Canyon Ha'. To start climbing an hour before sunset was a joke. And the three-pitch new climb we made before dark was a joke – two up, one across and down. Gill was entertaining wild goats while, above, we decided if the route would go and where, given the shrinking but marvellous light, and our own high spirits at this madness under the pressure of darkness.

We leapt up blocky ledges of the vertical left wall above a pool. Easy, exhilarating and steep. Good to have the harness on after two weeks of book-writing here on a make-or-break push, a year behind contract. I was climbing with Chris, the American archaeologist who'd tempted us here, to the remote north-east village of Mochlos where he was site-foreman of a dig by American Classics students. (They were to prove helpful in reading chapters, as I finished them, of the *Pastoral* book (Gifford 1999) I was trying to complete.) I'd met Chris at my slide lecture on 'British Soft Rock' for a gearstore in North Carolina two years earlier. He said he was about to come to Sheffield for the MA in Landscape Archeology. You know how the climbing village works. So here we were in Crete, doing what we could against the heat and the light – in earnest exploration of the bottom of one of the most spectacular gashes in Crete that's visible from the road – the Ha Gorge.

What surpised us was the bolt. We climbed the left wall and traversed in above a pool that's fed, in spring, by a smooth undercut shoot. As we stepped down onto this dry water shoot we met a bolt. Was it placed for climbing, or for a gorge descent? I went to the back of the shoot and found another pool with water-smoothed concave walls. No way up there. The Ha Gorge is a 1,000ft crack produced, not by erosion, but by tectonics – the stretching of the fault-scarp. In spring it must be one long bottled waterfall (that once fed eight watermills below) – hardly suitable for a safe gorge descent. The answer must be someone prospecting, like us, but with the European disease of bolt brains that is now diagnosed as BSE – Boltline Spongiform Encephalopathy.

Chris suggested that he ascend the right wall above the lip of the first pool. An exciting and well-protected (with British nuts) position led to a fine pitch to a ledge. If we were going to step left into a steep groove the grade was going to go up, Chris pointed out tactfully, just as, I replied tactfully, the sun was going down. So I led out right across loose rock and descended the arête that led down to the rock-carved leat that had fed the ancient watermills. A brilliant sunset had taken place already over the olive groves below and the shadow of the Eleonora's falcon, that had been cruising them when we arrived, had passed over my shoulder to roost somewhere in the upper mysteries of the Ha.

So here is a little foray into the Ha Canyon at Hard Severe, suitable for the last two hours of an August day and capable of further development. Elsewhere in Crete, rock climbing has only been developed by the young custodians of the Austrian hut above the Samaria Gorge. Although Chris could not last the three months of the dig each year at the Minoan settlement on the island off Mochlos without a bit of cragging. So he has put belay bolts in the cliff at the back of the island to create two pitches of marvellous climbing up from the sea. Even he had difficulty finding them when he introduced me to his island secret after our adventure in the Ha.

Chris was also doing a project on watermills, so he arranged a weekend trip to the last working waterwheel at Zaros, at the southern foot of the central mountains. Whilst he interviewed the elderly miller, we would climb the Zaros Gorge with Jason, whose classical knowledge and meticulous notes on my text was improving my slowly growing book. We slept out beside the lake above the fish restaurants for which the village is famous. We got a late start, partly due to the wine and conversation of a warm evening, partly due to the entertainments of the morning. Chris caught a cicada and released it into the bivi-tent of the sleeping Jason, with the expected results as they met each other.

From the taverna at the back of the lake, signposts indicate the steep path up to the monastery that sits astride the bottom of the gorge. The path goes round the back and in by a small improbable back-door. Here we entered a living community of monks, pigeons, vistas and running water. Crossing the large balcony and up the steps – shallow, to slow life down – we passed the last source of water. Although springs are marked along the way and there is a famous stream and meadow at the top of the gorge, none of these proved to be flowing in early August.

The path is not hard to follow and winds up in a pattern of narrowings and openings that changes the ambiance of the walking. If in doubt, take a left. At an overhanging roof where crag martins nest, take a road left rather than continue right up the gorge. This brings you to a path with a rustic alpine hand-rail that climbs the side of the canyon and re-enters it by several bridges and ladders. As the river bed levels out it is hard to find the exit right to the meadows. We took a slope of open rock just beyond some red paint marks that doubled back right and which we probably should have taken. This led us to a church and below it the fetid stream where several Cretan families were picnicking and sleeping out for the weekend.

The lack of water here became an obvious problem, as our late start put us out in the strongest sun of the summer during the descent. I have never had a dizzy spell before in Crete, but I was dehydrated by the time we returned to the monastery and struggled over the last uphill bit before the final descent to the lake.

Our third canyon of the summer we had not intended to descend at all. We actually didn't know it was there, despite a huge map of it on the end of the main street we'd not yet visited. It certainly was the most delightful of the four. For the second half of the summer we'd moved to the south coast and the village of Makryalos. We took a bus up to the mountain village of Pefki with the intention of wandering back down by a different road. The village was deserted and it was lunchtime. Only one family was sitting outside in the shade.

'Is there a taverna nearby?' we asked.

'Yes. It's here,' came the reply.

The table was wheeled away from granddad who, it turned out, had made shoes for British soldiers who were on the run during the war. Chairs were found and beers, grapes and watermelon produced.

After we'd paid and said our grateful goodbyes we walked through the still deserted village and suddenly found a new sign inviting us to descend to Makryalos by the Pefki gorge. It turned out to be an ancient paved donkey trail which wound down through olive groves, past a mill and into a narrowing where new iron ladders dramatically descended into the final open hillside. A path through newly renovated houses came out onto the village main road.

We were walking along the Makryalos beach at the end of one afternoon when the former Peak District guidebook editor, Dave Gregory, suddenly popped up, like the ubiquitous gnome that he is, surrounded by grandchildren engaged in various kinds of gymnastic poses. We immediately recruited him for our final canyon descent, the Faragi Perivolakion. It was the shortest, but the toughest, requiring some careful scrambling and a commitment to solving the puzzles of its form.

We left our hire-car in the village of Kato Perivolakia, intending to hitch home from the bottom and collect the car later. In the early morning light a winding valley was pleasant. In fact, the twists of this canyon not only make it longer than it looks on the map, but hint at its sudden dry waterfalls. As the boulders and bushes got bigger route-finding became a team effort. We had little time to look up for a soaring vulture. There were no red paint spots up here. Technical down-climbing was increasingly required. At the first undercut big waterfall we made the mistake of attempting to take the steep slope on the left. A nervous return on marbles eventually confirmed that the scramble over a horn of rock on the right was the better way.

At the second impassable undercut rock-step, a cairn up on the boulder-field on the right led us across some unstable rocks, until a steep gully could be down-climbed to the canyon floor. By now it was the hottest part of the day and the outcome was still a bit in doubt. Turning around was barely an option. This all added to the tension that the best expeditions are fed by.

Actually it emerged that all the difficulties were over and an increasingly definite path took us down the left side of the gorge, beneath the impressive Kapsa monastery and under trees to the biggest fridge in the world stocked with cold drinks. This Tardis was no mirage. It was left from the weekend celebrations of the monastery's saint's day and guarded by a charming young woman who sold us several rounds and promised us a lift home. But first we crossed the road to the sea we'd been dreaming about. We stripped off to end, in the best possible way, this least idealized and pastoral walk of the six weeks I'd devoted to writing about pastoral literature. After a walk like that, when you enter the sea you know you've found Arcadia. It is really located in the waters of Crete at the foot of a gorge where the vulture of death lurks for the unwary. As death seems to be saying on that Poussin painting in Chatsworth House, Et in Arcadia Ego: in Arcadia I am also there.

CHAPTER 8 US ROCK

The VS climber's Guide to Tuolumne Meadows

'I think you're finding excuses because you've bottled out of climbing in the Valley.' Tim's accusation did perhaps have an element of truth in it. I'd been seduced by the brilliant fortnight we'd just had in the Meadows, leading through together, mostly at 5.6 and 5.7. And there were still things to do up here, the ever-present Cathedral Peak, for example, and the soaring Eagle Dihedral. Just recently we'd driven down to Yosemite Valley for a first look. Whilst Tim had been turned on by it, my reaction had been rather different.

When we stepped out of our hire-car's air-conditioning to stand in awe of El Cap, we were hit, not only by that breathtaking wall of rock, but a wall of breathtaking heat. But it was immediately clear that short climbs, even in the shade, would be missing the point of what the Valley is all about – climbing big walls to the rim. Even the easiest classics of this kind are 5.9, the grade at which we both had begun quietly freaking out when following a guest leader. The more I saw of the Valley Floor Tour (a mobile loudspeaker lecture) and the crowded barrenness of Camp Four, the more I was sure that Snake Dyke (5.4) on Half Dome was really the only justification for camping in this desecrated Valley.

I believed that for the VS climber visiting Yosemite National Park in August, whilst the Valley must be seen to be believed, it is in Tuolumne Meadows that most fun will be found. When eventually I sat on the top of the highest pinnacle of Cathedral Peak with Keith and Ira, who had kindly roped me in with them, we talked about tuning-in to the character of each of the domes we could see below us. What they all offer is superb friction on sparkling white granite with long run-outs between bolts. Here, in descents as well as ascents, you have to over-ride your eye's information and have faith in the evidence of your feet – you can stand up on that steep angle of friction. So you learn to read the different texture of each dome, not looking for 'holds' because, as Johnny Dawes once said of gritstone, 'It's all one hold.'

The nearest crag to our Lake Tenaya campground (currently being 'rested' from use), for example, was simply named Stately Pleasure Dome. The ultimate roadside crag, it provided the stately pleasure of balancing up glacier-polished granite, in a progress up the grades, with a swim between every route. You could start with the unstately Hermaphrodite Flake, the Lockwood's Chimney of the Meadows, in which you could discover the knee-bar resting position. At 5.4 it's one of the easiest climbs in the area. The continuation of Hermaphrodite Flake is 5.7 slab-padding with only one bolt in a full holdless run out. One look up at Eunuch might be enough for you to prefer the early abseil, and learn instead from the Great White Book (5.6). For 'book' read 'corner' in California.

This was our first climb in the Meadows. It reassured us with the familiarity of gritstone-type toe-stubbing across a closed crack, followed by Etive-style laybacking on friction, then Cornish chimneying past rounded boulders. Above the boulders Tim stepped right, on to the upper slab and learned to read the cover of the book. The slightest indentations in this sea of sparkling slab provided a fluid journey of movements uninterrupted by fiddling with protection. For my lead, next pitch, I preferred to have my fingers back in the spine of the book. But at the next double-bolt belay Tim decided to up the grade another notch and take the 5.7 horizontal traverse that follows a chest-high step in the sheer granite for 50ft, foot-padding and palm-slapping on different slabs. You walk it because you have to, eyes level with the equally smooth upper slab.

Perhaps a better introduction to this kind of 5.7 'face climbing' on friction is the middle section of White Flake. For this climb it might be worth suggesting that you reconsider the British habit of tying into the belay with the climbing rope. If you don't, you might live (let's hope) to regret it when you're quivering, out of rope and just out of reach of the next belay bolt. I took to using a 'daisy chain', and dark glasses to help distinguish the bolts from the crystals.

The next trick we learned on South Crack (5.8), after Larry had arrived from San Francisco bearing grapes and a bucket. A finger-locking crack reveals its crux to be the traverse above, where Larry found that the hanger had been removed from the protection bolt. He cunningly placed a wire over the protruding thread, jammed up the head of the nut and clipped a long sling. It stayed on, but thereafter he carried a spare hanger on his harness.

Larry decided that we had tuned-in so well that we could climb the 5.9. Dyke Route on Pywiack Dome that had a character, apparently, so delightfully smooth, 'You can't even sling a crystal.' Not that we actually had so far, despite all the hype in the guidebook (Reid and Falkenstein 1986) about typical Tuolumne protection provided by 'slinging chicken heads' or 'knob tie-offs'. This would be painful, if it weren't mostly mythical. Of Dyke Route I can only report that I found I had been concentrating so hard on the texture of glacier polish, that when I reached the top I felt I had had an emotional experience. The VS leader might prefer Pink Turds (5.8).

I did not feel the same on Fairview Dome's Regular Route (5.9) where the character of the rock is 5a crack climbing and you sort of know where you are. And I did not feel the same during our only epic, when Tim went walkabout on Walkabout (5.7) creating an unprotected 5a variant traverse high on Pennyroyal Arches, although I had to climb up to his first nut after he ran out of rope on his friction traverse towards a crack system. This dome is characterized by the refreshing smell of the Pennyroyal mint. It came in handy.

BEST VS I'VE EVER DONE

But I did feel I was reading unique rock on the golden page of Hobbit Book (5.7). A friend had said to Tim, 'Best VS I've ever done, but it takes some finding.' Well, it's spotted easily enough from the road, an open corner cutting a huge curve up the face of Mariuolmne Dome. The trick is finding the bookshelf, the ledge that leads across the upper face to the start of Hobbit Book. The clue is a clump of trees. As we roped up at the start of the ledge traverse, Larry was pointing out to me the way the Mountain Hemlock bows at the very top, and how to tell the Lodgepole pine by its grey bark. So reading the trees too, will help you to open the Hobbit Book.

The 'golden' face pitch of this majestic route is a unique puzzle of huge projecting crystals, each provided with a black vertical lip. You link them together in your own personal pattern, the whole of the High Sierra watching over your shoulder, beneath your feet, pumping your heart. On the way down we paused at the secretive Lake of the Domes, a high breezy hollow, and a calming place.

Perhaps the most bizarre climbing in the Meadows is the challenge of the Watercracks (5.7 and

5.8) on Lembert Dome. The left chute of water-polish shot me out at a first attempt. Larry showed us that you come in from the right and wedge a left foot across the back of the smooth runnel, then press down with a right palm on the rounded edge. Tim bridged, and others I'd seen hold a crucifix position to lift feet over the few steps. The climber who told me, 'You have to swim up the Watercracks,' didn't say which stroke was best.

And so to Cathedral Peak, the well-named structure which dominates Tuolumne Meadows and was first climbed by John Muir in 1869. 'No feature', he wrote, 'of all the noble landscape seen from here seems more wonderful than the Cathedral itself, a temple displaying Nature's best masonry and sermons in stones.' I'd learned a lot in the Meadows from the rock and the reading of it. I didn't need to go pulling on everything in sight to have 'ticked' some of the *Fifty Crowded Classic Climbs* in Yosemite Valley. I needed one more 'sermon in stones' up in the meadows. I was going to solo the 5.4 route up Cathedral Peak, vaguely described in the little green Roper guide. It does not exist. Fortunately Ira and Keith tied me in with them as I was doing up my rock boots. Since no pitch by pitch description of this 5.6 sermon exists in any of our holy books, I offer it below. On the topmost pinnacle I blew children's bubbles. Keith was embarrassed – at first – but eventually let himself go and had a blow too. Ira laughed like a parrot, and nearly fell off his perch.

After a religous experience of uplift like that, one should come back to a bucket. It was for a bum-wash. Only one tap existed at the Lake Tenaya campground, and using soap in the Lake will bring an armed Ranger across the beach. This is a delicate wilderness patrolled by the priests of John Muir, so borrow a bucket for the perfect climbing holiday in Tuolumne Meadows. And get your own sermon from Cathedral Peak.

ROUTE DESCRIPTION:
CATHEDRAL PEAK SE BUTTRESS (5.6)

(1) 150ft up the right side of the buttress, books and flakes lean back and a belay tape is visible above. Head towards it, but cross a smooth intrusion of rock left and pull steeply through an undercut V on to the face of the buttress. This route's threaded belay tape is actually left and below the tape visible from the start (5.5).
(2) A hollow flake above the belay leads left to a ramp and a big flake. Step off this on edges to the right (5.6) leading up to huge crystals and then a corner on the left. Pull over to a spacious belay ledge. (From here escape is possible to the left up easy gullies missing all the fun.) 150ft.
(3) Traverse right along a horizontal groove whilst pinching crystals. 40ft (5.4). Belay below the obvious chimney.
(4) Climb the crystal-edged chimney by the inside, or the right face, or by bridging the knobs. Layaway up on the undercut flake to finger locks inside a chimney. An exposed quilt of crystals steepens to a ledge. 150ft (5.6).
(5) Cross right to the foot of a crack. At the top down-climb left under flakes to ascend a V-groove in the summit pinnacle. 130ft (5.5).
Descend via John Muir's ascent of 1869, down-climbing the V-groove and turning to the N side, then W along below the ridge until it's possible to cut back to cross the NE ridge at a surprisingly high point for the descent to the Budd Lake trail.

Allen Steck: The Silver Fox Of Yosemite

'It's up the hill on the right, the house with the red tiled roof', said the quiet, laid-back voice on the phone. I drove up from San Francisco Bay through the tree-lined residential streets of Berkeley. As I pulled up, the door opened and there stood the silver-haired man I'd come to see – a man with a route

Allen Steck, the Silver Fox of Yosemite, at a snowy Froggatt.

named after him. The Steck-Salathé route on Sentinel Rock winks down on Camp Four in Yosemite Valley. 'A magnificent route', Dermot Somers had said, looking at the calendar photo of it in my kitchen after the previous Festival of Mountaineering Literature. I was now in Allen Steck's kitchen to persuade the 67-year-old co-editor of *Ascent* that he should come to Britain in November for the 1993 Festival.

'John Salathé used to say that climb should be called "Steak and Salad",' Steck told me. 'John Salathé was a vegetarian.' In June 1950 when they created one of America's most famous climbs, Salathé was 51 and Steck was 24, a Berkeley postgraduate student of German.

'Did you bring your climbing shoes? Too bad. We could have gone to Indian Rock. It's five minutes away. In the '50s we used to practice leader falls there. Tied directly round the waist, the leader would go three feet above a peg and jump off, held by a hip belay. Will Siri, a biophysicist, would come out with a dynometer to measure loads on the ropes. He found that abseiling with the rope over an edge halved the body weight on the anchor.'

'Sounds dangerous to me, Al,' I suggested. 'Weren't you afraid of abrading the rope?'

'Well, we were all just students trying things out. Actually, Will got us funding from the military for several trips to do high altitude research. We were flown out to attempt the first ascent of Makalu in a military aircraft.'

'When was this?'

'In 1954. We were Boy Scouts out there. We got to 7000 feet on the south-east ridge, but we were all just kids from California – Willi Unsoeld, Bill Long and others. We couldn't get over the fact that it snowed every day. At first we would wait until it stopped snowing to start climbing! The first piece I ever wrote was about that trip. I sent it to *The Saturday Evening Post*, an East Coast magazine, and a telegram came back: 'Article barely acceptable'.'

The man who has edited, with Steve Roper, the most innovative regular climbing publication over the last 30 years, loves telling stories against himself. After university Steck worked at The Ski Hut, a Berkeley gear shop. There he made the first waist belts for Werner Braun's early big wall climbs. 'Can't think why I didn't take the leap of putting leg-loops on them. Pretty dumb, eh?'

What was not so dumb was setting up America's first trekking company, World Travel, and becoming a guide specialising in South America and Greece. A passion for Greek dancing and for wine (*Ascent* had its own label) tells you a lot about the man. But I was interested in Steck the Himalayan climber. A little probing produced a typical Steck story of his being the sole American guiding the Pakistani Alpine Club's first ascent of Paiju Peak.

'I was called their Technical Adviser. They were all well educated military men and spoke the King's English. When we came down victorious from the mountain they were asked who was the white infidel with them? I was introduced as their American Liaison Officer! A general's car came to pick us up, flag flying, and for a while Steck was god.

'I'd wanted only Pakistani names on the summit team, so I waited 50 metres short of the top. But as I stood there I weakened and asked them to throw a rope down. It didn't reach – there was a traverse involved – so my plan succeeded in spite of myself. We had an unplanned bivy on the descent. I'd brought no stove. I'd had to give an eight day climbing course to those guys before the ascent and now six of our abseils were in the dark. But they managed them with dignity.'

That last phrase is characteristic of Al Steck's generosity of spirit. While he was staying with us in Sheffield, we watched the traumatic TV documentary about Ed Drummond's marriage break-up. More than anyone else, Al has been an admirer and encourager of Drummond's writing, contributing the Foreword to his book. Al was certainly not starry-eyed about the Drummond in that film, but his first response was to think of the implications for Lia and Edwin's children watching this public bitterness in the future. His later response was to write to Drummond, an old friend who was clearly in deep distress.

When I took him to a snow-bound, frozen Froggatt for a couple of climbs on wet rock, Al certainly coped with dignity himself. He took the opportunity to use the thumb-up-between-two-fingers jam he'd invented to enter The Peapod on Curbar a few years ago. His deft smearing, his solid hands and thoughtful approach told you that here was a wily old fox of a laid-back, self-mocking Californian climber. With the faintest of smiles from under his moustache he asked if we really climbed every Sunday, or just when Californians came over. With the broadest of grins I confessed that, these days, I only went to Froggatt on a Sunday when it snowed.

Next day we were walking away from taking a look at The Rasp when Steck made me realize how *Ascent* had retained its ability to be continually surprising over 30 years. A creative mind cannot put itself on hold. Even as we shivered back through the snow to the road Al was saying, 'The key to a climb like that would be to work out a hands-off rest, with a knee-brace maybe, or a shoulder wedge across a corner.'

We pondered on the possibilities for a while before he said, 'Not that I've ever used any of those things myself.'

I looked across at him and I wasn't so sure. He was capable of inventing any technique, however unorthodox, to get himself out of a tight spot.

I was sorting my slides for a lecture on John Muir's California when Al's eye was caught by the Thank God Ledge in a view down the vertical 1,800ft North-west Face of Half Dome. 'You know, I led out to the middle of that ledge where it narrows and there's nothing for your hands. Your heels stick out over a 1,600ft drop. It was getting dark and I couldn't move. I had to do something.

So I decided to jump off backwards and catch the ledge with my hands. It worked. I swung along to the end of the ledge, then descended to those large ledges below. I had a comfortable night laid out with my head on my hands while Dick Long and John Evans sat it out at the belay.'

Steck doesn't always have it so comfortable. His fellow-editor, Steve Roper, who lives half an hour away from Steck, calls him 'El Vago' – the vague one. Joe Kelsey (1989) wrote: 'Allen is forgetful – at least, that was Steve's oft-mentioned theory for his being in Joshua Tree without a sleeping bag. I, however, believe that he starts up a lead without the runners, misplaces his hand-forged objet d'art of a nut remover in the sand, or removes foil-wrapped zucchini from the fire long after it would attract an archaeologist, because he has too many interests – many of them women.'

You might almost hear Al laughing at himself as he edited this for *Ascent* in 1989.

He left England with a Scottish salmon for a Thanksgiving dinner at his girlfriend's house near Boston, fired up to get the next *Ascent* out more quickly than the four year gap between the last ones, and steeling himself to broach his diaries for an autobiography.

The Steck-Salathé route is graded 5.9, the grade, I confessed to him, at which I had usually found I was about to fall off.

'You know,' he said sympathetically, 'it took me a lot of work to get beyond 5.9. I started going to a gym and then bouldered until my forearms screamed.'

'How old were you then?' I asked.

'I guess I was in my sixtieth year,' he said.

John Muir: Nature Reader, Conservation Writer

'Two years ago, when picking flowers in the mountains back of Yosemite Valley, I found a book.' So began the first article, written in 1871, that opened a life-long campaign to reunite people and nature.

The book was the metaphorical 'great open book of Yosemite glaciers', the finder John Muir, who was to be the inspirational, campaigning interpreter of not just these Yosemite pages, but also those of Western landscapes from Arizona to Alaska. Muir, a Scot, went on to become the founding father of the American conservation movement and inventor of National Parks.

But Muir was slow to turn to writing books. In 1992 Ken Wilson's Diadem Books published *John Muir: The Eight Wilderness-Discovery Books* in an order which told the story of his remarkable life. But he didn't write his first book, *The Mountains of California*, until he was 55, and his second, *Our National Parks*, took another nine years to appear. In the last stressful decade of his life he completed the manuscripts of four more. So Muir's books are essentially an older man's writing, often at its best when drawing directly from the freshness of the younger enthusiast's journal writing, the vitality of his letters and the elegance of his articles.

Most of this original material has been unobtainable since it was first published, which in some cases was over 100 years ago. In bringing the original letters and articles together for the modern reader in *John Muir: His Life and Letters and Other Writings* (Gifford 1996, Bâton Wicks), we wanted to offer an opportunity not only to rediscover the relevance of Muir's conservation beliefs and tactics, but also to rediscover Muir as a writer.

The collection of Muir's letters and essays reveals that he was perhaps at his strongest as an essayist. It is significant that his first three published articles, together here for the first time, were compiled from letters to friends. But just as the letters are close to reflective essays, so the essays are subtle reflections on the scientific and conservation issues of the time. Ronald H. Limbaugh's study of the article which became the popular book *Stickeen* reveals how even the writing of a magazine story about a dog was carefully crafted by reference, not only to Muir's original journal, but also to pencilled notes made in 105 books from Muir's personal library ('*Stickeen*' *and the Lessons of Nature*, University of

Alaska Press, Limbaugh 1996). In this essay for *Century* magazine Muir wanted to distil his post-Darwinian thinking about his fellow creatures. Within a popular, accessible form Muir wanted to nudge the reader into asking, 'If this little dog displays sentient intelligence and individual character, does it have a soul? If it has a soul, does it also have rights?' It was through his letters and essays that Muir sought to influence people to value the rights of nature in an age that still retained and institutionalized the pioneers' exploitation of natural resources.

Between the ecstatic aesthetics of Muir's nature writing and the empirical observations of his scientific essays, there was a preservationist agenda that could only be served by his keeping within the reach of the influential readers of *The New York Tribune*, the *Overland Monthly* and *Century*. To read nature through Muir's informed, celebratory letters and essays was to be enlisted in his campaign for the conservation of America's living distinctiveness – its dynamic, diverse landscape and all its inhabitants, from bees to trees.

LETTERS, ESSAYS AND MEMOIRS

In recent years Muir's relevance to our crisis in our relationship with the planet has been recognized by the appearance of four major biographies. The first was compiled in the form of selected letters with a linking commentary by Muir's literary executor and Sierra Club friend, William Frederic Badè. *The Life and Letters of John Muir* has been out of print following its publication in 1924. It is much quoted by Muir scholars and, although it has been the source of four recent US-published themed selections of his letters, most readers have not, until now, been able to read these passionate, eloquent letters as part of Badè's near-contemporaneous biography. Scottish readers will be fascinated by six letters from Muir's European trip of 1893 during which he made his first return to Scotland. These were not included in Badè's selection and have now been published for the first time.

Badè's essential *Life and Letters* has formed the corner-stone of our attempt to make available again as many original Muir essays as we could find, in the form in which Muir intended them for first publication. Although Muir himself drew from some of these essays for later books, these earlier versions were written nearer to the actual explorations they report and have long been recognized as some of the best things Muir ever wrote.

The essay series known as *Studies in the Sierra* was thought important enough to be republished as a book by the Sierra Club in 1950, but has long been out of print. No dry scientific writing, these essays are a vivid presentation of glaciology in a controversial context, refuting the contemporary professionals' theory of the cataclysmic formation of Yosemite Valley. Michael Cohen's brilliant analysis of Muir's evolving metaphors in the *Studies* concludes by observing that Muir's drawings provide the key to his proto-ecological vision: 'with their smooth rocks, wavelike granite pavements, and arrows showing the direction of glacial flow, they are reminders of the cycle of Nature' (*The Pathless Way*, University of Wisconsin Press, 1984). From a 'glacial book' to the tree of life, Muir's attempts to find metaphors for his vision of continuous ebb and flow, destruction and creation in nature, are ultimately revealed in his idiosyncratic sketches, published as early as 1874. Included in an addendum with Muir's first three articles is the historically important essay 'California Agriculture', never before published, which shows that Muir the practical man was as much concerned with cultivation as conservation.

Muir's belief that tourism could be educative, and that public education would lead to the political impulse towards preservation, led to his editing *Picturesque California*, which turned out to be a designer's disaster, the illustrations breaking up the text so much as to render it virtually unreadable. Retaining some of the illustrations, we have tried to make readable for the first time Muir's major essays introducing the Sierra mountains to the book-buying public.

They are followed by two campaigning essays published by *Century* magazine as part of the lobbying strategy devised by Muir and *Century*'s editor Robert Underwood Johnson: 'Treasures and Features of the Proposed Yosemite National Park'. Two weeks after the publication of the second of these essays President Benjamin Harrison signed a bill to create the first National Park for the protection of wilderness. Although used later for parts of his books, these elegant essays act as a guide not just to the features themselves, but to Muir's holistic vision of 'divine harmony' that is being threatened by 'the ravages of man'. Muir's 'watershed' definition of biological community, which includes human presence, is a key concept in today's attempts to find a solution to the problems Muir thought of as best approached in terms of biotic communities. ('Watershed: Writers, Nature and Community' was launched as the theme of his tenure by US Poet Laureate Robert Hass in San Francisco on April 6, 1996.)

When Muir died he was trying to finish the manuscript of *Travels in Alaska*, but he had written about Alaska in earlier essays and books which we have brought together here to complete the Alaska ouvre. The authoritative *Notes on the Pacific Coast Glaciers* still manages to convey the 'gloriously wild and sublime', just as the entertaining narrative of Stickeen manages to convey a depth of respect for 'all my fellow mortals'. *The Cruise of the Corwin* was put together by Badè from letters Muir wrote for the *San Francisco Daily Evening Bulletin*, supplemented by scientific articles and journal material. It combines the tension of a search and rescue expedition with the excitement of exploring a final frontier's harrowing and exalting surprises.

Muir's memoir of the magnate Edward Henry Harriman might surprise some readers: why was a conservationist commemorating the boss of the Southern Pacific Railroad? Muir's faith that if the wildernesses were made accessible they would speak to the travellers of the need for their preservation, overwhelmed any scepticism he might have had about Harriman. He was sceptical about Harriman's wealth ('He has not as much money as I have. I have all I want and Mr Harriman has not.'), but Muir's generosity of spirit towards a patron of science gives an insight into his own moral stature.

Of course, the best revelation about Muir's character comes from those who lived with him through some epic adventures. Samuel Hall Young's lively account in *Alaska Days with John Muir* is compulsive reading for those who always wondered how the famously solitary sage would respond to a companion in a crisis. When both Hall Young's shoulders were dislocated in a mountain-climbing fall, he remembers that Muir's rescue attempt was accompanied by his whistling 'The Bluebells of Scotland'.

We can get to know Muir better through the directness of these letters and essays, but it is only in the memoirs of those who knew him that we can sense his personal impact on others. After his death his friends in the Sierra Club, knowing that a great man had passed from their company, attempted to convey the nature of his charismatic character in brief memoirs published in several issues of the Sierra Club Bulletin. Collected together and re-published here they express a deep sense that what Muir stood for was of vital importance to the future of a civilization that could live at one with its natural environment. Further, there is a commitment to carry forward those values into the conservation politics of the future.

CONTINUING INFLUENCE

When Muir found a book in the Sierra mountains and began to translate it for the readers of, first, his letters and later his nationally popular magazine essays, he had begun to heal a gap that had grown between our species and our home, between our species and all the others. He said that he only wanted people to look and to care. But in teaching his readers how to look, he was mediating a vision.

Michael Cohen argues that *Studies in the Sierra*, which he calls 'this Tao of Geology', is central to Muir's finding a unifying cyclic image for the destructive creative tensions at work in the universe: 'The power of the sun became the power of the ice which hid the Sierra from light, killing and creating life, at the same time all flow and cycle, all paradoxical, and yet whole.' But what recent commentators have taken up is Muir's inclusion of our species in that vision. Frank Stewart in *A Natural History of Nature*

157

Writing (Island Press, 1995) echoes Muir's biographer Frederick Turner in pointing out that, perhaps more than Thoreau and Emerson, Muir reconciled an individualistic love for land with a participatory democracy, urging his readers to recreate their links with their land through *Picturesque California*, for example, and to act for its protection through the arguments of 'Treasures and Features of the Proposed Yosemite National Parks.'

Today such action is continued in the name of John Muir by the Sierra Club throughout the USA and the John Muir Trust in Britain. The letters, essays and books included in *John Muir: His Life and Letters and Other Writings* were the means to an end that remains all too unresolved today. Their re-appearance to complement *The Eight Wilderness-Discovery Books* should provide further tools to continue the healing of the gap between humans and their home that Muir began as he approached the environmental crisis of the end of the opening of the twentieth century. It is to be hoped that this book will be used to help us engage with ours.

Ten Letters to John Muir

These poems were completed in early 1990, 100 years after the formation of Yosemite National Park. They are intended to update John Muir, founding father of the National Park, about places which Muir wrote about a century or more earlier.

To John Muir From Lake Tenaya

'Pywiack – lake of the shining rocks',
Said the Indian when you first saw it.

My first summer in the Sierra
I camp and climb by 'Lake Tenaya',
Wearing dark glasses against the glare.
The glacier polished granite still blinds
The Winnebagos each early morning,
Rounding the bends on their summer passage,
Tailboards declaring 'Cruise America'.

Between shining stone and pure water
Yours was a culture cut from wood,
The lumbermen cruising through the forests
Of America for wooden wheels, fences, towns.
'We all travel the milky way together,
Trees and men,' you said after climbing a tree
To travel with it through a storm.

Here at the walk-in campground of Lake Tenaya
Frontier families from Berkeley and the Bay Area
Have left their cars and carried in
For the nightly campfire, an ice-box
And an axe. The woods still echo
To the sound of old backwoods America,
Songs floating on the woodsmoke.
But it's the first summer down in Yosemite Valley

(Where you entertained Emerson at your sawmill)
That the fires are out, woodcutting banned.
Rangers investigate the few campfires.
And you tell me in your guidebook, without irony,
That this lake was renamed in honour of the chief
Who sold Yosemite to the frontiersmen.

From Mount Hoffman

26th July 1869: 'Rambled to the summit of Mount Hoffman, eleven thousand feet high, the highest point in life's journey my feet have yet touched.'

Your 'ramble' up from the Valley
To spend a night on this bare mountain,
A steep ascent of five thousand feet,
Left me breathless before I turned the page.
And even starting from Snow Flat
I was pleased to pause on a real chair
(My first in weeks of boulder-seats)
Left outside by the tree-stump table
Among the cabins of May Lake Camp.

Breathless from the final scramble
And the view, looking down on Half Dome,
Cloud's Rest, far glaciers and Tenaya Lake,
I sit quite still and meet the marmots
Smiling eerily like cats as they creep
Out from their crevices, expecting to be fed.
Disgusted by these half tame summit pets,
I turn and scree-slide down the dusty trail
To bathe my legs in the clear May Lake.

From Fairview Dome

Waiting on the white granite
Steepening north face
For the sun to hit
From behind the summit
With the blinding heat
We feared and wanted,

Waiting, too, for Nick
To stem or lieback

Past the little roof
Before white light hid
All holds above in a
Sudden sun-shaft,

There came this aura
Over the dome top
In which there danced
The insects of the air
Shining on silver wings,
True angels of light.

From Tuolumne Meadows

We are not counting two hundred plants
Within two hundred yards, reflecting upon
'The infinite lavishness and fertility
Of nature – inexhaustible abundance
Amid what seems enormous waste.'

We are counting coins
In the crowded car-park
At the Meadows
For a phone call to England.

We no longer look
Out in awe across the meadow
Flat as the cloudless sky
Empty and still, a place
That slows the urban pulse.

We turn instead into
The Tuolumne Meadows Store
To find an inexhaustible abundance
Of everything but quarters.

Outside there are no sheep,
Your 'hoofed locusts' now
Replaced by those dispensed from cars
Stepping off grass onto white granite
As though on roadside glaciers.

From the trunks of cars
Backpackers bring forth
A lavishness of equipment and
From bulging pockets a few more quarters.

When twenty-two have been begged
We stand in line in the sun
Waiting with infinite patience
To be connected by the voice
Of the Pacific Bell Telephone Company

And see a coyote cross the road.

From Cathedral Peak

'No feature, however, of all the noble landscape as seen from here seems
more wonderful than the Cathedral itself, a temple displaying Nature's best
masonry and sermons in stones.'

Over the top again, John Muir,
And I would be if I could solo,
Like you, up here, the easiest climb
Of our day – mine the South-East Buttress,
Yours the North-West Ridge.

But I'm glad of the offer
Of a rope from Keith and Ira
When we bridge a crack on crystals,
And on your summit I offer them
Children's bubbles to be blown.

Keith is not too sure
But blows, and rainbows rise
Over High Sierra peaks and domes
On an updraught of laughter
As Ira nearly falls from our perch.

Since the desecration of two bolts
Has been removed, we down-climb
Your first ascent and I realise
You invented the hand-jam
A century before Don Whillans or Joe Brown.

From Mono Lake

Down Bloody Canyon in a thunderstorm
A car hangs half over the edge
Of a wilderness flushing out the unwary.
Lee Vining (pop. 500) offers 'Burgers and Things'.

We breakfast at Niceley's, steamy and buzzing
With the first rain in a year to fall
On Mono Lake, shrinking in the desert
And sucked at by the City of Los Angeles.
We sign a petition and walk to the shore
That's danced upon by flies whose larvae
You saw the Indians eat. Laughing and chatting
They gathered wild rye, 'a hopeful people'.
But as we turn back, beyond the weird towers
Of tufa the sky is black, as with ash,
Over the volcanic mountains you wandered
With geologist Le Conte. Back in town
I buy an Indian pot washed with the colours
Of a sky where the sun set long ago.

From Lake Tahoe

Beside this inland sea of open water
Where you botanized along the shore
Vacationland has spread its wares
Between the ski stores and the casinos,
Shouting in lights its liquor and its licences
For anything, paid for in plastic (NO BLOOD TESTS).

And every small motel boasts a swimming pool
Beside the lake you called 'King of them all'.

From The Trail To Mirror Lake

– Where we turned back
In the ankle-deep dust
And choking horse dung
That is the path of a century
Of preserving by popularizing
Yosemite National Park
And your 'easiest trail
Out of the Valley'.

We had just hiked down
From the Meadows to the Valley
Zig-zagging the height of Half Dome,
Singing on the Snow Creek trail,
And turned left to follow tourists
Seeking our own image

In the stillness of Mirror Lake.
But instead we stuck our feet
In its outflow under the bridge.

Mirror Lake is silting up,
Fading like the photographs
Taken of tourists at sunrise
Reflected in the light of 1902.
From Harry Best's studio
Prints fixed after June
Would not last out the year.
Now the Valley is closing
A door you helped to open,
Or rather frame in print.

You would celebrate this change
In the living landscape, and you're right,
Something has shifted, clarified
In the inner landscape of ourselves.
Those presences, from Lake Tenaya
To Half Dome, have been processes in us
Both on and off the trail.
We cannot say we've seen your
'Spiritual, angelic mountaineers
That so throng these pure mansions.'

They are not so pure any more.
Crystal creeks and mirror lakes
Are infected by the presence
Of the living Giardia Lambia,
Carried through the mountains by humans
And perhaps a process we were part of
When we felt the healing power
Of 'champagne water' on sore feet
Beside the trail to Mirror Lake.

From Camp Four

'What,' says Shepherd Billy, 'is Yosemite but a canyon – a lot of rocks – a
hole in the ground – a place dangerous about falling into – a d-d good place
to keep away from.'

In the depths of night
Karabiners chink on harnesses coming or going
At six each morning
The garbage skips are emptied in mid-air.

Traffic starts early.
We step out into the barren black dust
To find four sleepers
In their bags behind our bear-box, but that's OK.
E1 Cap already glows
And the heat is thickening on our skin
Like the dust.
We interrogate the sky and the permanent pessimism
Of the forecast,
Deciding again if we go to Half Dome tonight.
The Valley Floor Tour
Begins the circle of its loudspeaker lecture.
The Londoner, now living
In Los Angeles doing hair transplants,
Leaves Camp Four
With his two American kids, carrying only
A video camera.
As he is descending from the fabled pool
Above Nevada Falls
We pass on our way up for a night's relief
Above the Valley floor.

From Half Dome

When we arrived below the southwest face
The sun had already set, and looking up
I saw a rocket launch out from the top
Of your 'Tissiack' – a golden sun-lit jet
Following the sky-trail to San Francisco.
All night they winked above us as we lay
Where you would have watched only shooting stars.

Climbing crystals in the early morning chill
We saw the sun creep round the dome
To set alight our ladder of jewels,
This Snake Dyke of quartz and felspar,
White and gold nuggets big enough to pinch
And pull on for five hundred feet
Until the angle eased. We reached a tree.

In the endless unroped padding towards
A top that kept unreeling back, my mind,
Turned (by too little water, too much sun)
Back to eighteen seventy five and you
Climbing up the opposite side, first person
To pull up Anderson's new rope, despite
His warnings and the fresh November snow.

No Brocken Spectre below the summit edge
For us, but three despondent Brits hanging
From that sliced hank of beef – the Northwest face.
They're on their second day and find it's tough.
Out on the flat top there's a fairground crowd
Heady from their pull up the chains that now
Replace the rope you climbed to meet us here.

North Carolina Climbing

You've gotta go. Easter would be a good time. August is too hot and sticky they say. But North Carolina climbing has for a long time been a well-kept secret, even from the rest of America. It's traditional climbing of superb quality on varied types of rock and the locals love the chance to climb with visitors from the UK. They've been so cut off for so long that even a Brit of dubious ability was given that quiet Southern hospitality.

THE MAN

If you're going to fall off a crag in a US Wilderness Area, you might do worse than to make sure you're held by a local. Mine was a snuff-dipping, steely fit local guy with a greying crewcut going by the name of Howard. He served behind the counter of the Outdoor Supply Company in Hickory, greeting everyone by name as they pop in from the sun/mist/snow/ice/sun that was January in North Carolina. On campus at Lenoir-Rhyne College my students confided to me, 'Howard is the man.' Whatever that meant, he certainly was as far as I was concerned. After taking me bouldering in the leafless backwoods of late January, on the first Sunday in February we hit one of the major crags outcropping on the rim of the Linville Gorge, location for the filming of *The Last of the Mohicans*.

Howard was the nearest thing to a native I was likely to meet. He lived in a wooden farmhouse that his great-grandfather built in 1886. He'd put up new routes (which he pronounces as 'rowts') in the Linville Gorge, but never been west of the Mississippi. His pride and joy was his brand new silver 4x4 pick-up truck. He cleaned it *before* each Sunday's climbing trip.

THE FALL

His shining silver truck came ghosting out of the dimness just before dawn to pick me up. Beside Lake James, where the Linville River emerges from the ravine, Howard pulled off onto a track, jumped down to engage the hubs of the 4x4, and eased his baby gently over six miles of ruts. Then there was two miles of hiking up to the rim where we bushwhacked to a place which looked like any other, but where Howard knew we would emerge between knarled low trees that crouch on the very edge of the gorge.

'Dang! Ice!' Howard says as we begin to downclimb the steep descent gully. The lingering smooth ice sculptures do not hinder our progress down wet loose blocks. 'Any good at tree climbing?' says H. Sliding down a log across a gully is not a familiar British climbing skill. Finally a short rappel from a tree over a wet cave gets us to the trail round to the front of this magnificent wall. Fortunately the trees are still bare and allow an appreciation of this 500ft white granite cliff that is seamed with horizontal lines, rough textured and rich in features that give a variety of types of climbing with not even the thought of a bolt allowed by these fiercely independent North Carolina climbers. I don't know it yet, but H. is the master of the bombproof six point hanging belay. He doesn't know yet that he's going to need it.

Our line is a starred 5.6 called Little Corner that falls back into the cliff after a bulge that hides the first belay.

We're geared up and H. is tied in for the lead when he says to me, 'This sounds crazy, but I haven't climbed with you before. Can I see you tie a figure of eight?' For a moment I don't quite understand. I've been climbing for over thirty-five years. I chuckle to myself and wonder if I'd have thought to ask that. My respect is growing by the minute.

The corner itself is a little vegetated, but there's a fine crackline on the right that leans back. H. makes short work of it, placing what comes to be his regular four runners in a full run-out. He rounds the bulge with the small bush in it by making big steps up right. With only ten feet of rope left he takes a long time fixing a belay at every stance. Here he doesn't like the insitu threaded tape, he tells me.

The first pitch is deceptive. The edges turn to slopers, the crack narrows and forces the use of a raised slab on its right, which then runs out of edges just as the left side rears up smoothly. There's nothing for it but a blind layback with feet testing the friction. It's better than it looks. Then steep pulls right of the bush turn into mantles onto ledges leading left into the little belay ledge. I notice that H. has equalised all his belay points to perfection. I'm climbing with an old-fashioned craftsman.

He's done the 5.10 on the left that comes in close here and knows the topo shows a 5.8 crack up left, so he heads up towards a roof, stemming wider and wider until he's pulling up the wall on its right. Soon after he belays, taking even longer this time. I should have guessed what that meant.

My problem is that after bridging up to reach a good edge for my right hand, I'm then committed to the right overhanging wall and when I reach round the roof with my left hand I find nothing. The corner has closed up. H. found some edges here to pull up on. I retreat and try again. But there's nothing new to be found and my arms are screaming 'Not enough training!' On my third try I fall off. I'm turning in space on H.'s two 10.5mm ropes (he only clips one) and sit above the wooded winding river way below. Failure on a 5.6 first time out is embarrassing.

H. is a model of Southern politeness about it all. He lowers me down to the belay. I clip in and untie from the rope H. has been leading on. The other rope we've both tied into, but H. has been trailing it, ever cautious with this unknown partner, for possible rappels. Now it can be used to top-rope me through the crack on the left that goes easily at 5.6. This was obviously where the route should have gone, but we've both learned that H. is so much better than me that he can take a straight line and I simply can't. Shaken, but not stirred, I can relax at H.'s expertly improvised belay as he cruises on up the corner, pointing out a steep 5.6 crux stepping into a bottomless V on fist jams. I find this tiring in my strained state, but it's all there and, in the next two pitches I can appreciate the brilliant sharp edged quality of this rock.

THE CRAGS

So I'd topped out after a little too exciting an introduction to the Linville Gorge's Shortoff Mountain, the most southern in a line of crags before the gorge dips down to Lake James.

Howard hung in with me. A few weeks later he took me up the best 5.7 in North Carolina just a few metres south of Little Corner. Maginot Line is an overhanging corner that has horizontal slots for perfect stemming in balance all the way past a hanging belay to a wall, a roof and a final steep wall, all on terrific holds. I did this on a Sunday in late March after it had rained on the Wednesday, but the route had dried in the early North Carolina sun. In fact, the whole crag showed no signs of drainage.

The next crag to the north along the rim, North Carolina Wall, has the best 5.6 in the state, The Daddy, which I'd done on an Easter trip in 1994 when carrying water was crucial to our sunbaked, vulture-watched, success on this 500ft exposed buttress which keeps its crux for the final overhang. Further north across the other side of the Amphitheatre descent for The Daddy is the starred ridge of The Prow at 5.4 and then the overhang of The Open Book at 5.11.

So there is quality at all grades here, as there is at Table Rock further north again and the distinctive feature of the landscape for miles around, from which the North Carolina Wall routes are approached. The key to Table Rock is finding out in advance whether the gate to the access road has been unlocked for the season.

If you like the wilderness ambience, Looking Glass Rock is a dome in the forest of fine friction and exposed leads. (There are official little camping spots on the road up to Looking Glass from Brevard towards the Blue Ridge Parkway.) The Nose is the classic 5.8 and better protected than most things here. Jimmy and Lilace Guignard led me up this with a thunderstorm bearing down on us. I didn't get to climb on Rumbling Bald, but Jimmy showed me his panicing poem about a 'runout' 5.8 route there.

Stone Mountain is another, beautifully streaked, 600ft friction dome, with two classic cracks, above a meadow close to the road. Belays are bolted here, but don't expect many bolts in between. (Check out *Climbing* 192, March 2000, pp. 52-62 for a crag profile.)

I really liked Crowder's Mountain, a monolith overlooking the skyscrapers of Charlotte. There are both traditional routes on amazing rock flutings and overhanging sports routes. Avoid the weekends when it's crowded.

THE PLAN

My recommended sports plan (at the time of writing) would be to fly into Charlotte, hire a car and call up Blueridge Mountain Sports, 803B Friendly Centre Rd, Greensboro, NC 27408 (910 852 9196) to get the local news about access and camping. Then head for Moore's Wall where discrete wild camping is allowed. The store climbers will want to meet up with you there and show you around the superb routes on some of the finest, marble-like rock I've ever climbed on. The Wailing Wall (5.6) on the left of the Amphitheatre went through some unlikely but sharp-edged rock for its grade.

Then you should call up the Outdoor Supply Company, 3006 North Centre St, Hickory, NC 28601 (828 322 2297) to check whether the road is open (depends upon the lateness of snow up there) before going up to Table Rock to camp wild. Howard will be delighted to climb with you or recommend appropriate crags for the weather conditions.

The local climbers climb every weekend all around the year. They don't get many visitors finding these magnificent crags in the backwoods and they're only too willing to be helpful. Buy the latest edition of *The Climber's Guide to North Carolina* by Thomas Kelley and get out there, y'all.

GLOSSARY

Explanation of severity of climbs

BRITISH GRADING SYSTEM		AMERICAN SYSTEM
ADJECTIVAL[a]	NUMERICAL[b]	
Easy (E)		Class 1
		Class 2
	1a	Class 3
Moderate (M or Mod)	1b	Class 4
	1b	Class 4
Difficult (Diff)	1c	Class 5.0
Hard Difficult (HD)	2a	Class 5.1
Very Difficult (V Diff)	2b	Class 5.2
	2c	Class 5.3
Hard V Diff (HVD)	3a	Class 5.4
Severe (S)	3b	Class 5.5
Hard Severe (HS)	4a	Class 5.6
Mild Very Severe (MVS)	4b	Class 5.7
Very Severe (VS)	4b	Class 5.7
	4c	Class 5.8
Hard Very Severe (HVS)	5a	
	5b	Class 5.9
Mild Extremely Severe (E1)		Class 5.10a
	5c	Class 5.10b
Mild Extremely Severe (E2)		Class 5.10c
		Class 5.10d
Extremely Severe (E3)	6a	Class 5.11a
	6b	Class 5.11b
Extremely Severe (E4)	6c	Class 5.11c
		Class 5.11d
Hard Extremely Severe (E5)	7a	Class 5.12a
		Class 5.12b
Hard Extremely Severe (E6)		Class 5.12c
		Class 5.12d
Hard Extremely Severe (E7)		

[a] rating based on level of protection available.

[b] grade of the hardest technical move.

Abseil Means of descending a fixed rope.

Anchor Means of fixing a belay to the rock.

Arête Sharp ridge of rock.

Back-and footing Climbing up a crack with your back on one side and your feet on the other.

Belay (noun) A combination of the point on the rock where the rope can be secured, the belay method (i.e. the way in which a rope is held or arranged allowing a fall to be stopped) and the belayer (person who manages the rope in order to brake a climbing partner's fall).

Belay (verb) To secure a rope by winding it round a peg or spike and manage the rope in a way that allows a fall to be stopped.

Belayer Person managing the belay.

Belay plate One form of belay device.

Bergschrund Gap between snow and rock.

Bowline Knot formerly used for attaching the rope to a climber.

Bridging Spreading the legs to use holds on opposite walls of rock.

Cam or **Camming device** A device for placing in cracks with sprung wheels or cams that bite the rock. The first had the tradename **Friend** and they are available in different sizes.

Chapbook Collection of popular tales.

Chimney A deep crack wide enough to admit a person.

Chimneying Means of ascending a chimney.

Chockstone A stone naturally wedged in a crack or chimney.

Chop (to get the chop) to die.

Classic Rock Book listing supposedly quality easier climbs in the UK (Wilson, K. (ed.) (1978) *Classic Rock*. London: Diadem.).

Cornice Windblown overhang of snow.

Crab Common UK word for carabiner, alloy snaplink.

Crux The hardest section of a climb.

Daisy chain A sling attached to the harness having a series of loops in it.

Descender (*descendeur*) Device for descending a fixed rope.

EBs Antique form of light rock boots.

Finger lock Way of twisting a finger into a crack to be able to pull up on it.

Flake A thin piece of rock that is detached or partially detached from the main face.

Friend The original and still popular camming device for placing in cracks.

Glissade To slide down snow standing up.

Hanger The plate hanging from a bolt into which a crab is clipped.

Heel hook The hooking of a heel, usually above the hands.

Hex A hollow wedge that has hexagonal sides [for placing in a crack]

Hitch A knot (e.g. Italian hitch).

Ice-axe arrest Arresting a slide by lying on the axe head.

Incuts Holds that dip down as though made for fingers.

Jam Means of wedging a hand or fingers in a crack.

Jug Perfectly shaped large handhold.

Jumar Method of ascending a fixed rope either using a device called a jumar or a knot such as a prusik.

Knife-blade Metaphor for something that looks like this.

Krab See **crab**.

Layaway A hold or move requiring leaning back with legs braced, as in a layback.

Layback Hands used in opposition to feet in a horizontal position.

Leader Person who climbs the route first.

Leading through A term for doing alternate leads.

Mantle (mantleshelf) Pressing down with two hands to get a foot to join them.

Moac Trade name for an ancient form of metal wedge.

Nut General term for metal wedges of different numbered sizes to be placed in cracks.

Peg Metal spike with an eye that is usually left permanently in place when hammered into a crack.

Pinch grip Making a hold by pinching a piece of rock.

Pitch The distance between consecutive stances (ledges where climbers can anchor themselves, and belay their climbing partners). Climbs may be single-pitch or multi-pitch.

Piton See **peg**.

Prusik Knot that slides up a fixed rope, but not down.

Prusik loop Carried to make the above knot if needed.

Quickdraw A short tape with a crab at each end, one of which is to be clipped to a bolt or nut. Through the other the rope runs.

Rappel (Rap) American for abseil.

Route finding Route-finding ability is the skill in finding the best way up a cliff or mountain when there is no description, or the way is not obvious.

Runner A method of placing something on or in the rock through which the rope can run in the middle of a pitch to reduce the length of a fall. Sometimes these can be **poor,** or merely **psychological runners.**

Run out The running out of the rope in the lead.

Second The climber who follows the leader of a pitch.

Serac A precarious block of ice in a glacier that could be about to sheer off.

Side pull A hold requiring a horizontal pull.

Slab Easy angled rock.

Sling A loop of tape (nylon webbing).

Spike A sharp projecting point of rock.

Stance Where a belay can be made between pitches.

Step cutting Using an ice-axe to cut holds in snow.

Sticky boots Light rock boots with adhesive rubber soles (formerly, light rock boots did not have these).

Tape Nylon webbing. Slings and harnesses are made of tape.

TD Très Difficile (an Alpine grading).

Thread Making a runner by threading a sling around a chockstone or through a natural hole in the rock.

Three star climb A subjective assessment of the highest quality of route (good but lesser quality routes are referred to as a one or a two star climb).

Thrutch A colloquial term referring to a method of climbing akin to scrabbling in which any method is used to move the body upwards.

Topo A guide to the routes on a crag that is diagrammatic only and does not describe it in words.

Top-rope Lowering a rope so that leading is not necessary.

Trundle To roll a boulder down.

Tuber Trade name of a type of belay device.

Wallnut Trade name of a type of nut.

Wire The smaller nuts are fixed on wire and are sometimes called 'wires'.

REFERENCES

Beetham, B. (1953) *Borrowdale*. The Fell and Rock Climbing Club of the English Lake District.

Bell, J. H. (1950) *A Progress in Mountaineering*. Edinburgh: Oliver and Boyd.

Bennett, R., Birkett, W. and Hyslop, A. (1979) *Winter Climbs in The Lake District*. Milnthorpe: Cicerone.

Bouvier, J-P. (1984) *Rock-climbing in France*. London: Diadem.

Brailsford, J. (1987) *Ecrins Massif: Selected Climbs*. London: Alpine Club.

Brunner, H-D. and Lochner, M. (1988) *Deutschland Vertikal*. Munich: Meyer.

Carr, H. (1926) *Climbers' Guide to Snowdon and the Beddgelert District*. Climbers' Club.

Cleveland Mountaineering Club (1985) *Climbs on the North York Moors*. Leicester: Cordee.

Cohen, M. (1984) *The Pathless Way*. Wisconsin: University of Wisconsin Press.

Coxhead, E. (1938) *June in Skye*. London: Cassell.

Craggs, C. (1988) *Costa Blanca Rock*. Milnthorpe:Cicerone.

Cram, G., Eilbeck, C. and Roper, I. (1975) *Rock Climbing in the Lake District*. London: Constable.

Desroy, G. (ed.) (1989) *Yorkshire Gritstone*. Yorkshire Mountaineering Club.

Drasdo, H. (1959) *Eastern Crags*. Fell and Rock Climbing Club.

Fell, J. (1990) 'Gingilos'. *High* **94** (September issue), 41.

Furguson, D., Jones, I. A. and Littlewood, P. (2000) *Tremadog*. Climbers' Club.

Fyffe, A. and Nisbet, A. (1995) *The Cairngorms*, Volume I. Scottish Mountaineering Club.

Gifford, T. (ed.) (1992) *John Muir: The Eight Wilderness-Discovery Books*. London: Diadem Books.

Gifford, T. (1996) *The Rope*. Bradford: Redbeck.

Gifford, T. (ed.) (1996) *John Muir: His Life and Letters and Other Writings*. London: Bâton Wicks.

Gifford, T. (1997) *The Climbers' Club Centenary Journal*. Leicester: Cordee.

Gifford, T. (1999) *Pastoral*. London: Routledge.

Gilbert, R. (1983) *Memorable Munroes*. London: Diadem.

Gilbert, R. (1994) 'The Letterewe Accord – A Great Leap Forward'. *High* **136** (March issue), 24.

Godfrey, J. and Karslake, E. (1994) *Landscapes of Western Crete*. London: Sunflower Books.

Griffin, H. (1970) *Still The Real Lakeland*. London: Robert Hale.

Hankinson, A. (1988) *A Century on the Crags*. London: Dent.

Haskett-Smith, W. P. (1986) *Climbing in the British Isles* (Reprint of the 1895 guide). Glasgow: Ernest Press.

Heaton Cooper, W. (1984) *Mountain Painter*. Kendal: Frank Peters.

Hooper, J., Hancock, N., Ohly, S. and 9 others (2000) *West Cornwall*. Climbers' Club.

Howett, K. (1990) *Rock Climbing in Scotland*. London: Constable.

James, R. (1970) *Rock Climbing in Wales*. London: Constable.

Jenkin, G. (1986) *Swanage*. Climbers' Club.

Jones, O. G. (1897) *Rock Climbing in the English Lake District*. London: Longmans.

Kelly, H. M. (ed.) (1935) *Rock Climbing Guides to The English Lake District*, 1st series. Fell and Rock Climbing Club.

Kelsey, J. (1989) 'The Best of Times, The Worst of Times', in Steck, A. and Roper, S. (eds) *Ascent*, 27–43. San Francisco: Sierra Club.

Limbaugh, R. H. (1996) *'Stickeen' and the Lessons of Nature*. Alaska: University of Alaska Press.

Littlejohn, P. (1979) *South-west Climbs*. London: Diadem.

Livesey, P. (1980) *French Rock-climbs*. Leicester: Cordee.

MacInnes, H. (1971) *Scottish Climbs* (2 volumes). London: Constable.

Mill, C. (1987) *Norman Collie: A Life in Two Worlds*. Aberdeen: Aberdeen University Press.

Mitchell, I. (1997) *The Mountain Weeps*. Glasgow: Stobcross.

Murray, W. H. (1951) *Undiscovered Scotland*. London: Dent.

Murray, W. H. (1979) *Mountaineering in Scotland and Undiscovered Scotland*. London: Diadem.

Noyce, C. W. F. and Edwards, J. M. (1939) *Lliwedd*. Climbers' Club.

Pretty, M., Milburn, G. and Farrant, D (1989) *Tremadog*. Climbers' Club.

Pritchard, P. (1997) *Deep Play*. London: Bâton Wicks.

Ratcliffe, D. (1980) *The Peregrine Falcon*. Waterhouses: T. & A. D. Poyser.

Reid, D. and Falkenstein, C. (1986) *Rock Climbs of Tuolumne Meadows*. Denver: Chockstone Press.

Renouf, J. (1997) *Alfred Heaton Cooper: Painter of Landscape*. Grasmere: Red Bank Press.

Robertson, M. (ed.) (1955) *Mountain Panorama*. London: Parrish.

Salkeld, A. and Smith, R. (eds.) (1990) *One Step in the Clouds*. London: Diadem.

Sauvy, A. (1995) *The Game of Mountain and Chance*. London: Bâton Wicks.

Stainforth, G. (1992) *Lakeland*. London: Constable.

Stainforth, G. (1994) *The Cuillin*. London: Constable.

Stewart, F. (1995) *A Natural History of Nature Writing.* Washington DC: Island Press.

Sumner, J. (1988) *Mid-Wales.* Climbers' Club.

Thomas, D. M. (ed.) (1970) *Granite Kingdom: Poems of Cornwall.* Penryn: Tor Mark Press.

Turnbull, D. G. and Turnbull, R. W. L. (1973) *Climbers' Guide to the Northern Highlands Area*, Vol. II. Edinburgh: Scottish Mountaineering Trust.

Williams, P. (1982) *Snowdonia Rock Climbs.* Sheffield: Extreme Books.

Wilson, K. (ed.) (1978) *Classic Rock.* London: Diadem.